BOWLING GREEN STOCK CAR RACING

On the Front Cover: The 23-year-old Marshall Love Jr., the official track photographer at Beech Bend Park and a stock car driver, took this self-portrait in 1951. Marshall took this photograph to send to his girlfriend, Irene Sparks, who lived in Gradyville, Kentucky, which explains why he looks as if he is dressed for a date. The race car is a 1934 Ford. (Courtesy of Marshall Love Jr.)

Cover Background: This 1951 photograph illustrates the tremendous early popularity of stock car racing in Bowling Green. The crowds motivated Charles Garvin to continue adding seats. Ultimately, up to 7,000 fans could attend the races. (Courtesy of Kentucky Library and Museum, Western Kentucky University [WKU].)

Back Cover: The Regional Championship Race was the final race of the 1951 season, held on October 21, 1951; Larry Graham won the race driving Upton's Garage No. 22, which was built by Lattney Upton. Shown here at the trophy presentation are, from left to right, unidentified track official; Lattney Upton; Dottye Nuckols, Miss Kentucky 1951; Larry Graham; and Wayne Norris, the flagman. (Courtesy of Sadie Upton Blind.)

BOWLING GREEN STOCK CAR RACING

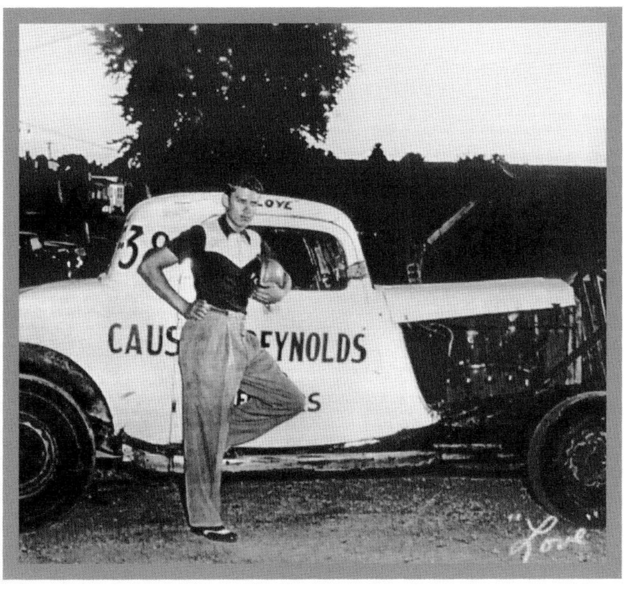

Larry Upton and Jonathan Jeffrey

ARCADIA PUBLISHING

To Larry H. Graham, who has been an inspiration to three generations of the Upton family; Yvonne and Wayne Guy for their generous support of this book; and Marshall Love Jr., Beech Bend's official photographer, who went everywhere in Bowling Green in search of stock cars and drivers to photograph. Finally, to all those drivers who raced at Beech Bend Park in 1951, launching the story of Bowling Green as the city of speed.

ISBN 978-0-7385-8583-3

Published by Arcadia Publishing
Charleston SC, Chicago IL, Portsmouth NH, San Francisco CA

Printed in the United States of America

Library of Congress Control Number: 2009940824

For all general information contact Arcadia Publishing at:
Telephone 843-853-2070
Fax 843-853-0044
E-mail sales@arcadiapublishing.com
For customer service and orders:
Toll-Free 1-888-313-2665

Visit us on the Internet at www.arcadiapublishing.com

CONTENTS

ACKNOWLEDGMENTS

The publication of this book is a testament to the commitment of the staff at Kentucky Library and Museum at Western Kentucky University to build a collection of early-day stock car racing in Bowling Green. Unless otherwise noted, all images appear courtesy of the Kentucky Library and Museum, WKU. Of special mention is the work of Marshall Love Jr., a professional photographer and stock car driver, who made the effort to take photographs of all of Bowling Green's stock car drivers and their stock cars in 1951.

In addition, a special thanks to Hugh Porter Causey, who built the first stock car in Bowling Green; Carolyn McClard Honchell, the daughter of Raymond McClard, who provided many of the photographs and information about motorcycle racing at Beech Bend Park; Wayne and Yvonne Guy; Mary Jo Cook; Donald Upton; Dallas Jones; Dick Webber; David Garvin; Elmo Guy; Betty and Lattney Upton; Justin Upton; Judy McDonald; Mark Reynolds; Kevin McReynolds; and Larry Graham. Also, Jim Baird, the current photographer at Beech Bend Raceway, took a personal interest in this book and was instrumental in providing photographs and documentation for present-day racing in Bowling Green. Steve Cavanaugh of Nashville, Tennessee, deserves special mention for his chronicling of the career of "Bullet" Bob Reuther, a Nashville regular at Beech Bend Park, who went on to race with NASCAR and was later inducted into the Tennessee Motorsports Hall of Fame. In addition, Steve Cavanaugh introduced this project to Russ Thompson of Nashville, Tennessee, who has spent a lifetime collecting over 10,000 photographs of stock car racing with an emphasis on stock car racing at the old Nashville Fairgrounds track. Thompson was able to document many of the Nashville drivers who raced in Bowling Green. Finally, without the gentle, persuasive persistence of our editor, Amy Perryman, this book would never have been completed.

INTRODUCTION

Bowling Green, Kentucky, founded in 1798, is a beautiful Southern city nestled adjacent to the Barren River and set amid the undulating foothills of south-central Kentucky. Long before Bowling Green was known as the home of Western Kentucky University, the General Motors Corvette assembly plant, the National Corvette Museum, and the birthplace of Duncan Hines of cake mix fame, the town forged a progressive but not aggressive attempt to become a community of consequence. The Civil War hampered this progress, but the march quickened after the difficult years of Reconstruction. Transportation was always an important component of this growth. Over the years, Bowling Green enjoyed access to good roads, river traffic via steamboats and barges, rail service on the Louisville and Nashville Railroad, and, by the late 1930s, a developing airport. This transportation infrastructure placed Bowling Green on solid footing to benefit from the economic boom after World War II. Interestingly, transportation remains a theme for the city today. Besides the Corvette's allure and the city's presence on one of America's most heavily traveled interstates, Bowling Green is the home of Beech Bend Park, where racing and other automobile-related events are held on a regular basis, bringing tens of thousands of guests to the community. This photo journal documents all types of racing at Beech Bend Park, with stock car racing being the fan favorite in the late 1940s and 1950s. Beech Bend Park is known to many as an important component of Bowling Green's emergence as a high-speed entertainment center.

Until recent years, stock car racing was a Southern sport. Those who partook in this sport were so-called rednecks and moonshiners—at least that was the image promulgated by NASCAR in its early days. Today the stock car racing craze has exploded nationwide, and the sport downplays its moonshiner roots. That early rustic image may have been an advertising ploy, because it certainly was not the foundation for stock car racing in Bowling Green. Numerous stock car racetracks popped up in the vicinity of Bowling Green and Nashville after the end of World War II. They were owned and promoted by businessmen looking to capitalize on the nation's pent-up demand for entertainment after 15 years of Depression and war. Furthermore, people had money to spend, and no excitement competed with racing the family car.

The stock car drivers came from diverse walks of life far removed from the hillbilly or moonshiner element. In Bowling Green, for example, there were young men such as Tommy Smith, the son of a business owner and inventor, who went on to graduate from Georgia Tech and become a millionaire businessman; Marshall Love Jr., the owner of a photographic studio; and Larry Graham, a descendant of Kentucky's honorable Judge Asher Graham, who became an U.S. Air Force officer during the Korean War, later relocating back to Bowling Green as a local businessman and farmer. Hugh Porter Causey, the young man who built the first stock car in Bowling Green, continues to this day to operate an auto wrecking business in the city. Lattney Upton, another car builder, was the great-grandson of Elijah Upton, a hero at the Battle of the Thames in the War of 1812 and the progenitor of a prominent farming family in Richardsville, Kentucky. Most, if not all, of the local drivers came from solid family backgrounds that had no link to the mythologized moonshine racers of NASCAR fame, a reputation that seems to have attached itself to anyone who raced stock cars on dirt tracks in the sport's early days.

In 1941, an enterprising man named Charles Garvin purchased a gently rolling section of land covered with beech trees located about 2.5 miles northeast of Bowling Green. The property, being used at the time as a dairy and farming operation, was situated in a big U-shaped bend of the Barren River. Its proximity to Bowling Green, combined with the cool shade of the beech trees and the quiet solitude of the slow-moving river, had made the area a camping and picnic haven from the long, hot days of summer since the 1880s. Locals have always called the place Beech Bend, and the name itself denotes peace and serenity; however, the stock car racing fever would soon change that, at least on Sunday afternoons.

Garvin saw the potential for more than just camping and picnicking. He soon renamed the area Beech Bend Park, charged 10¢ admission, and initiated the gradual development of a complete amusement park. The first addition to the camping and picnicking activities was a live pony ride. A swimming pool in 1947, pavilions for dancing, and a large Ferris wheel quickly followed. Eventually, Beech Bend became one of the largest amusement parks in Kentucky.

On a summer day in the mid-1940s, three teenagers from Bowling Green, brothers Elmo and Wayne Guy and their friend Billy Hudson, headed their motorcycles toward Beech Bend. At the gate, Garvin collected his usual 10¢ fee, and the boys roared their motorcycles through the park's dirt roadways. Entering a large meadow near the Barren River, the boys ripped through the grass and weeds, racing each other in a large oval, which gave them an idea.

When Elmo, Wayne, and Billy returned to the front gate, they asked Garvin if they could make a flat racetrack for their motorcycles in the meadow. Billy Hudson, whose father was the head of the Warren County Roads Department, said that he could get access to a road grader to carve out a track. Garvin quickly agreed but told the boys that they had to do the work. Garvin soon teamed up with Raymond McClard, the local Harley Davidson motorcycle dealer and a Bowling Green politician, and staged their first motorcycle race in 1946.

Garvin and McClard did not know it yet, but the real entertainment dollar in the years following World War II was going to be in stock car racing. Bowling Green was not yet on the racing map, but stock car racing was already taking root in towns throughout the region. Hugh Porter Causey, a young, local garage owner and car lover, decided to build a stock car that he could race in nearby Russellville and other surrounding towns. Going a step further, McClard tried, with limited success, to promote a track outside the town on the Russellville Road. Clearly, momentum was building.

As the 1940s drew to a close, Garvin and McClard believed that the time had come when the public was ready to support stock car racing in Bowling Green. They promoted their first stock car race at Beech Bend in 1948, the same year that witnessed the birth of NASCAR. Aware of Hugh Porter Causey's interest in racing and the fact that he had built a race car, Charles Garvin called Causey and asked him to help assemble a group of people willing to build stock cars and support racing at Beech Bend. Causey was soon running advertisements on radio and in the local newspaper, the *Daily News*, inviting interested parties to contact him. He also used his own extensive network of mechanics and car aficionados to help him. According to Causey, "Pretty soon it seemed like everybody in Bowling Green was building a race car."

Charles Garvin and Raymond McClard, supported by key men like Hugh Porter Causey, organized the Bowling Green Sporting Association to sponsor the races. Garvin also improved the one-third-mile track by adding a pit area, flagman's and official's booth in the infield, concession stands, and a grandstand. Before the first race, Garvin even announced that he was going to build a roof over the grandstand for the comfort of the fans. By mid-year 1951, all was ready.

The first race was announced for Sunday, August 5, 1951, with time trials beginning at 1:00 p.m. and the first of eight races scheduled to begin at 2:00 p.m. Admission was set at $1 for adults and 50¢ for children under 12 years old. The schedule called for four heat races, each consisting of six cars racing eight laps; an Australian pursuit race, in which cars line up single file (slowest in front to fastest in the rear) with cars being eliminated as they were passed; a consolation race; and an undisclosed special event in addition to the feature race. To insure that they had a good field of cars, Garvin and McClard sent out invitations to drivers competing at neighboring tracks.

In an interview with the *Daily News*, Raymond McClard identified the local car owners and drivers expected to participate in the inaugural event as the following: Causey and Reynolds Garage, Tommy Smith, driver; Mayhugh Motor Company, A. W. Nolan, driver; Wingfield Auto Service, Marshall Love Jr., driver; and Wright's Welding and Machine Shop, Elmo Guy, driver. McClard stated that several other businesses committed to participating that first Sunday included Wallace Motor Company, Cohron Motor Company, Upton's Garage, Tunk's Garage, Burch's Golden Tip Service, and Dixie Garage.

The first race at Beech Bend Park was a resounding success. An overflow crowd of 2,500 people watched a field of 19 cars put on an exciting show, including five crack-ups, two of which were spectacular rollovers with no injuries. People from out of town dominated the events beginning with Elmer Tapp of Owensboro, Kentucky. He set the first time trial record at 25.3 seconds around the one-third mile dirt oval, with an average speed of 47.43 miles per hour. Bowling Green drivers Billy Hudson, driving for Mayhugh and McReynolds Motor Company, and Elmo Guy, driving for Wright Machine Shop, were the only local winners, winning a heat race and the Australian pursuit race, respectively. The unexpected high fan turnout prompted the Bowling Green Sporting Association to announce that racing would continue each Sunday afternoon until the onset of bad weather. The promoters also announced that they would construct an addition to the grandstands to accommodate larger crowds.

As the season wore on and the crowds became more enthusiastic, the racing brothers, Elmo and Wayne Guy, became the local drivers to beat. Elmo became the local favorite by finishing near the top each week to the more experienced out-of-town drivers. Finally, on September 30, 1951, Wayne Guy surprised Elmo by becoming the first local man to win the feature race; he made it a clean sweep by also winning his heat race and the Australian pursuit race that same day. In a 2003 interview, when asked what he liked about stock car racing, Wayne replied, "I just liked being there! And I always wanted to beat Elmo!"

With the weather changing, the Warren County championship was scheduled for October 14, 1951. This race would be open only to local drivers. According to the local newspaper, Wayne Guy was the designated "marked man" due to his surprising triple win two weeks earlier. Elmo Guy was also mentioned as a top choice to win. As it turned out, Elmo Guy was the Warren County champion, and Larry Graham was a close second.

On October 21, 1951, Beech Bend Park held the last race of the season, which was billed as the Regional Championship, with all drivers welcome. The championship race was extended to 25 laps. The Bowling Green Sporting Association announced that for the first time trophies would be presented by a special guest of honor, Miss Kentucky 1951, Dottye Nuckols. Again Elmo and Wayne Guy were considered the local favorites to cop the championship.

In races prior to the Regional Championship, however, another local driver, Larry Graham, a 22-year-old student at Western Kentucky University, had been making a move toward the top. Graham had missed out on traditional sports in his youth due to a bout with polio, so he viewed stock car racing as a chance at a level playing field. Graham had raced Raymond McClard's "The Thing" a few times but was looking for something with more power. Lattney Upton, owner of the Upton's Garage No. 22, was looking for a driver. Graham knew the car had lots of power but considered the 1938 Dodge with the 1936 Cadillac V-8 something of a Rube Goldberg setup. It was a car out of the mainstream and had never been a winner; however, Graham decided to give the car a try.

Les Williams broadcast the race over local radio station WLBJ. In spite of all the out-of-town competition, the race was dominated by Elmo Guy, followed by Wayne Guy and Larry Graham. These three held off the field as the race approached the 20-lap mark when, suddenly, Elmo Guy got a flat tire. He continued to race but was losing ground as Wayne took over first place with Graham in second. Although Graham was pressing him, the race appeared to be a cinch for Wayne Guy until, with two laps to go, Wayne met Elmo's fate as a tire went flat. Larry Graham vaulted past him to victory lane. Beech Bend Park's inaugural season was over.

The fan excitement and support was so overwhelming that stock car racing at Beech Bend became a fixture until drag racing surged to the fore 10 years later. During the early 1950s, crowds of 7,000 became common as Garvin continued to expand the facilities.

1

First There Were Motorcycles

Racing is the most ancient of sports, dating beyond the dim past of humankind's earliest scribbling. The desire to compete, to prove ourselves, to be the best, and to win seems to be a natural part of our human makeup. We have made a contest of everything from horse racing to horseshoes to chili cook-offs. In many ways, life itself is an internal contest of sorts, an endurance test or, in the words of Shakespeare's Hamlet, "Whether 'tis nobler in the mind to suffer the slings and arrows of outrageous fortune or to take arms against a sea of troubles." Let it be said that stock car drivers always elect to take up arms against the sea of troubles. Racing, if one thinks about it, is a metaphor for life, containing all the elements that make life interesting, exciting, frustrating, challenging, and fulfilling. It really does contain the "thrill of victory and the agony of defeat."

It was inevitable that man's need to experience every emotion in every possible situation would eventually extend to automobiles. The earliest tracks were asphalt and hosted expensive open-wheel sports car races, which were considered very high-class events. Stock car races, however, originally catered to the "common people" primarily in the South and were shunned by the upper classes.

But before the stock car, motorcycles took center stage at Beech Bend Park with the first race held in 1946. Charles Garvin, a former prizefighter and the owner of Beech Bend Park, and Raymond McClard, the Harley Davidson motorcycle dealer in Bowling Green, were superior promoters of the races that took place at the park. Both were fearless, a trait required of a promoter, but were also likable, trustworthy, and well connected to the community. Garvin worked behind the scenes while McClard, also a Bowling Green politician, worked as the front man. They made an excellent team. But like all good things, it did not last. Ultimately, McClard pulled out of the partnership. Nevertheless, the two men launched something special in Bowling Green. Motorcycles had a monopoly for most of the period from 1946 until 1951, when stock car racing and unbelievable crowds took Beech Bend Park to another level.

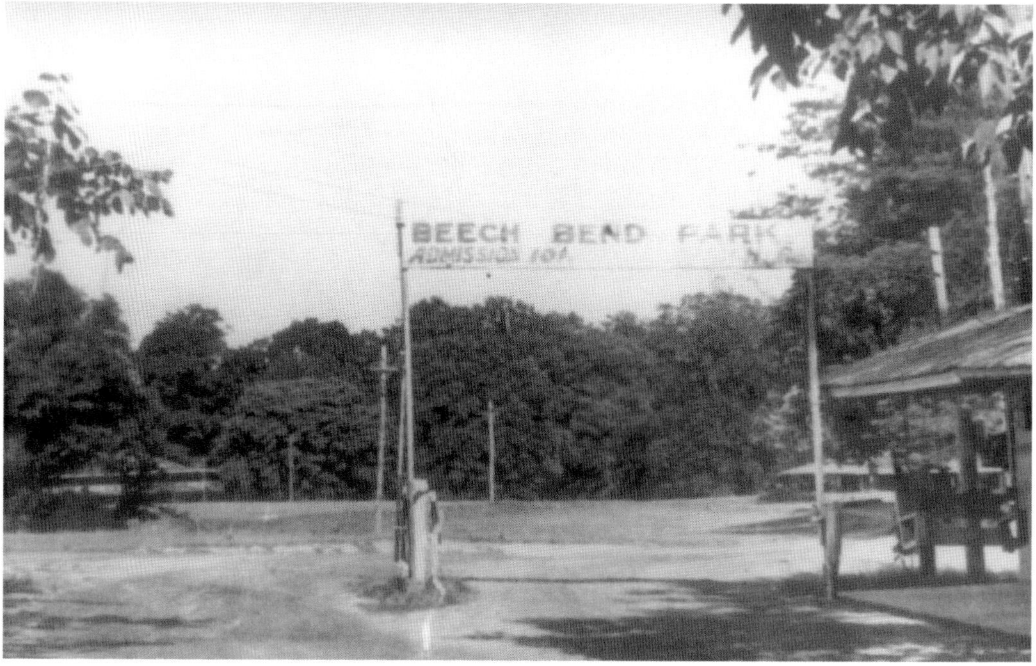

Above is the original entrance to Beech Bend Park, which was used by the first stock car drivers. Below is an improved entrance from the 1970s with the ticket booth on the right. During Charles Garvin's reign, the entry fee was always a dime. Prior to the building of the formal ticket booth, Garvin stood in front of his home, near where the mailbox is located, to collect his dimes. (Above, courtesy of David Garvin.)

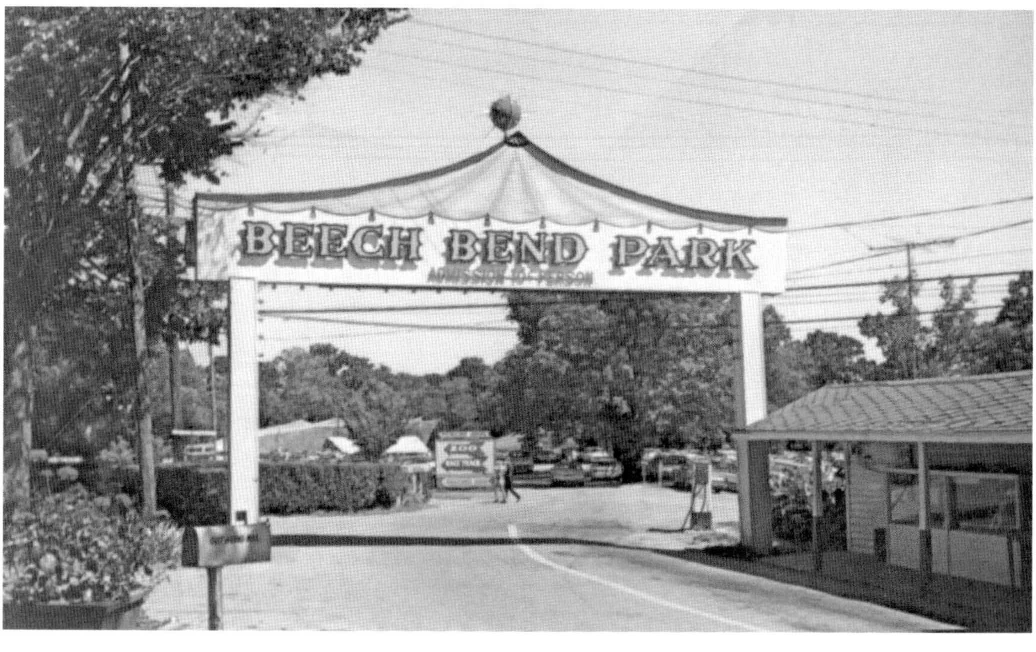

Charles Garvin stands with the reward of his labors: a sack of dimes. Of course, once in Beech Bend Park, one paid a fee for various carnival rides and other entertainments; nevertheless, it is unusual that any business would maintain the same small entry fee of a dime over the course of so many years. (Right, courtesy of David Garvin.)

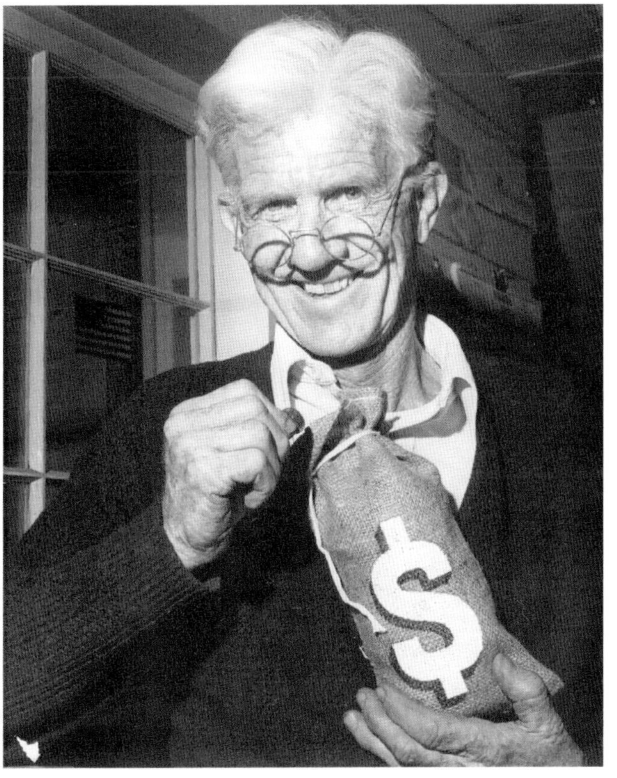

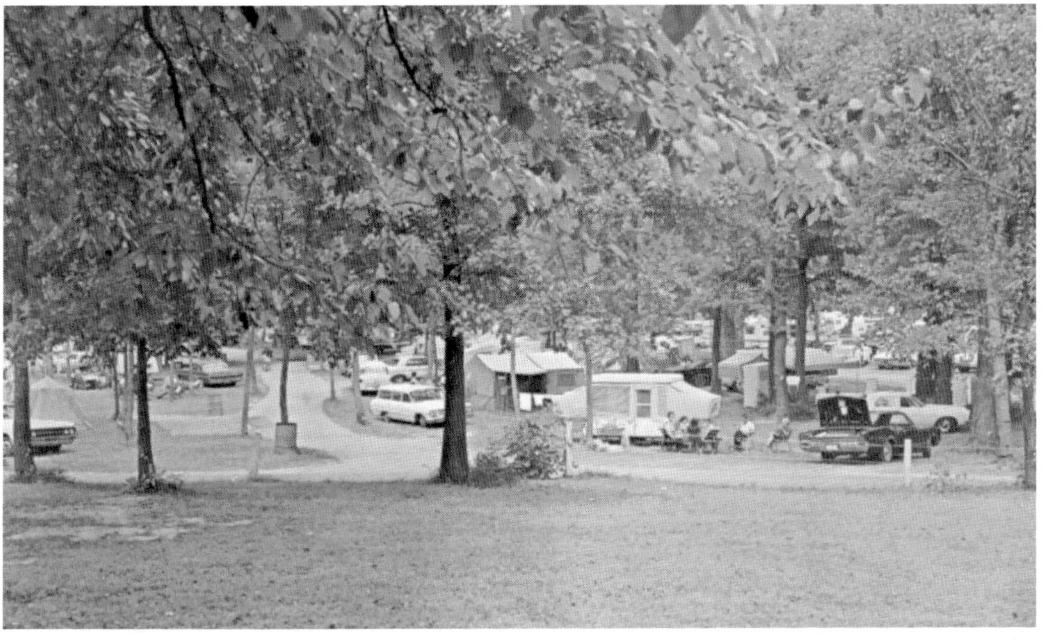

Although this photograph is from a more recent time, camping, fishing, or just relaxing was the original lure of Beech Bend Park. Charles Garvin, throughout his ownership of Beech Bend Park, charged just a dime to come through the front gate.

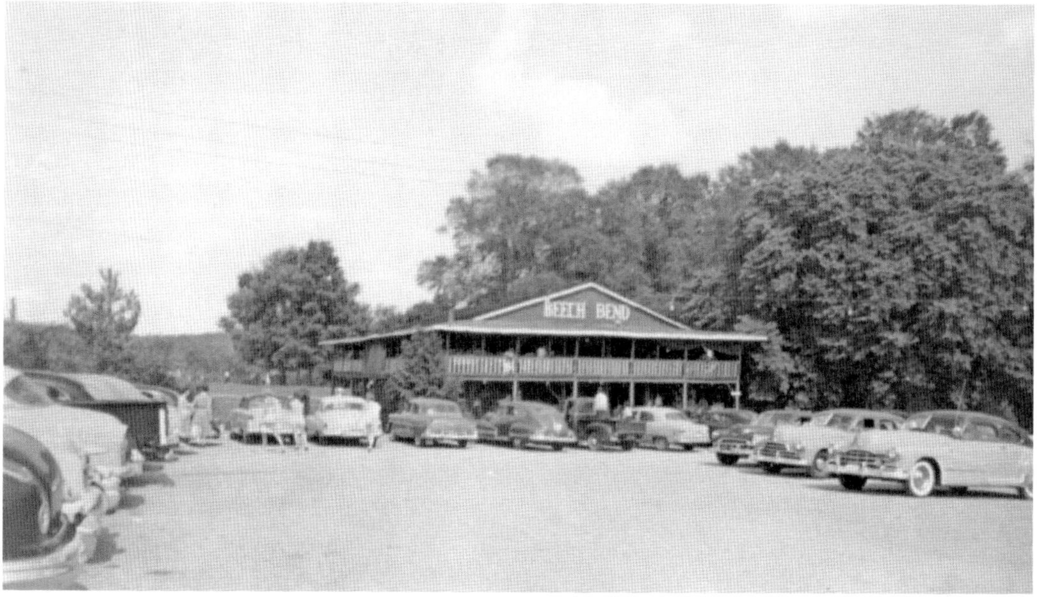

The dance pavilion at Beech Bend Park dates from the early 1900s and was always popular with anybody that liked to dance. It served as a social getaway during World War II and the Korean War for young soldiers stationed at military posts near Bowling Green. Men in uniform were regular visitors at the dance pavilion.

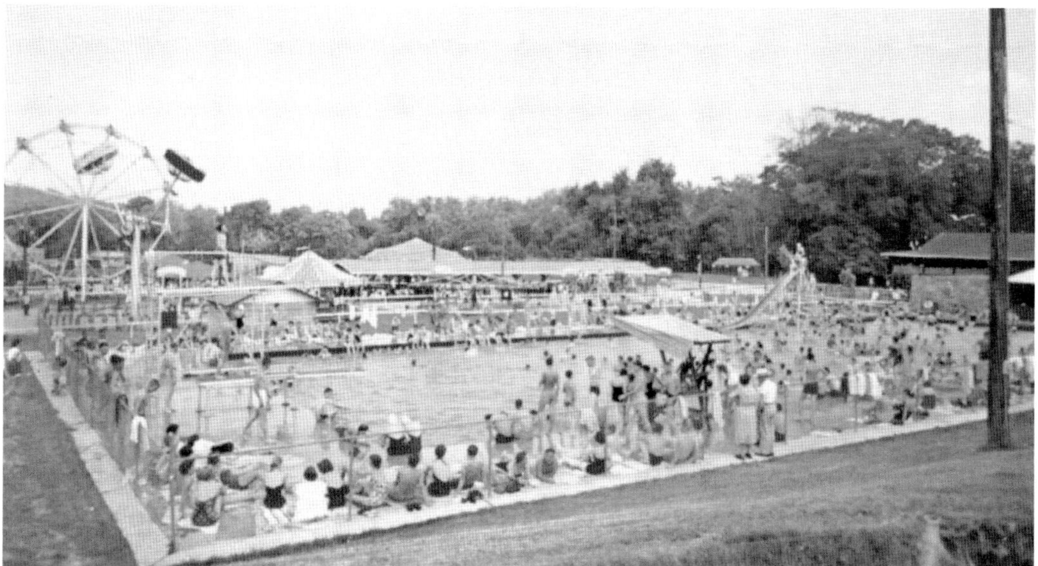

One of the first major attractions at Beech Bend Park was the opening of its public swimming pool in 1947. It was only the second outdoor swimming pool in Bowling Green, coming a few years after the opening of the pool at Western Kentucky University. Beech Bend Park's pool was large, 140 feet long and 60 feet wide, and had diving boards and a slide. It was a summertime favorite attraction at 25¢ per session plus, of course, the 10¢ entry fee.

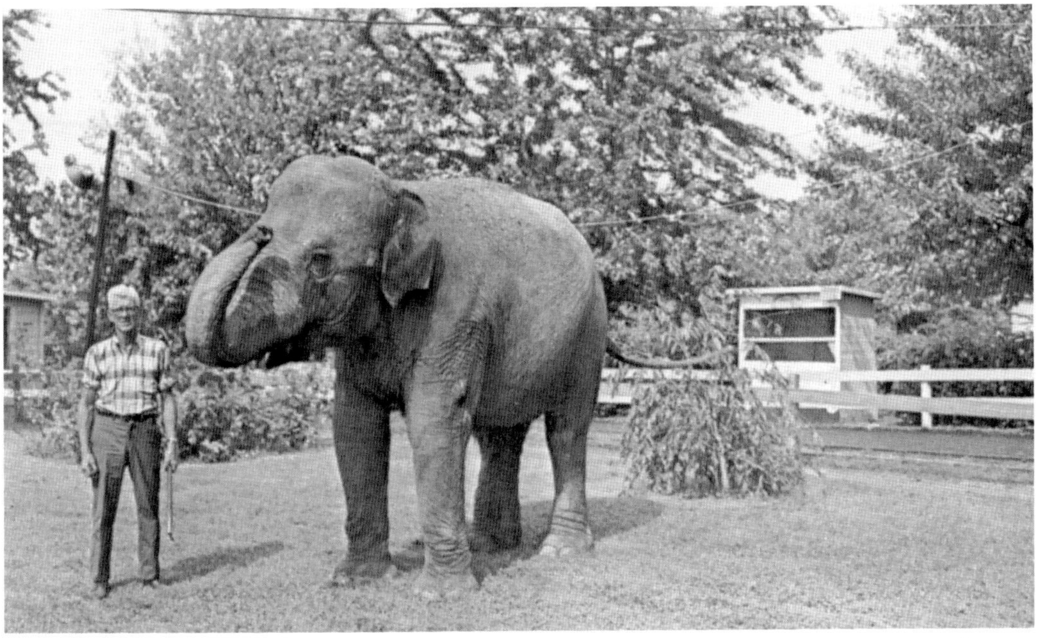

Charles Garvin, the owner of Beech Bend Park from 1941 through 1980, poses with one of his pet elephants in Beech Bend Park. Garvin, always with a flair for the dramatic, purchased his first eight elephants in 1958, and soon the pachyderms became fixtures at Beech Bend Park's zoo.

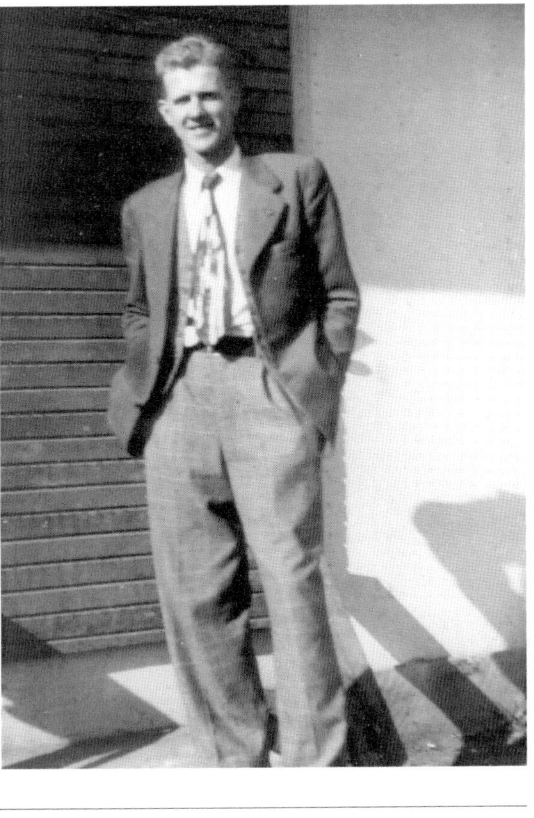

This is a photograph of Charles Garvin in the 1930s when he was working as the chief deputy clerk of the Warren Circuit Court. This was during the time in his life that he was laying the financial foundation for the purchase of the farmland at Beech Bend. Garvin was a professional boxer on the side and served in the Kentucky National Guard, where he learned he could make money acting as the soldiers' lender for short-term loans. (Courtesy of David Garvin.)

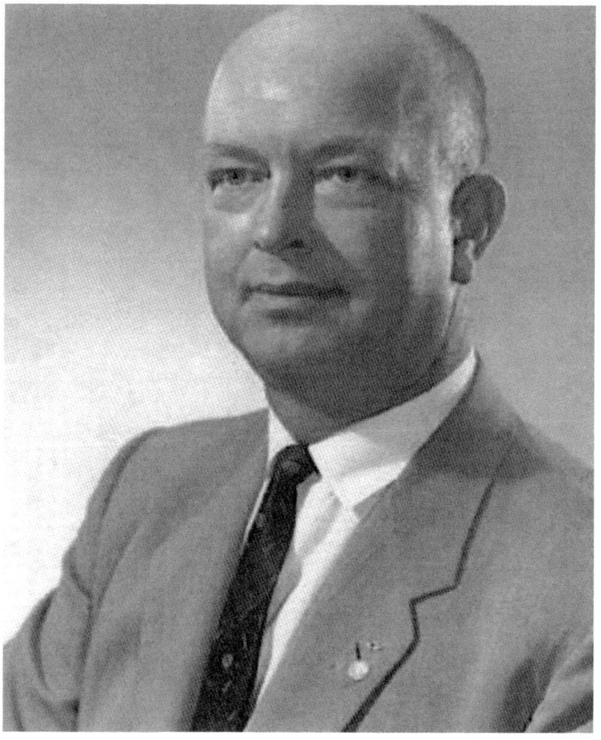

Raymond McClard is pictured here at the height of his business and political power. McClard had a penchant for politics, fueled by the charm of his personality and a natural fondness for people. He never lost an election. According to his brother, H. A. McClard, "Raymond never forgot a name and was friendly to everyone he met . . . He treated everyone with total respect." (Courtesy of Carolyn McClard Honchell.)

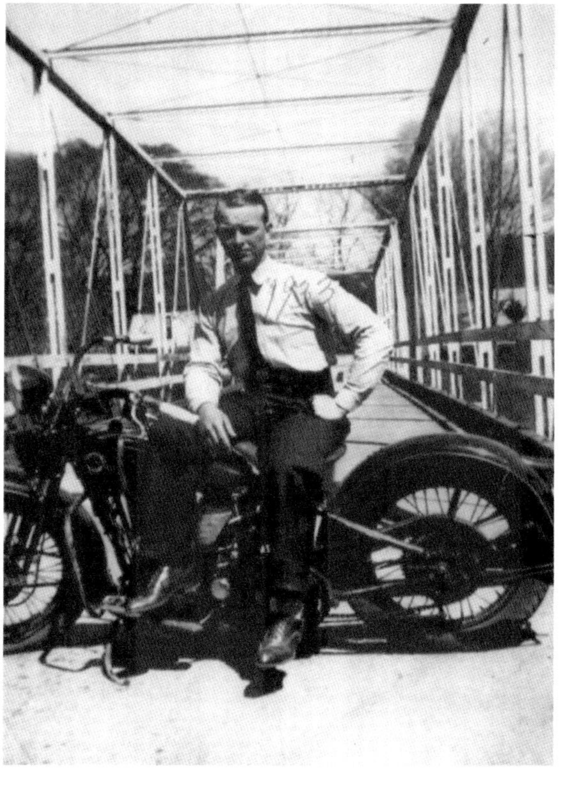

This photograph shows Raymond McClard in 1933 at age 15 sitting on his motorcycle. McClard liked cars but had a lifelong love affair with motorcycles, which ultimately led to his ownership of the first Harley Davidson motorcycle franchise in Bowling Green, Kentucky. (Courtesy of Carolyn McClard Honchell.)

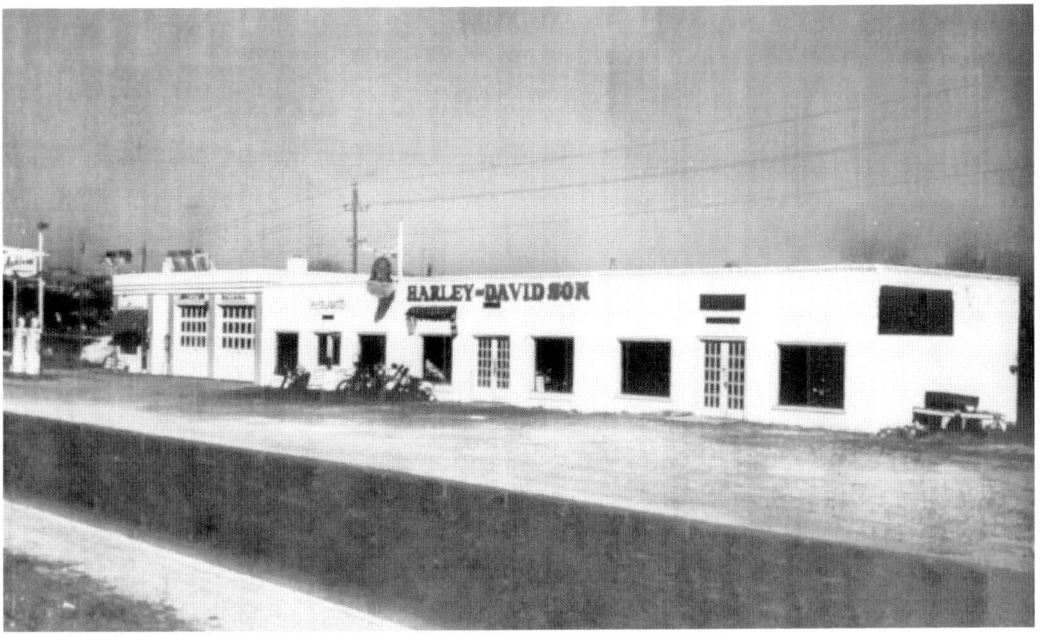

McClard's Harley Davidson motorcycle shop in 1950 was located in Bowling Green, Kentucky, on the Russellville Road. Raymond McClard constructed the building himself and, with his wife, Gladys, operated an Ashland service station, a bottle-gas business, and the motorcycle shop at this site. Gladys proved to have the business acumen to take over and operate the businesses. This enabled Raymond to do what he loved and was most adept at, making his foray into local politics and racing. (Courtesy of Carolyn McClard Honchell.)

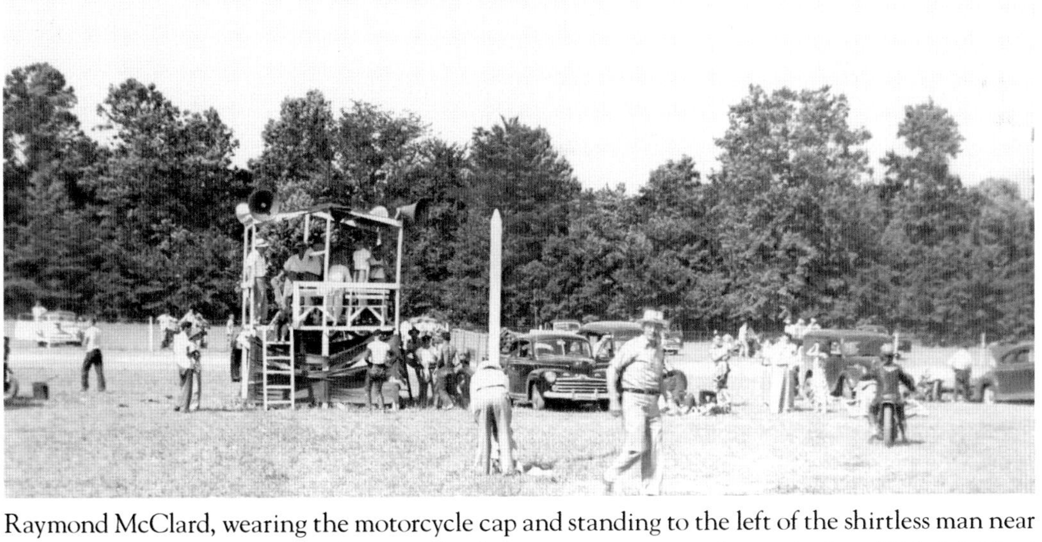

Raymond McClard, wearing the motorcycle cap and standing to the left of the shirtless man near the judges' stand, is in charge of making final preparations on race day in the late 1940s. McClard was a master at this type of work. The man standing in the far right of the judges' stand is testing the loudspeaker. (Courtesy of David Garvin.)

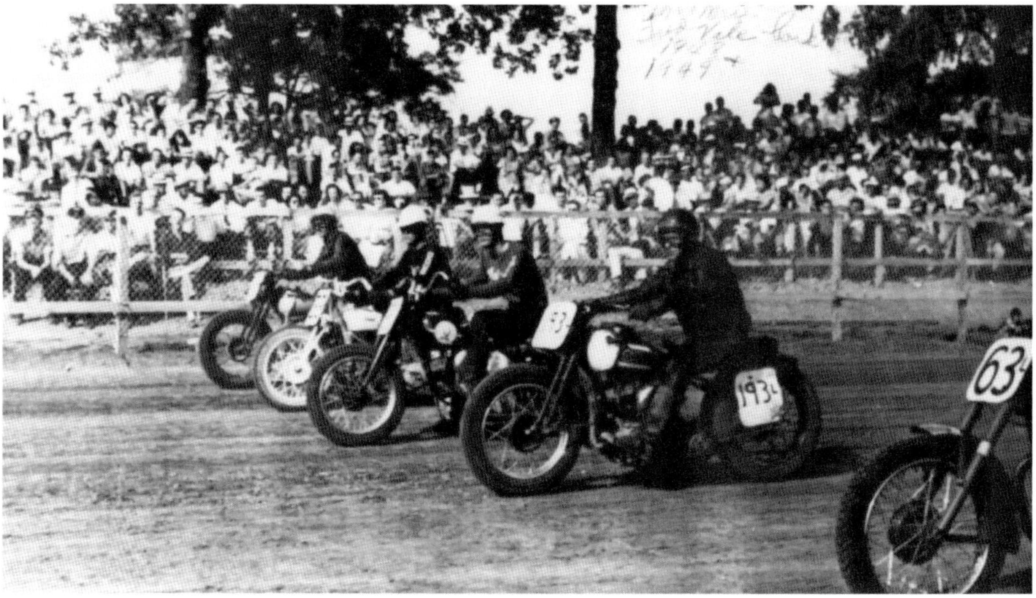

Motorcycle racing becomes a reality at Beech Bend Park in the late 1940s. In the photograph above, these young racers stare at the flagman as they are "on the mark." Publicity for the early races was spread throughout Bowling Green by word of mouth and flyers posted around the town. Charles Garvin and Raymond McClard used their contacts and resources to promote the events, and very little money was spent on promotion or prizes. Below, a race official gives instructions while No. 48 and No. 12 share a nervous laugh prior to the green flag. (Both, courtesy of Carolyn McClard Honchell and David Garvin.)

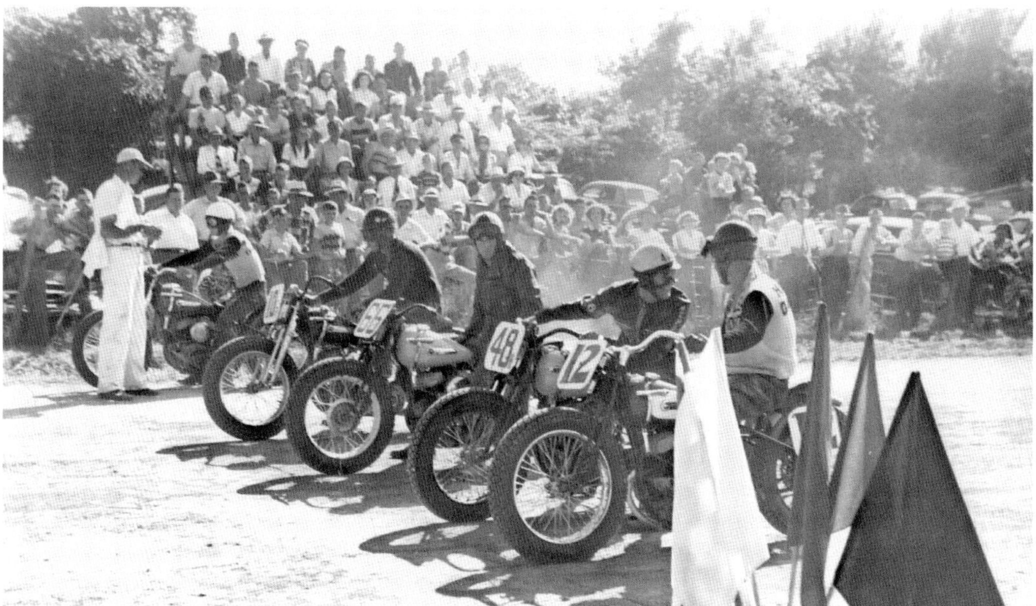

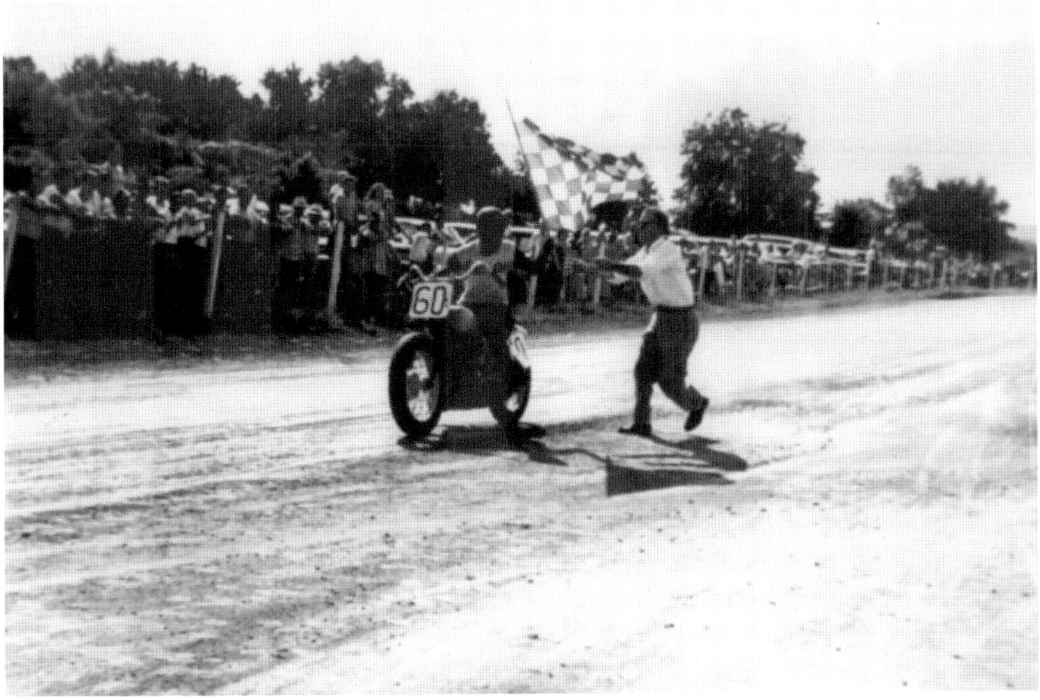

During the period of motorcycle racing at Beech Bend Park (1946–1951), there was very little money for the racers. The men who participated did so for the love of the competition, bragging rights, and the privilege of taking the victory lap with the checkered flag in front of their fans and friends. (Both, courtesy of Carolyn McClard Honchell and David Garvin.)

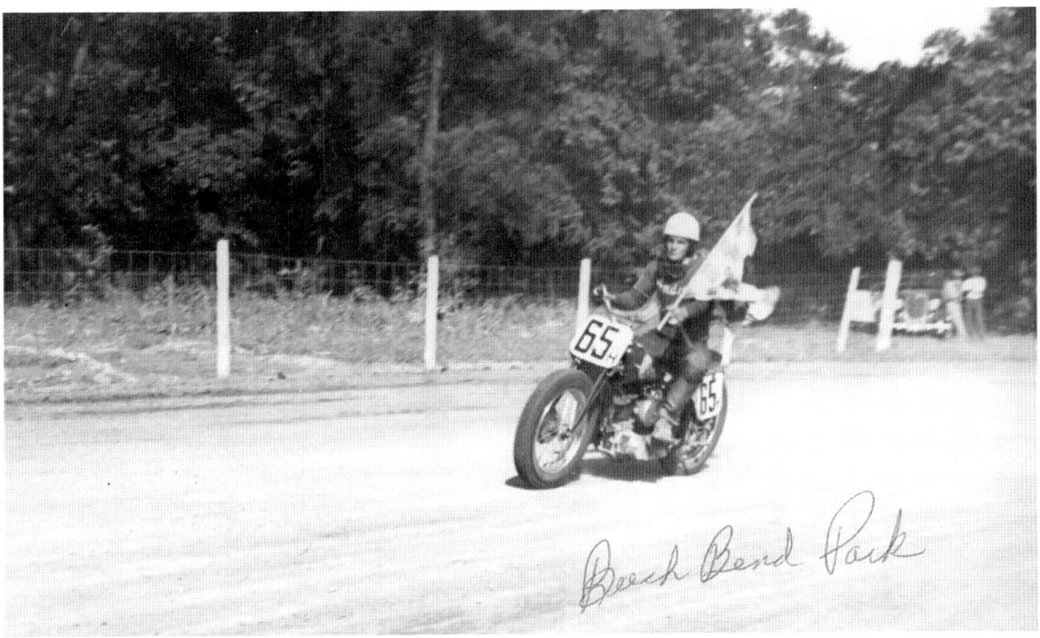

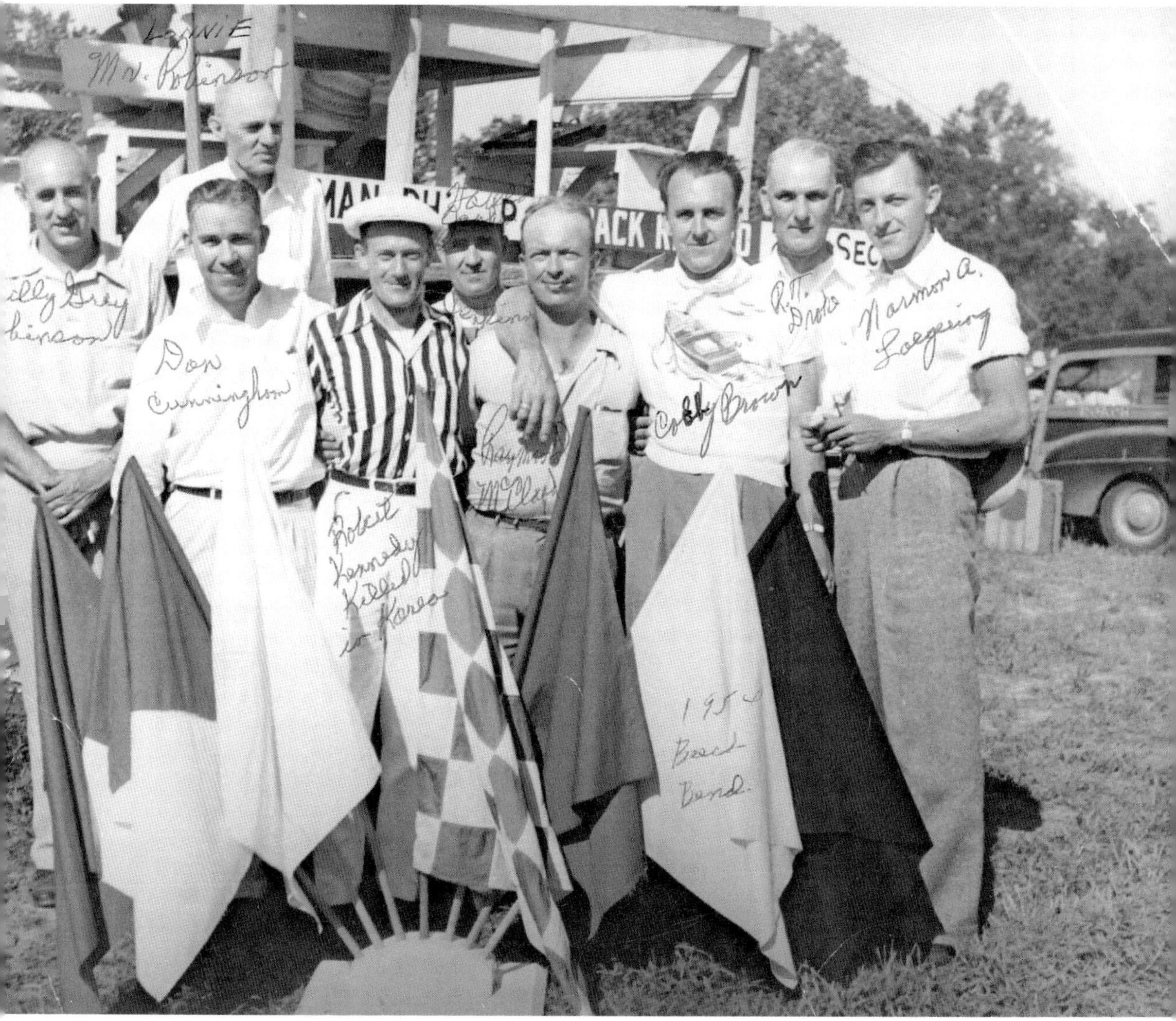

This photograph appeared in the *Daily News* in 1954. Carolyn McClard Honchell says that her family life revolved around motorcycles and racing. The family attended numerous dealer conventions in Kentucky and Indiana, and sometimes as far away as Illinois and Wisconsin. The dealers were all friends, and they visited and helped each other in promotion of motorcycle races and other events. (Both, courtesy of David Garvin and Carolyn McClard Honchell.)

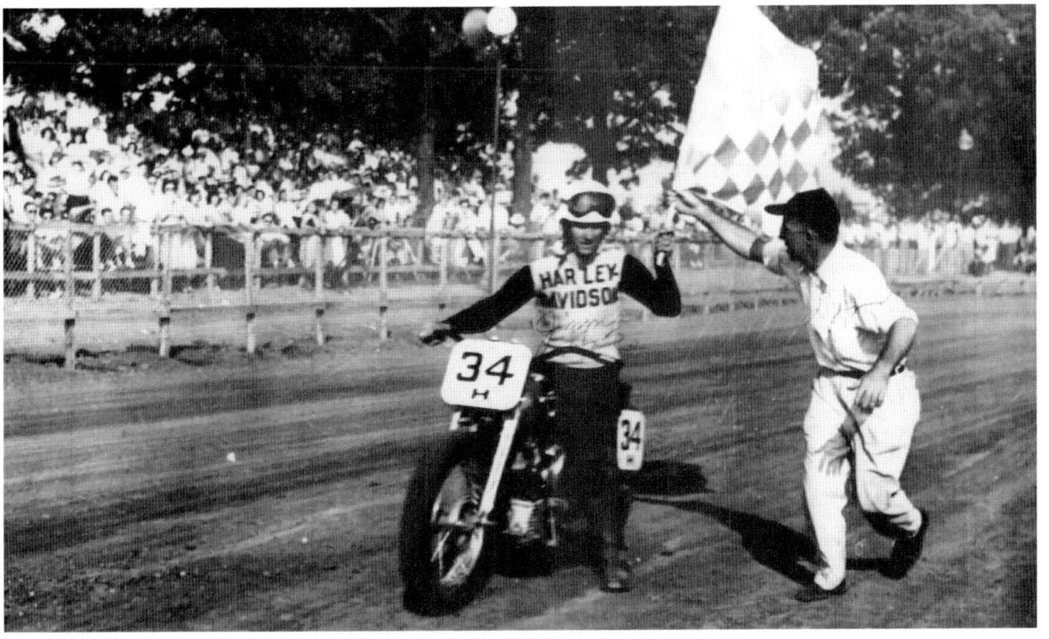

After winning a race at Beech Bend Park in 1949, Jimmy Hole, No. 34, takes the checkered flag from Dan Cunningham, the flagman and a Harley Davidson motorcycle dealer from Louisville, Kentucky. In the picture below, another winner is returning the checkered flag at Beech Bend Park. Carolyn McClard Honchell, the daughter of Raymond McClard, remembers the excitement in the air on race days. She recalls one event in which motorcycle riders rode beneath a platform under which hot dogs hung. The object was for the rider to take a bite of a hot dog while zipping under the platform. (Both, courtesy of Carolyn McClard Honchell.)

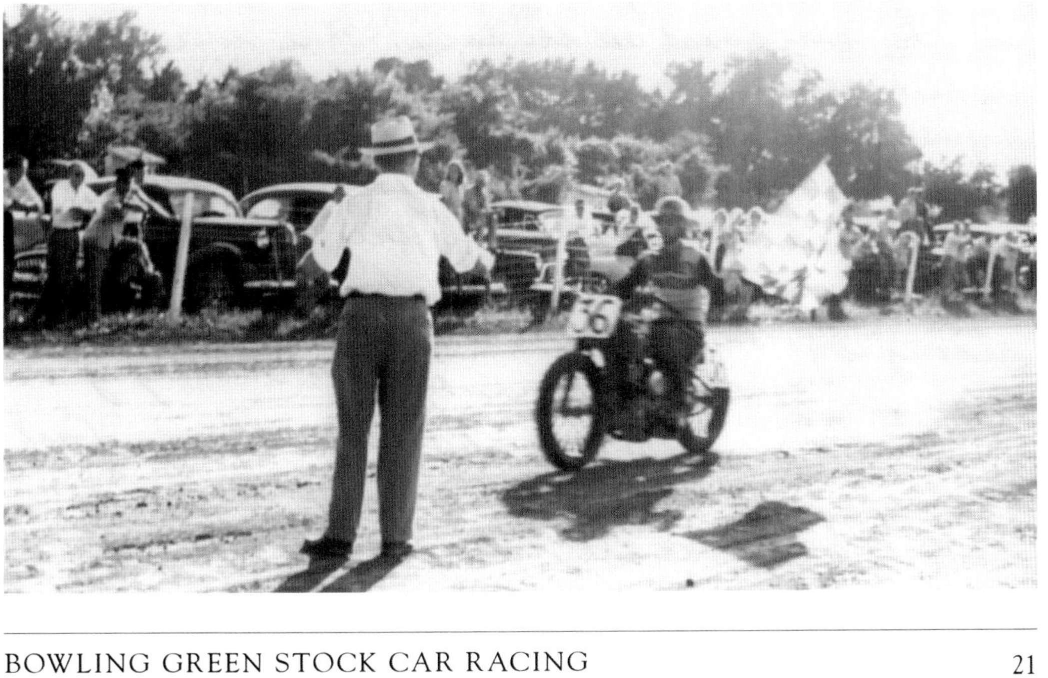

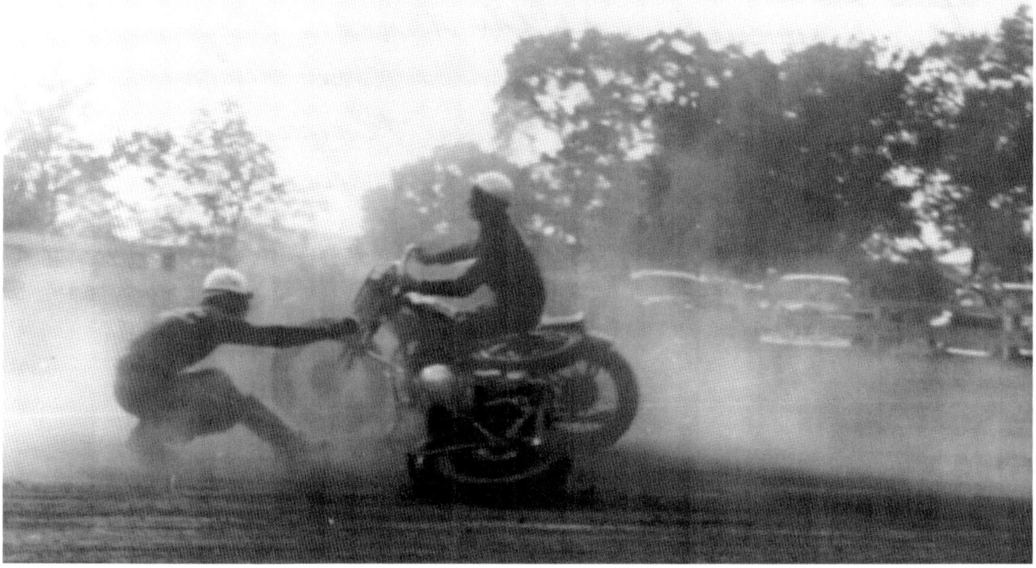

Motorcycle racing is a dangerous sport, and one gets some sense of that in this Beech Bend Park photograph that shows one motorcycle down as another rider roars past. The downed rider is trying to get his bike out of the way. One gets the rider's sense of desperation as he struggles with his bike. (Courtesy of Carolyn McClard Honchell.)

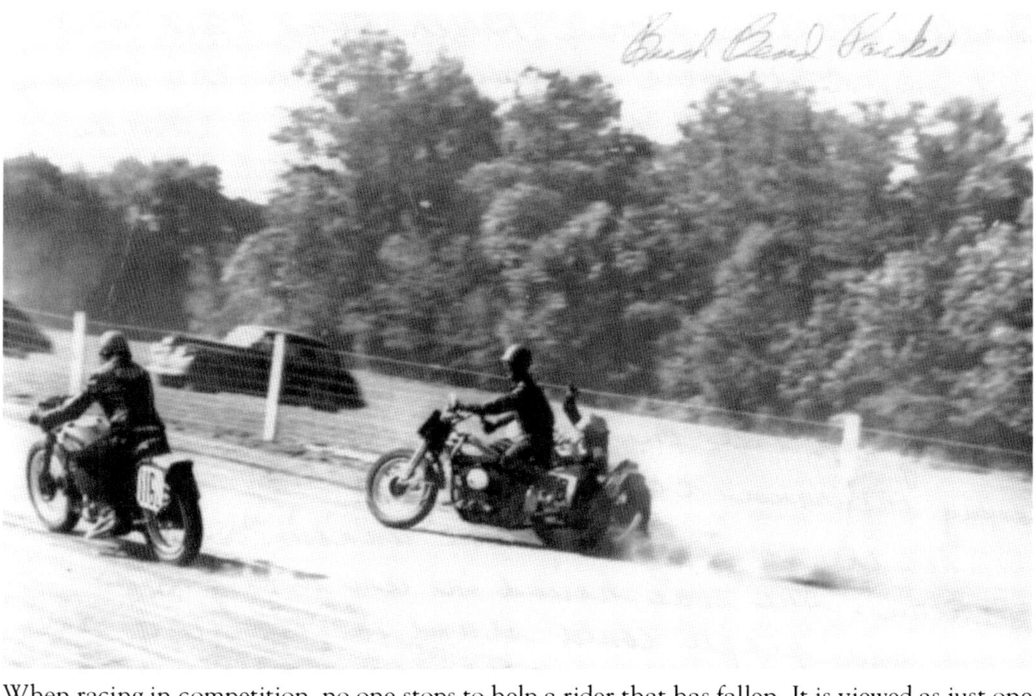

When racing in competition, no one stops to help a rider that has fallen. It is viewed as just one less competitor on the track. At the speed the two motorcycle racers are going, they barely notice the downed rider. (Courtesy of Carolyn McClard Honchell.)

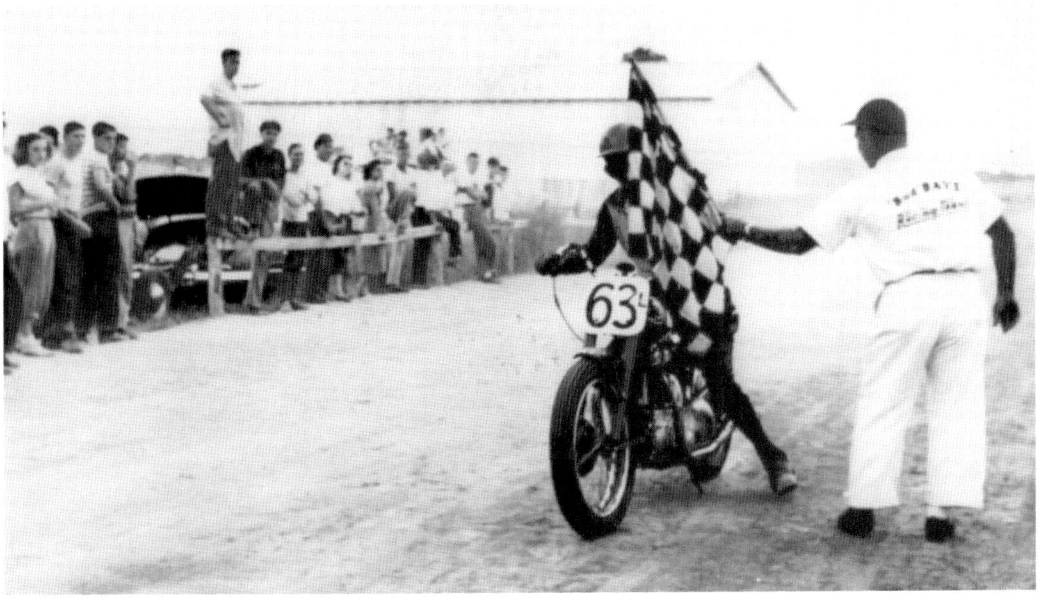

The Beech Bend Park motorcycle racers competed at other tracks in the general vicinity of Bowling Green. This race was a big "Bud Days" event in Owensboro, Kentucky. Owensboro was also one of the early entrants into stock car racing and sent several experienced stock car drivers to Bowling Green in 1951. (Courtesy of Carolyn McClard Honchell.)

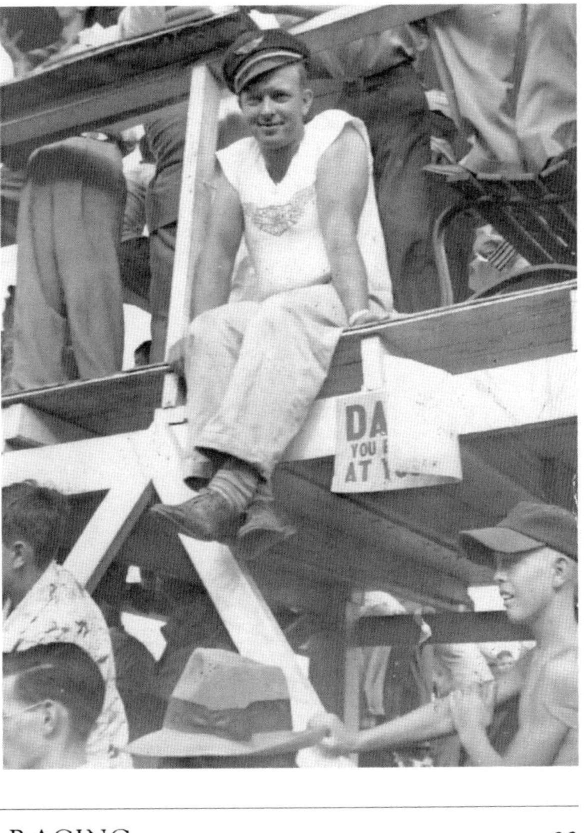

Raymond McClard, Bowling Green's Harley Davidson dealer, dressed in traditional motorcycle gear of the 1940s. McClard was a man who enjoyed life, and the jaunty tilt of the cap and the expression on his face in this photograph seem to radiate joy and contentment. (Courtesy of David Garvin.)

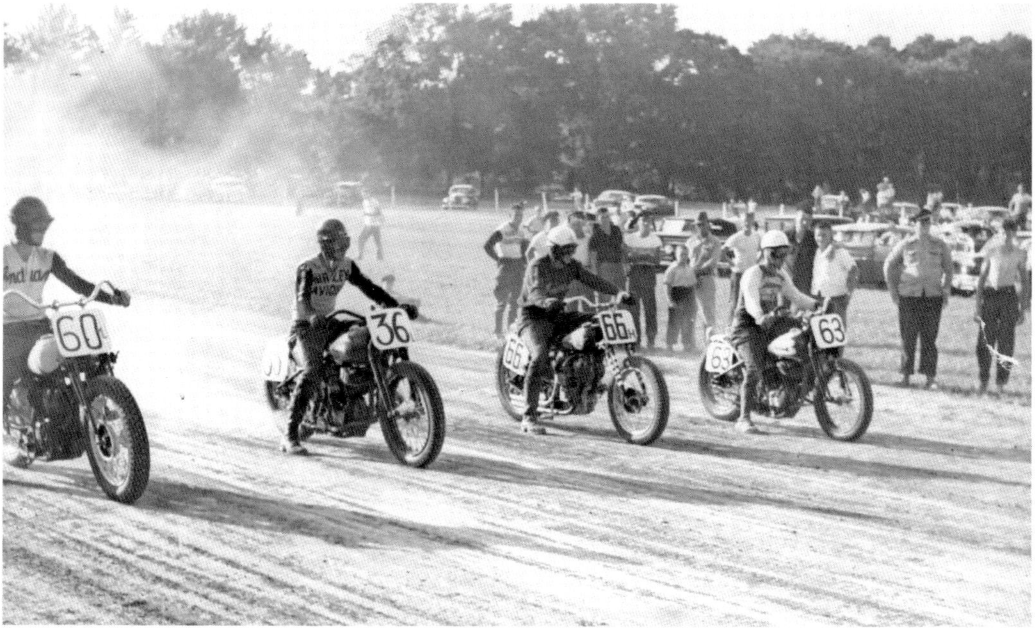

The racers are lined up with one foot on the ground awaiting the signal to begin the race. No. 60 represents Indian motorcycles, and No. 36 represents Harley Davidson. Notice the fans lined up at the edge of the racetrack, which has no barriers. (Courtesy of David Garvin.)

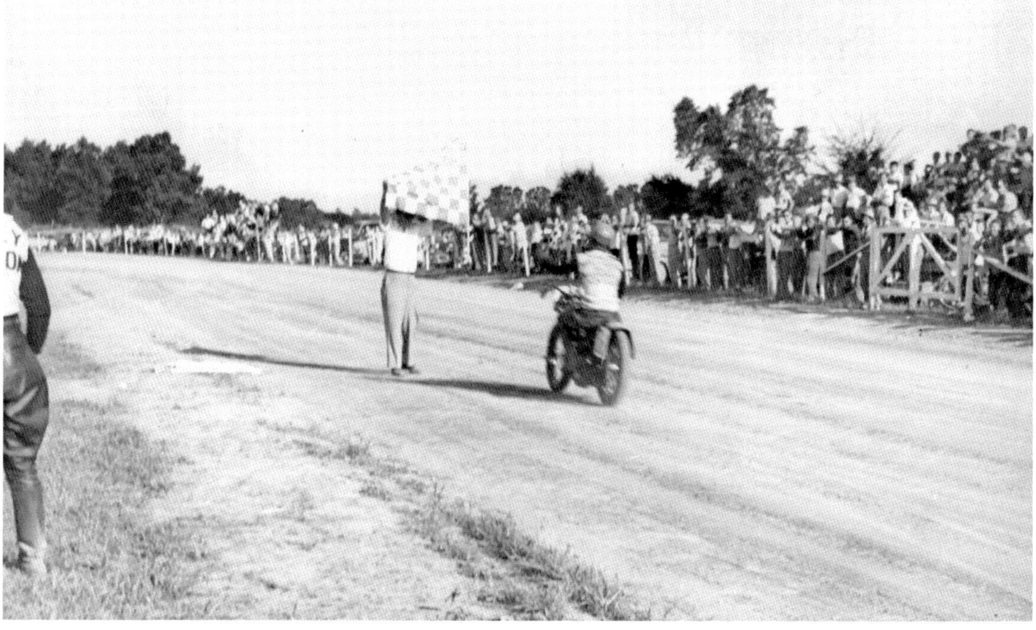

This racer is coming by for the checkered flag. Notice the rider at the far left of the photograph wearing early-day leather racing pants while on the right an extraordinary crowd of fans is lined up along the fence. (Courtesy of David Garvin.)

2

"There Are Only Three Real Sports"

Automobiles are wonderful—and dangerous. In the year 2004, there were 42,636 deaths from automobile accidents in the United States. In addition, over four million people required emergency room treatment. This is not a phenomenon of recent years; auto deaths and accidents accelerated throughout the 20th century, particularly since World War II, with the growth of America's love affair with automobiles. The 21st century promises more of the same.

These statistics, however, beg the question: why do men and women of apparent sound mind strap themselves into large, heavy projectiles, powered by high-performance engines, and race 20 cars at a time around a short, one-third-mile dirt track for a prize of a few dollars and a plastic trophy? It sounds foolhardy; however, these people do take precautions. They wear crash helmets and fireproof suits, shoes, and gloves to protect them from exploding tanks of high octane racing fuel; the cars contain roll cages; and the drivers are strapped in tight with a five-point quick release shoulder harness. Who are these people, and what are they thinking?

At the beginning of stock car racing in Bowling Green in 1951, racing was for men only, and they took almost no safeguards. Primarily, a driver's gear consisted of a football helmet, a handkerchief over the nose and mouth to keep the dust out, a T-shirt, Levi's, and work shoes. The seat belt was generally something from a World War II airplane. Larry Graham rolled a car only once in his career but was smart enough to carry a pocket knife so he was able to saw his way out of the car as he was hanging upside down. As Ernest Hemingway reputedly said, "There are only three real sports: boxing, bullfighting, and racing. Everything else is just a game."

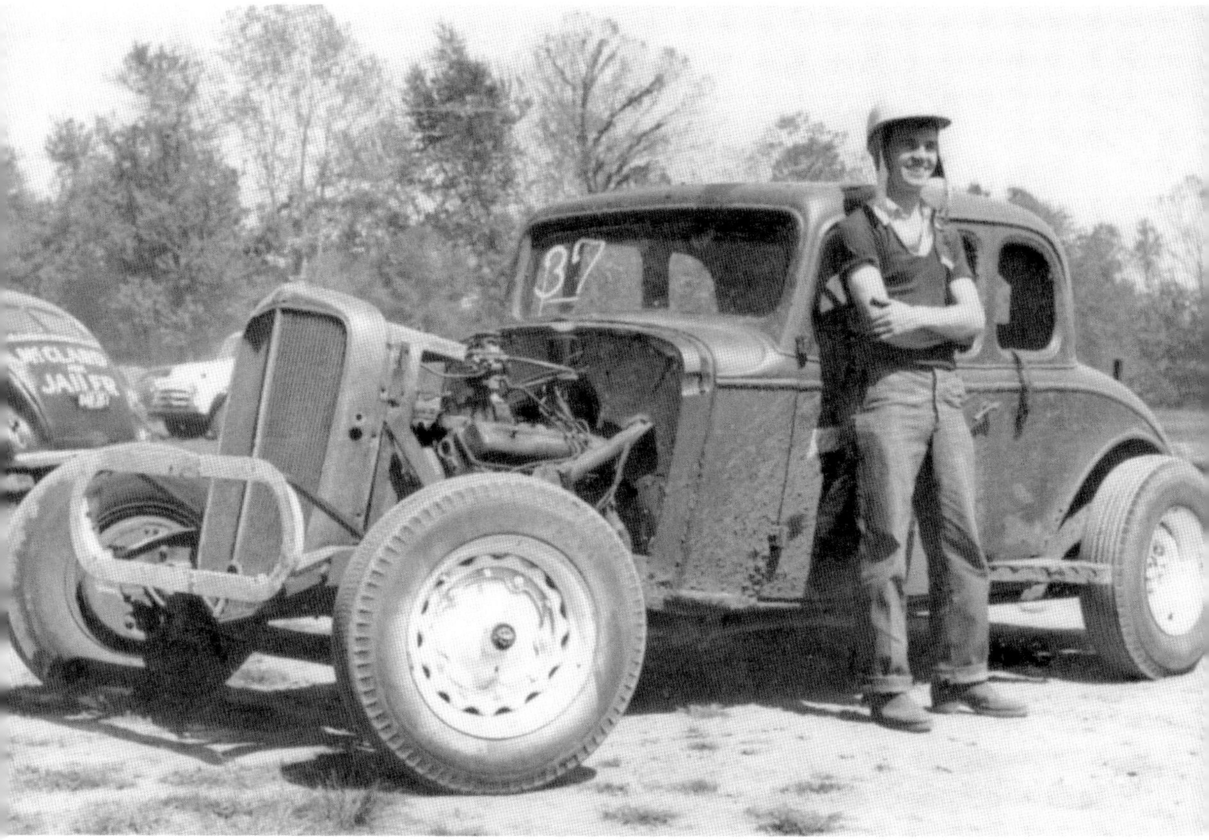

Elmo Guy was racing motorcycles from an early age and, as he said in an interview on March 18, 2004, the transition to stock car racing was easy for him. Ernie Wright, owner of Wright's Machine Shop in Bowling Green, approached Raymond McClard, owner of the Harley Davidson dealership, for a list of young motorcycle riders who might be interested in stock car racing. Elmo Guy was one of several men who were invited to test drive Wright's 1932 Chevrolet stock car. Guy did not even know how to drive a car. He was strictly a motorcycle man but was intrigued by the chance to race a stock car. The group of men met at the Beech Bend Park track, and Wright put them through a few test laps. Elmo's first reaction to the car was the feeling of stability created from having four wheels under him. It felt good! It felt safe! So he gave the car full throttle, and Ernie Wright had a driver for the No. 7-11 stock car. (Courtesy of Yvonne Guy.)

Wayne Guy (left) and Ray Mercer take a break from car building to admire their work. Building a race car required removing every comfort the manufacturer had built in. All excess weight was removed to allow for the extra weight of the roll cage and protective metal bars. The car builders used secret gear ratios to maximize both speed and power. If they raced on a different size track, they had to come up with another secret ratio. (Courtesy of Yvonne Guy.)

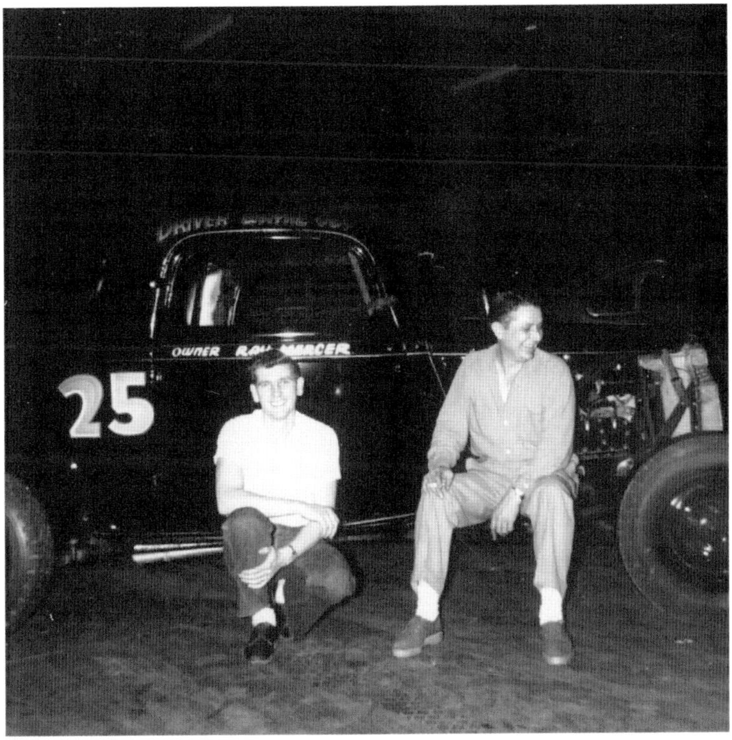

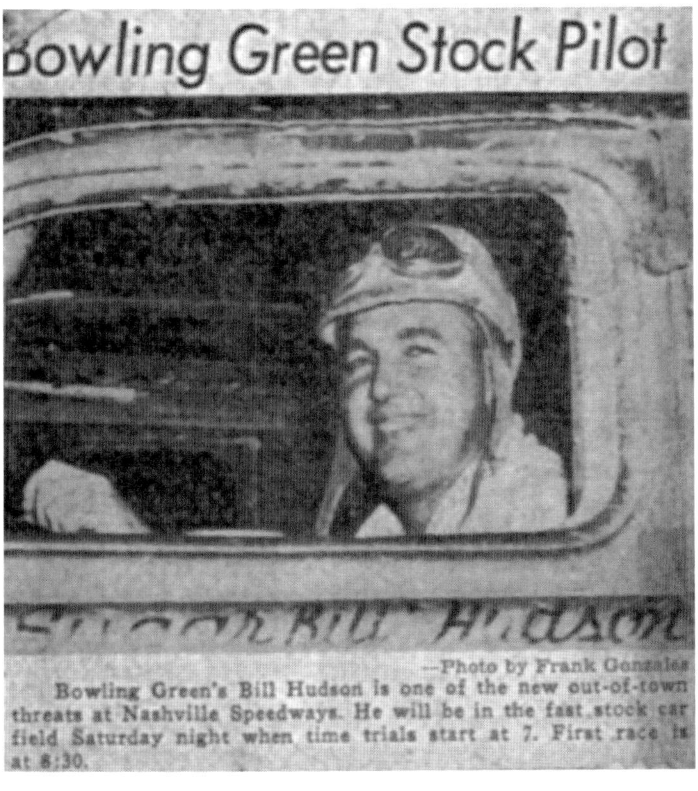

Bowling Green Stock Pilot

"Sugar Bill" Hudson

—Photo by Frank Gonzales

Bowling Green's Bill Hudson is one of the new out-of-town threats at Nashville Speedways. He will be in the fast stock car field Saturday night when time trials start at 7. First race is at 8:30.

This photograph of Billy Hudson of Bowling Green was featured in a Nashville newspaper, where he was described as one of the out-of-town threats at Nashville Speedway. Hudson, along with Wayne and Elmo Guy, planted the seed with Charles Garvin for motorcycle racing at Beech Bend Park in the mid-1940s. Note that Hudson had his nickname "Sugar Bill" painted on the car door. (Courtesy of Russ Thompson.)

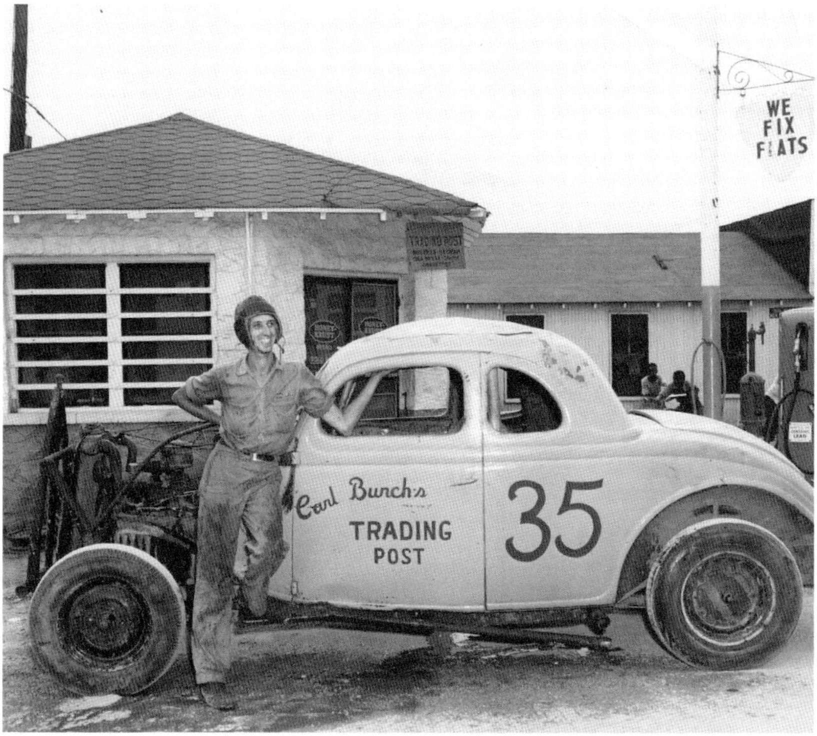

Carl Burch, owner and driver, is shown with his beloved 1935 Ford stock car. Burch was a very likable man and popular with the other drivers. Although the car did not have the horsepower to win, his fellow drivers were always pulling for him to win. (Courtesy of Marshall Love Jr.)

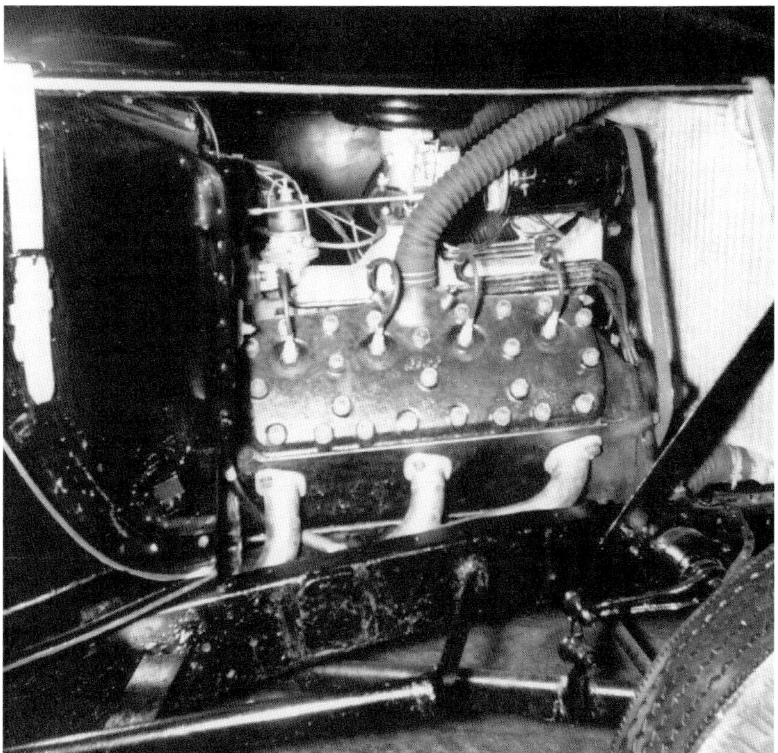

This is the 1946 Ford 239 cubic-inch flathead V-8 engine in Ray Mercer's No. 25 stock car. Mercer modified the engine with a 4-inch stroke, bored it to 3 7/16 inches, and added a full racing cam. This was considered a hot stock car in 1951. Mercer and Guy had no secrets when it came to their engine; they could win races regardless of who knew what about their car. (Courtesy of Yvonne Guy.)

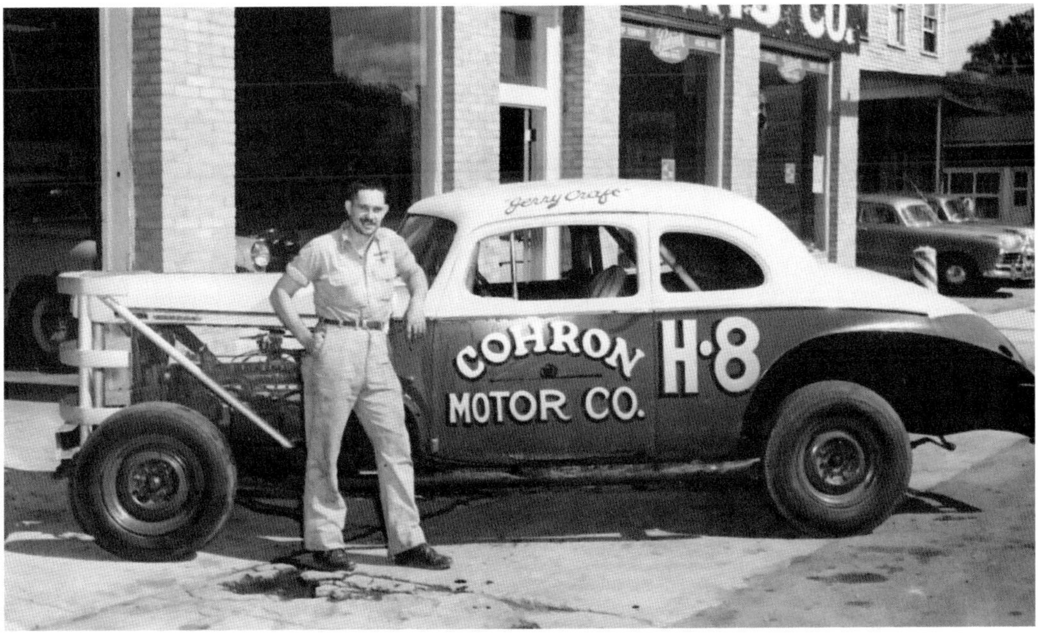

This is Cohron Motor Company's 1951 entry at Beech Bend Park. The man alongside the car is unidentified, although it may be Jerry Craft, the driver. (Courtesy of Marshall Love Jr.)

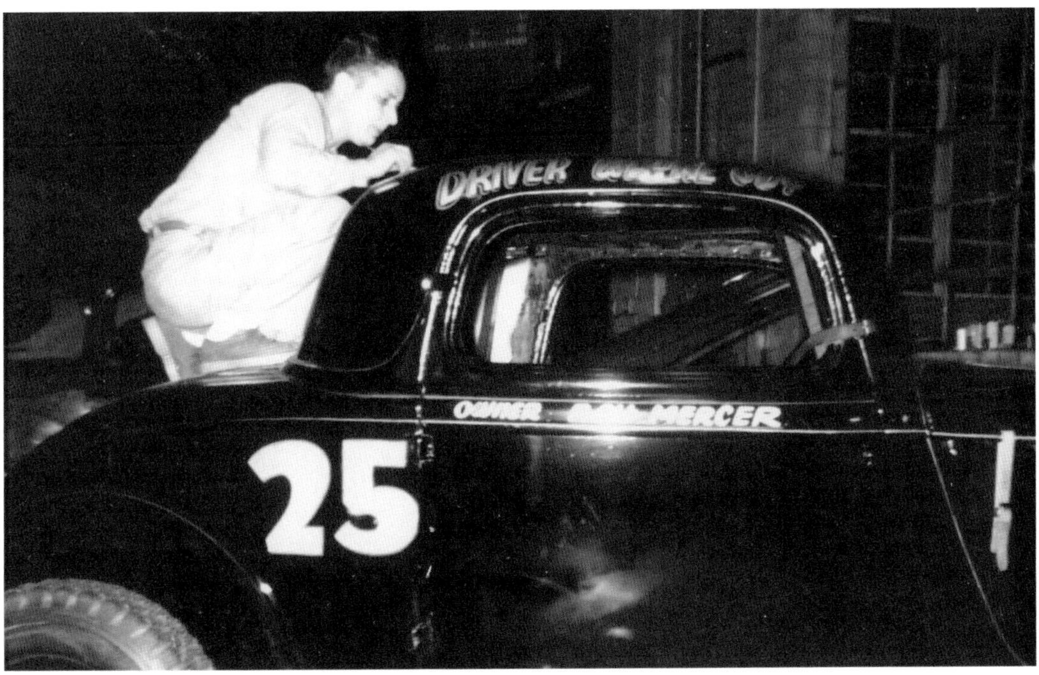

Ray Mercer, owner of No. 25, a 1934 Ford, puts the final touches on the car. According to Wayne Guy, the driver, Mercer was constantly experimenting with the car to improve its power and performance, sometimes with less than stellar results. Even though Guy might tell him the car was perfect, Mercer could not resist just one more adjustment. (Courtesy of Yvonne Guy.)

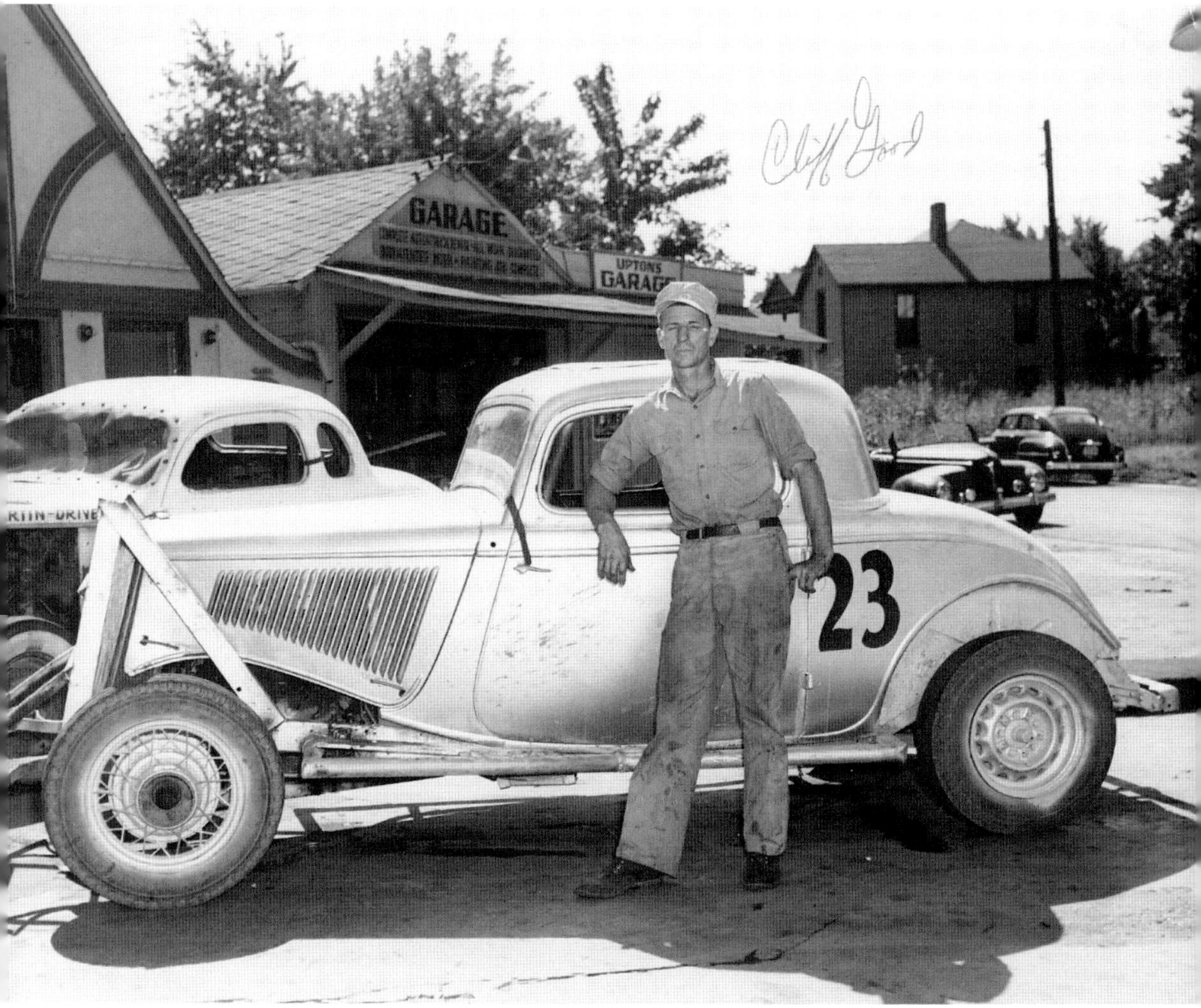

This photograph of Cliff Goad was taken in front of Upton's Garage at the corner of Sixth and College Streets in Bowling Green. At age 39, Goad was the oldest stock car driver at Beech Bend Park in 1951, so naturally the other drivers nicknamed him "Pappy." Most of the drivers were in their 20s with Joe Harrod the youngest at age 16. (Courtesy of Marshall Love Jr.)

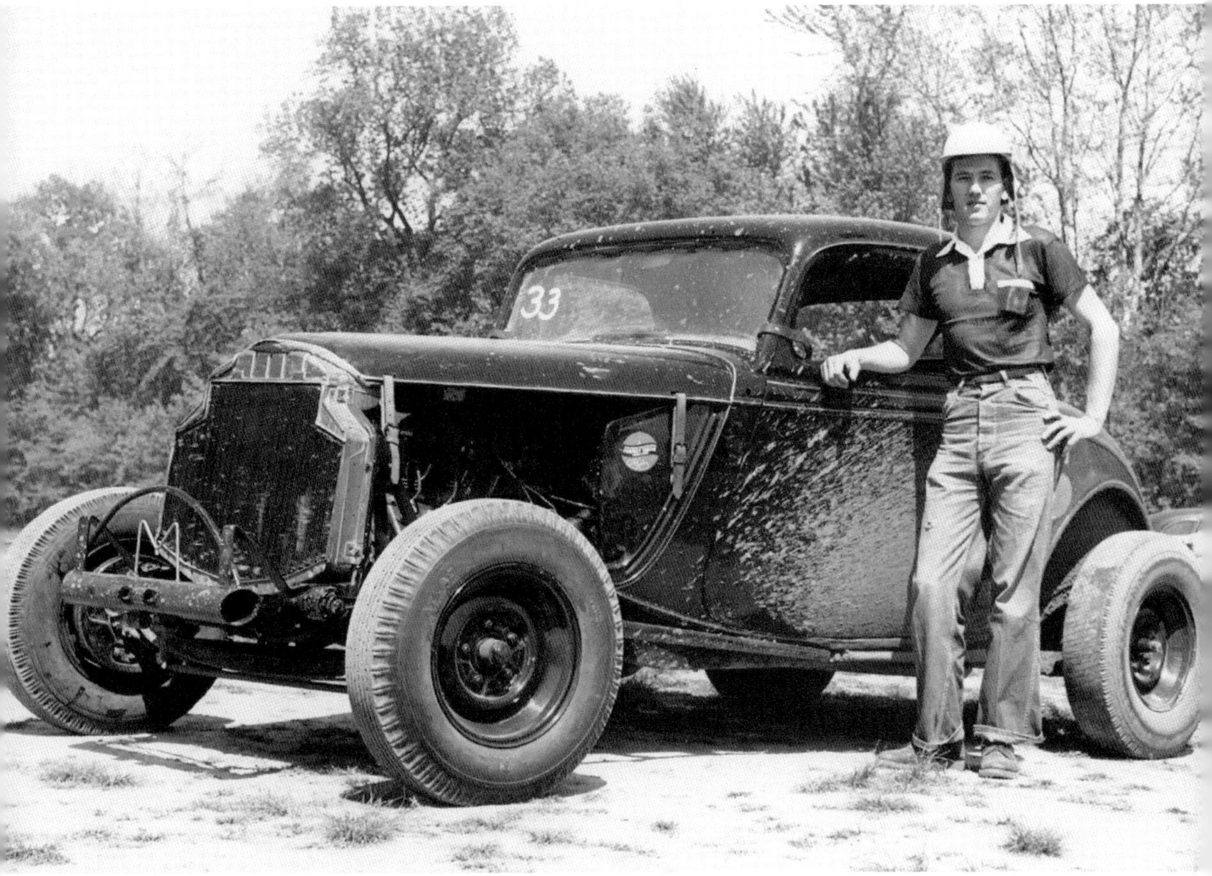

Wayne Guy stands alongside his 1934 Ford stock car. Wayne, along with his older brother, Elmo, grew up on motorcycles and speed, so the transition to stock car racing was almost natural. Guy got started in stock car racing when his coworker, Ray Mercer, the service manager at Wallace Motor Company in Bowling Green, approached him about driving his stock car. Guy and Mercer's deal was that Mercer would maintain the car. All the winnings would go into a bank account, out of which all expenses would be paid, and any surplus would be split evenly at the end of the season. As Wayne recalls, heat races paid $20 to win and the feature race paid $50. The first race was at Rich Pond, Kentucky, and Yvonne Guy, Wayne's wife, was under the impression that Wayne was a member of the pit crew for Ray Mercer until the track announcer reported, "Driving No. 25 today will be Wayne Guy." Guy's most vivid memories are of beating his brother, Elmo, because Elmo was the fiercest competitor in Bowling Green. (Courtesy of Yvonne Guy.)

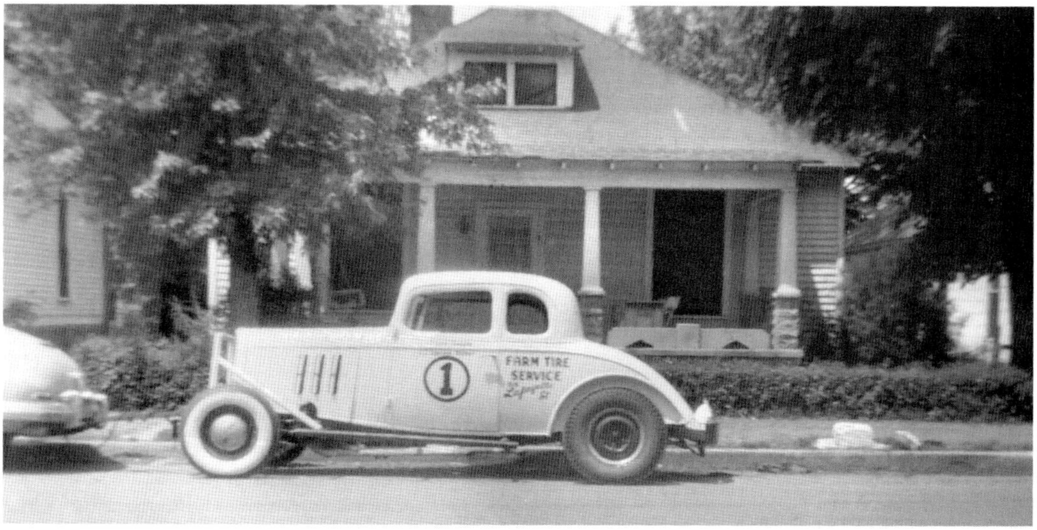

This stock car was owned and driven by Charles T. Upton Jr. of Nashville, Tennessee. Charles was the nephew of Lattney "Latt" Upton, owner of the Upton's Garage No. 22. Charles introduced Latt to stock cars when he took him to a race in Owensboro, Kentucky, in early 1951. The car is parked in front of the house of Mattie Porter, a neighbor to Lattney Upton, who lived at 605 Chestnut Street in Bowling Green. (Courtesy of Donald Upton.)

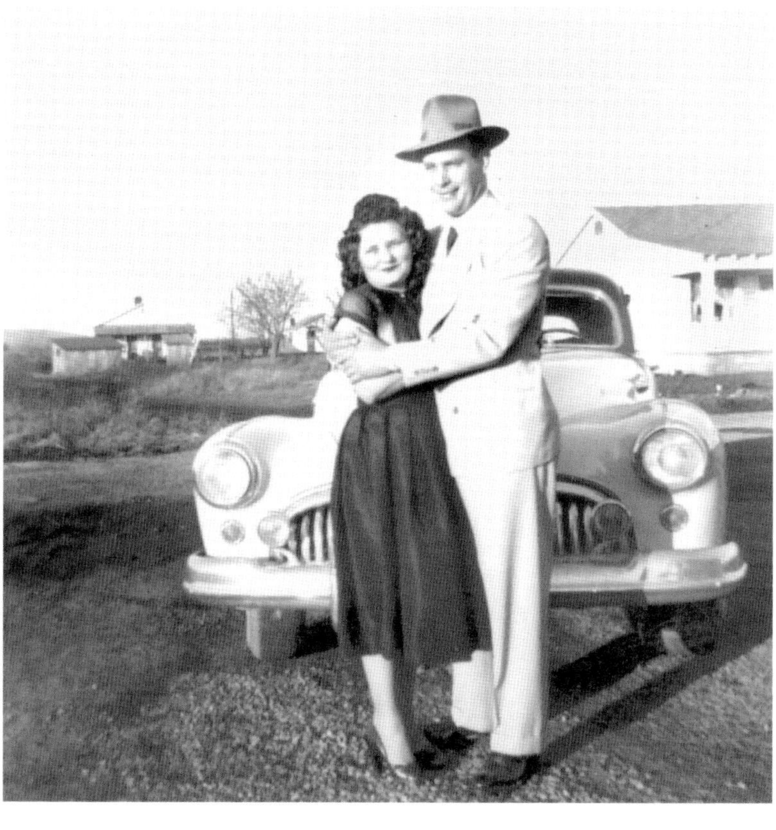

Norene and Charles Thomas Upton Jr. of Nashville, Tennessee, were frequent visitors to Bowling Green. Upton, a nephew of Lattney Upton, loved to race his stock car at Beech Bend Park. Though this photograph might suggest that the Uptons were returning from church, that is not the case. Sunday's best was commonly associated with stock car racing in 1951, at least in Bowling Green.

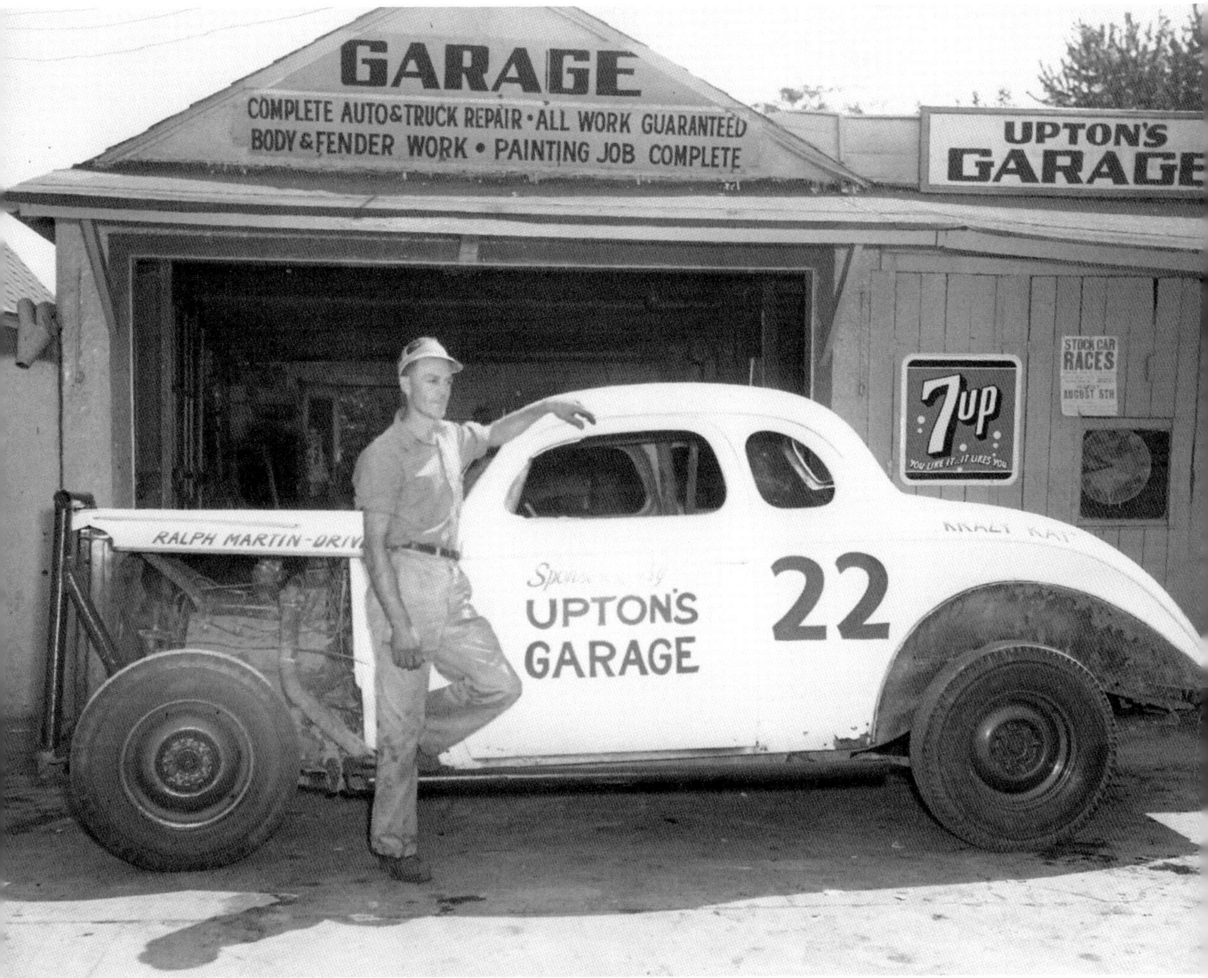

Lattney Upton was the builder of this 1938 Dodge. The notation on the hood says "Ralph Martin, Driver." Along the back fender is the name of the car, "Krazy Kat." Upton named the car after the 1940s cartoon character because so many of the other car owners and drivers thought he was crazy to field the heavy 1938 Dodge coupe with its 1936 Cadillac V-8 engine. Most of the cars were the lighter Fords with modified engines. In some ways, the other racers were correct; the car was powerful but heavy and unwieldy. Notice the poster on the wall of the garage, which advertises the first stock car race at Beech Bend Park on August 5, 1951. (Courtesy of Marshall Love Jr.)

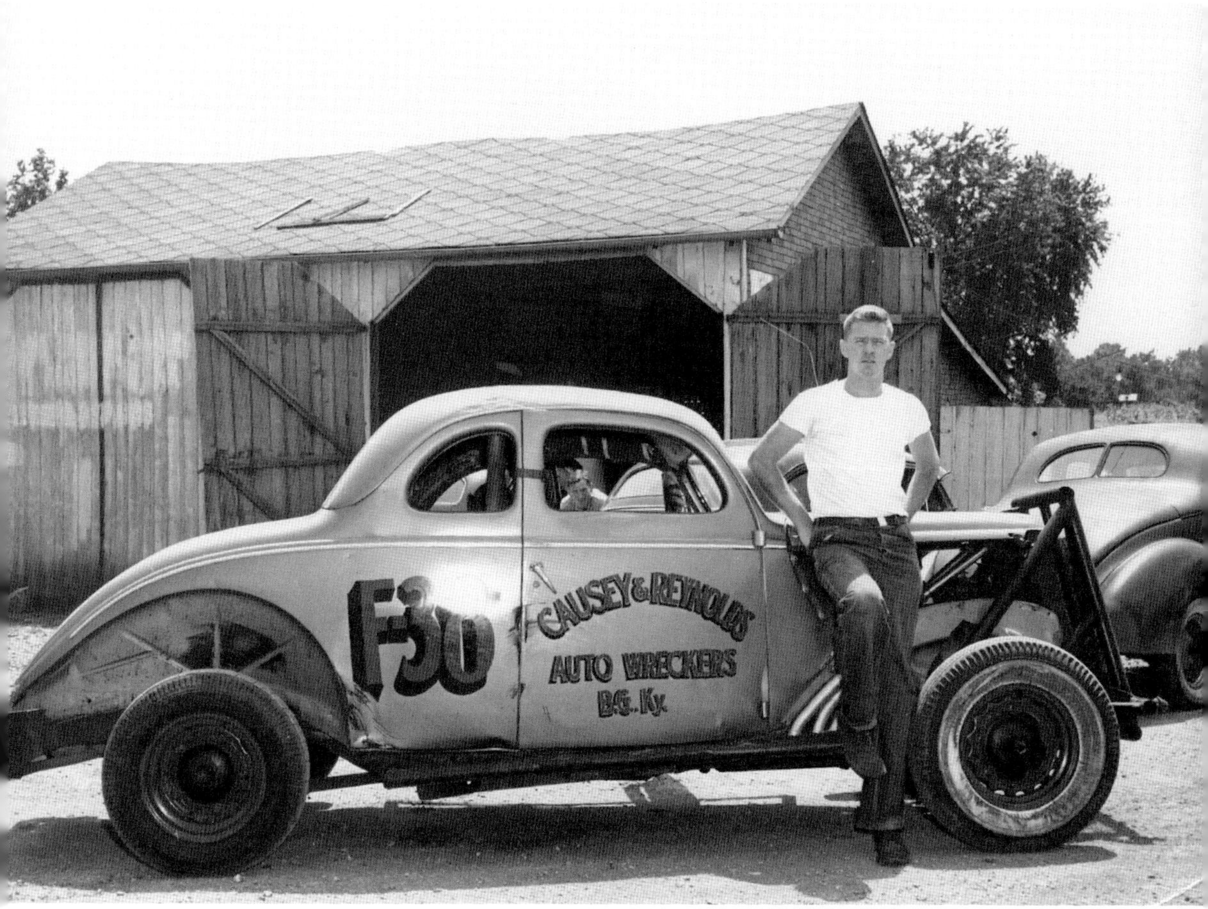

Hugh Porter Causey built the first stock car in Bowling Green, a 1936 Ford. In a 2004 interview, Causey said that Charles Garvin had noticed that the racetrack in Russellville, Kentucky, was drawing good crowds; Garvin asked Causey if he would help put together a group in Bowling Green that might be interested in racing at Beech Bend Park. Garvin later hired Causey at $25 a day to serve as pit steward at Beech Bend Park. Causey still owns the first tractor and fire truck used at the racetrack. Prior to the opening of Beech Bend Park track, Causey had hired Tommy Smith, a student at Georgia Tech University, to race his F-38. At one early out-of-town race, Smith and a Tennessee driver named "Little Smitty" banged doors on the track. When the cars rolled to a stop in the pits, Little Smitty bolted over to Smith's car, yelling at him to get out. When the 6-foot, 6-inch Smith climbed out the window and stood up, Little Smitty turned on his heel and went back to his pit.

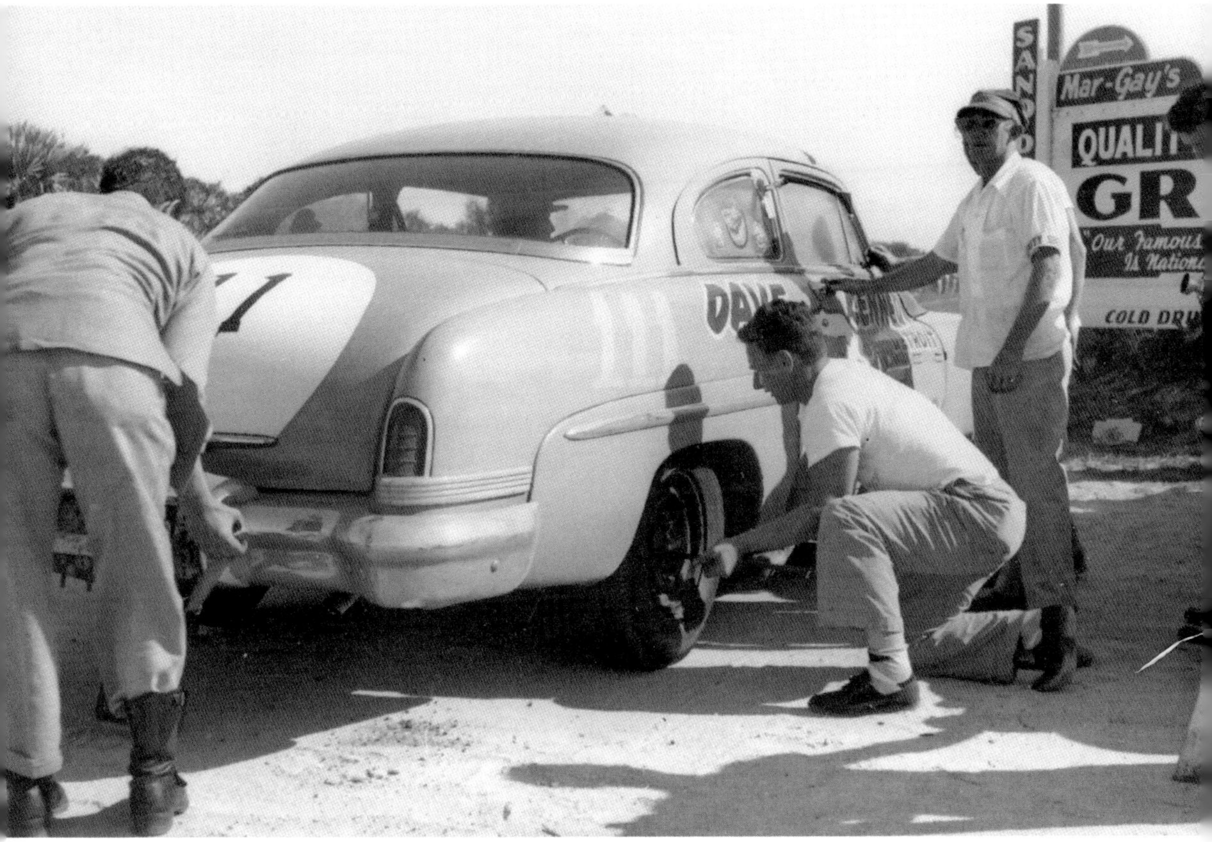

After graduating from Georgia Tech in 1952, Tommy Smith immediately went into the military during the Korean War. He was stationed in San Bernardino, California. This photograph is Smith in his 1952 Oldsmobile 88, which was sponsored by the military base service station. It is being prepared for a drag race in Pomona, California, where he set a speed record on April 4, 1954. The race story was big enough that it was published in *Hot Rod Magazine*. (Courtesy of Mary Jo Cook.)

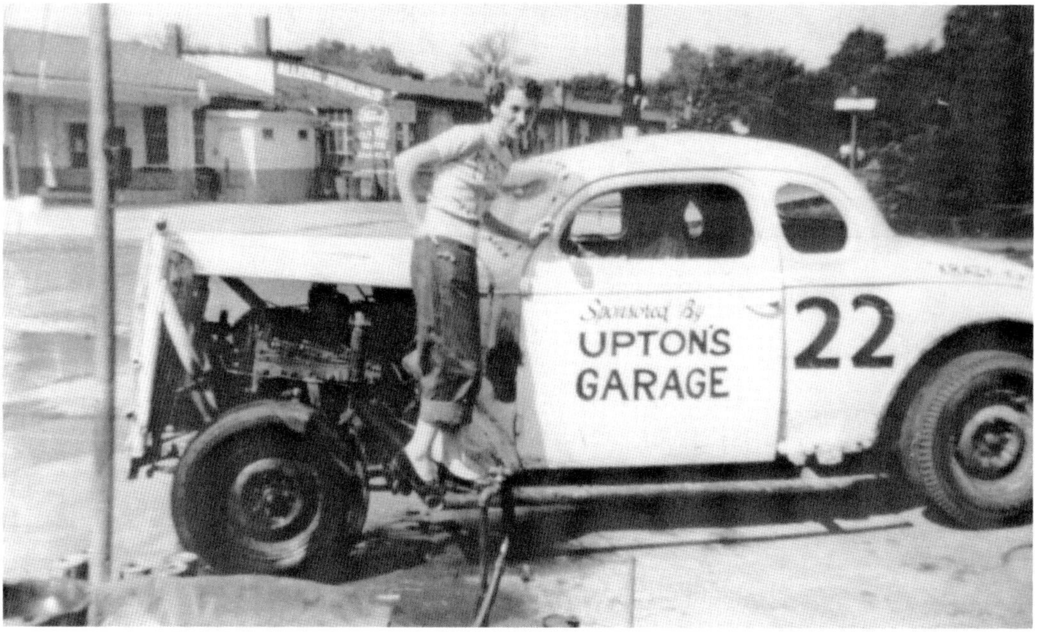

Betty Upton (top) stands on the protective railing of No. 22 in front of Upton's Garage at the corner of College and Sixth Streets. Her 10-year-old son, Larry, sits behind the wheel. Below is Lattney Upton's first entry in the 1951 season, which was sponsored by Lindsey's Gulf Service located at Fifth and State Streets in Bowling Green. Clifford Lindsey, the owner of Lindsey's Gulf Service, was Upton's brother-in-law. Sponsors were hard to come by, so car owners paid the expenses out of their own pockets or turned to friends and relatives for financial support.

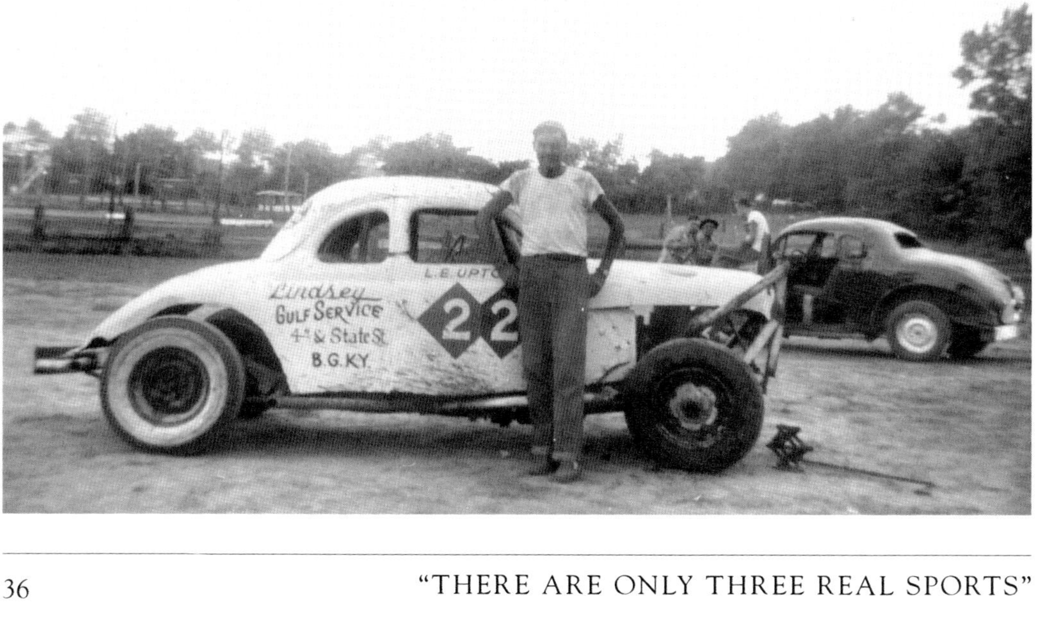

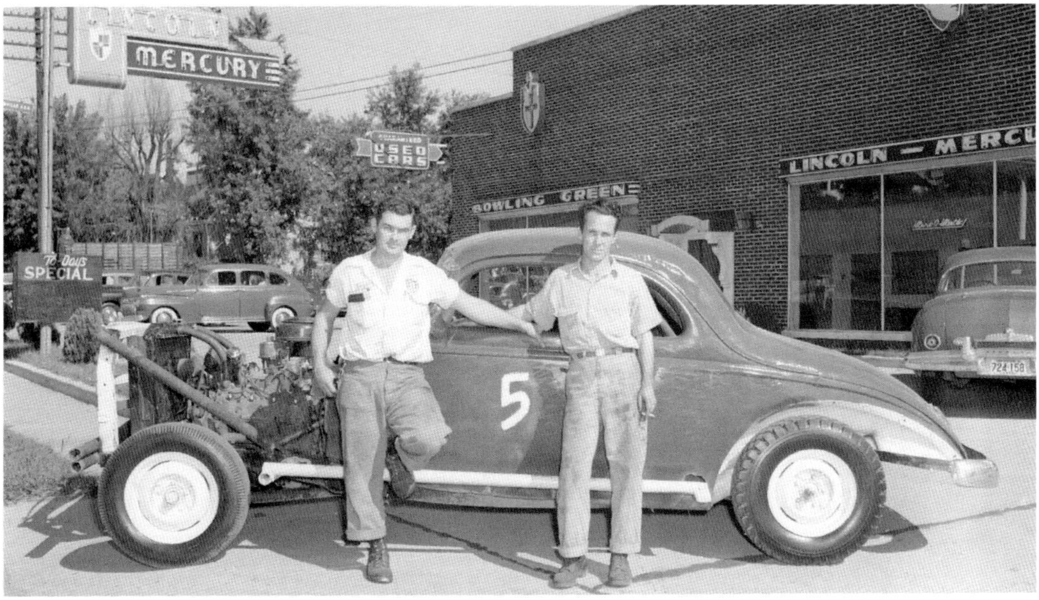

Jim Meeks (left), the driver of No. 5, stands alongside his unidentified mechanic. The car was sponsored by the Bowling Green Lincoln-Mercury dealership. Almost every automobile dealership and independent garage in Bowling Green and the surrounding area built stock cars to race at Beech Bend Park. (Courtesy of Marshall Love Jr.)

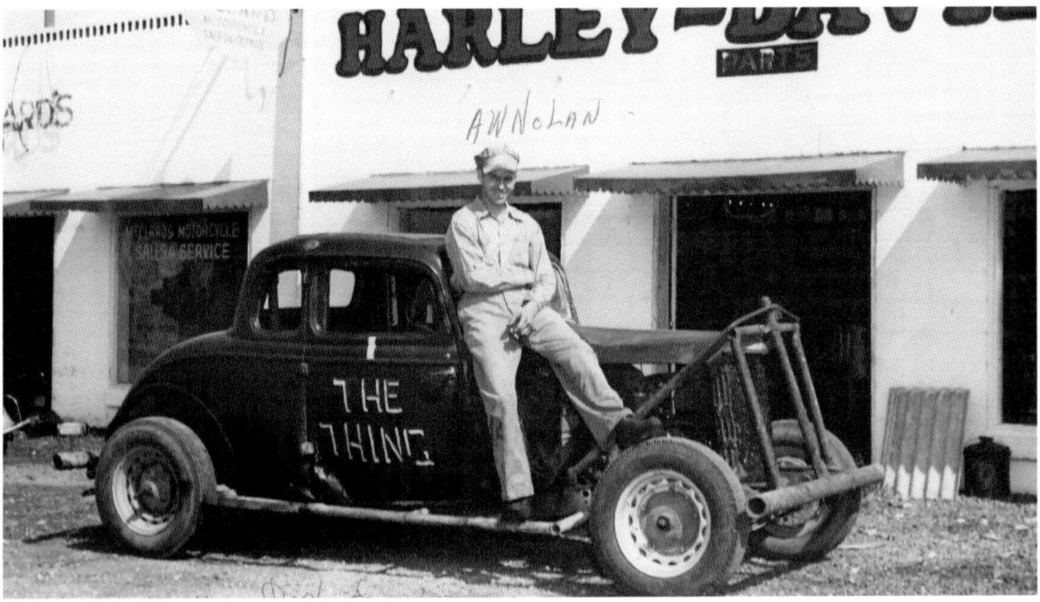

A. W. Nolan sits on the hood of "The Thing," which was owned by Raymond McClard. The car was powered by an 85-horsepower Ford "strictly stock" flathead V-8. It did not have a locked rear-end and, as a result, was hard to control. It never won a race. Strictly stock engines simply could not compete against a field of cars powered by modified engines. The early rules were that one could do anything to a race car as long as it looked like a stock car on the outside.

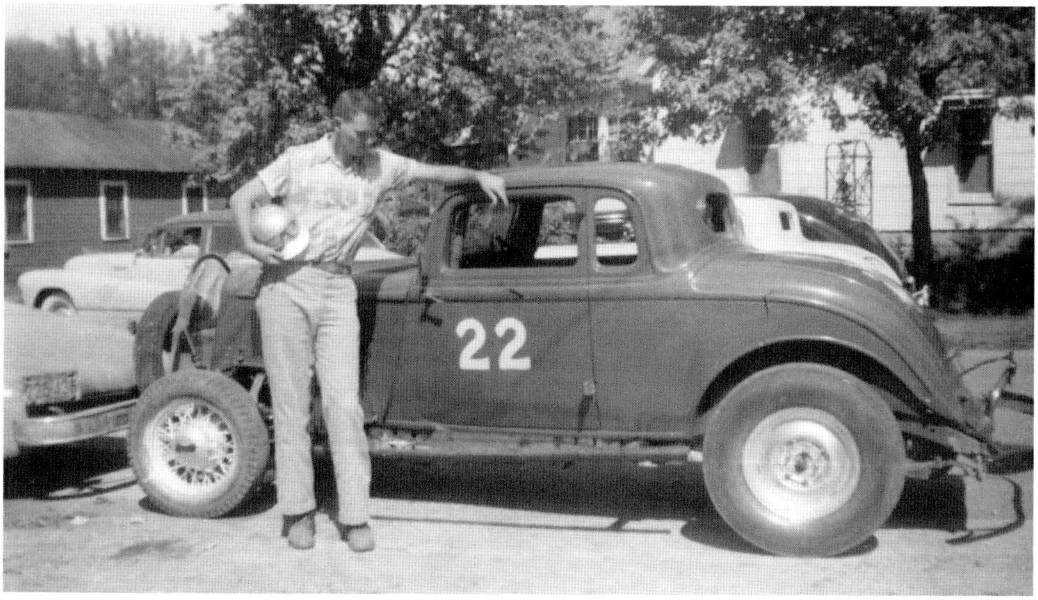

Randall Bales, holding his helmet, stands by his new ride at the beginning of the 1952 season at Beech Bend Park. The car is a 1933 Plymouth, which was built by Lattney Upton. In the background is Charles Upton Jr.'s No. 1 parked in front of Lattney Upton's house in Bowling Green, Kentucky.

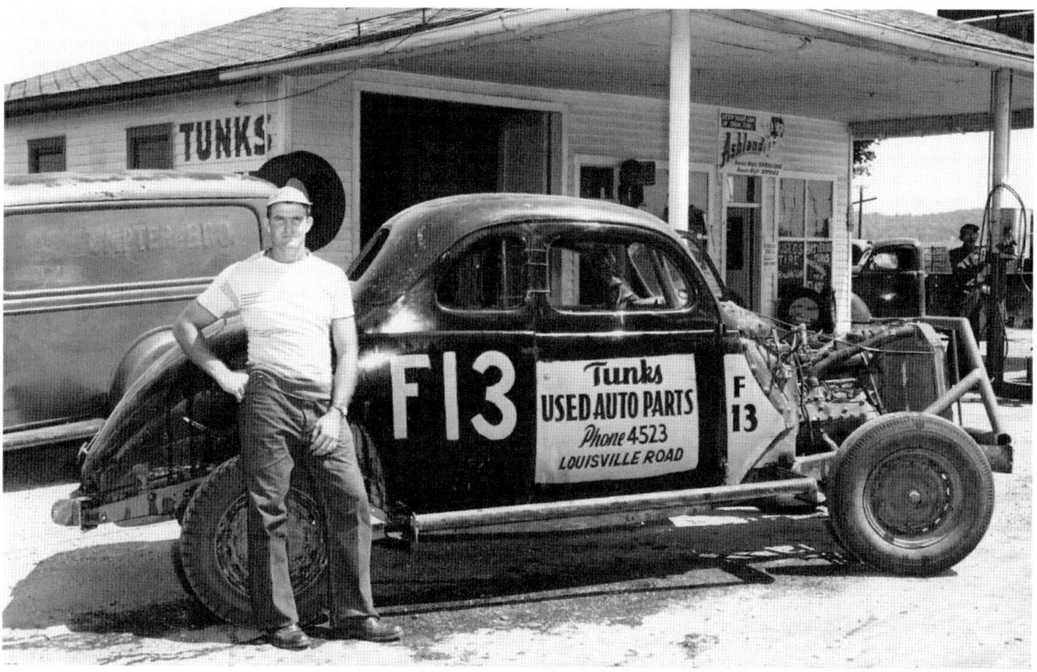

The unidentified man standing beside No. F-13, sponsored by Tunk's Used Auto Parts, Bowling Green, Kentucky, is probably one of the several drivers who raced Tunk's cars over the years. The car is believed to be a 1939 or 1940 Ford. (Courtesy of Marshall Love Jr.)

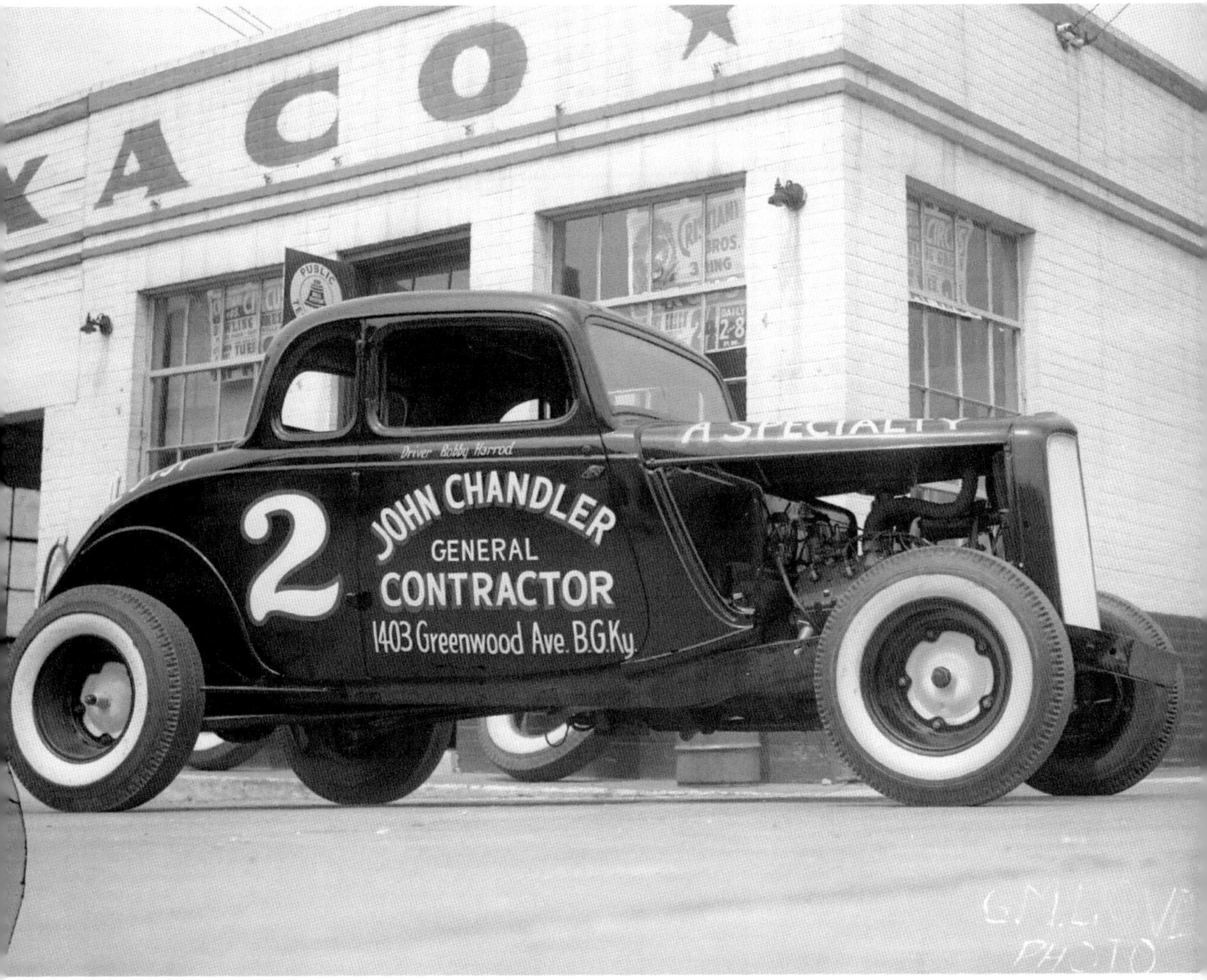

This 1934 Ford shows the pride of ownership that motivated most of the owners and drivers that raced at Beech Bend Park. This John Chandler–sponsored car was driven by Bobby Harrod, a native of Warren County, Kentucky. Harrod was 20 years old when he began racing in 1951. He worked as a mechanic at Causey's Auto Service, and when asked what he had done to the 1946 Ford V-8 engine that powered his car, he responded, "Secret!" (Courtesy of Marshall Love Jr.)

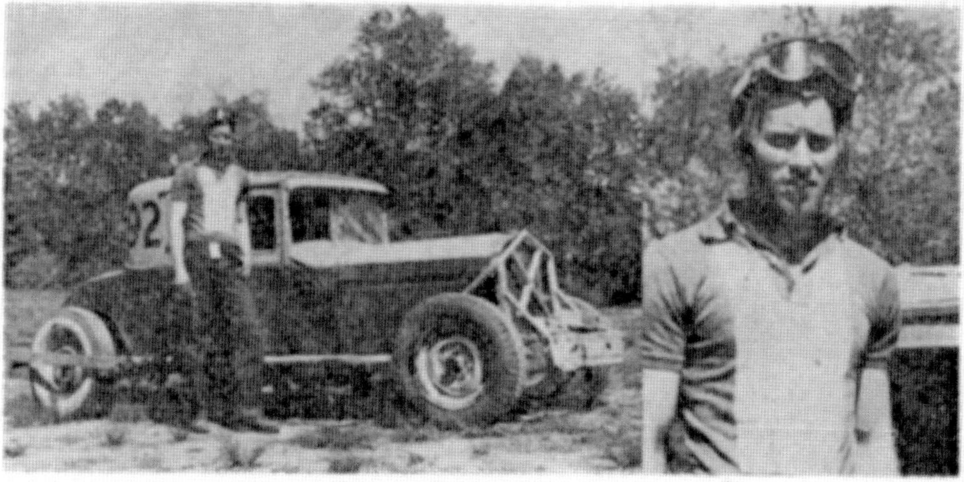

Photo by Earl "Preacher" Moore

NEIL CORNELL

Our featured driver today is Neil Cornell, driver of car No. 92. To better acquaint you with him and his family, the following information has been compiled. Neil was born in Whitesville, Missouri on June 1st, 1927 and when quite young moved to Wisconsin. Through the company he was then working for, his travels landed him in Bowling Green where he met his wife, the former Margie Miller. They were married in Rossville, Georgia on April 4, 1950 and now live at 115 College View Drive with their 2 year old son Timothy Cornell. Neil, or "Corny" as some of his friends have nicknamed him, is 6 feet 1 inch tall, weighs 180 pounds, has blue eyes, brown hair and his complexion is fair. He is self-employed as a poster advertising salesman and displayer. When not racing, his main hobby is hunting and we understand he is quite a good shot. Margie, his wife, during the two years that he has been racing has missed only 1 race and that was because she couldn't find a baby-sitter for "Timmy" when he was a baby. Neil's car, No. 92, is owned by Willie Miller and sponsored by the Miller & Richards Garage. It is powered by a 1948 Chrysler motor and the body and chassis is Essex. Neil has one turnover but has never been injured. And that's the story of Neil "Corny" Cornell.

This is a Beech Bend Park racing program broadside featuring Neil Cornell. (Courtesy of Yvonne Guy.)

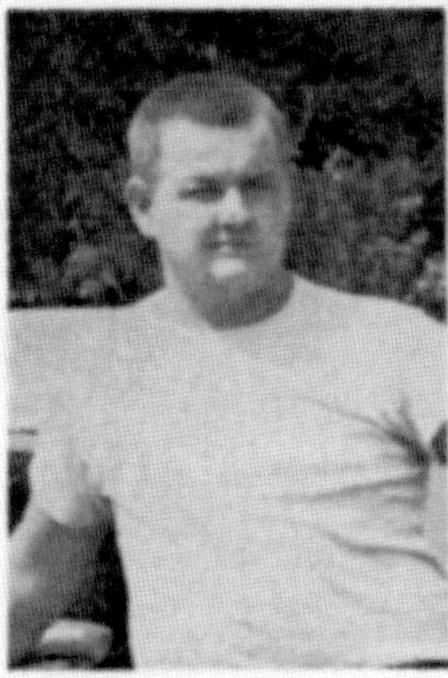 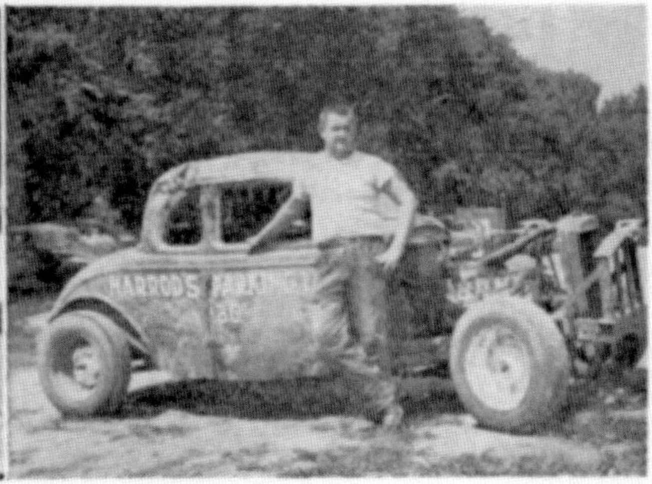

Photo by Earl "Preacher" Moore

JOE HARROD

Our featured driver for today is one of the youngest stock car racing drivers in this part of the country, if not the youngest. Joe was born in Warren County on February 24th, 1937 which makes him about 16½ years old. His physical description is as follows: height, 5'7"; weight, about 180 pounds; hair, brown; eyes, brown; complexion, fair. Joe Harrod has been working for the past year as a mechanic for Hugh Porter Causey at Causey's Auto Service, 408 7th Street. He just started racing in June of this year and veteran drivers say he has the makings of a top-notch driver. His car, No. 4, is owned by Joe and sponsored by Harrod's Service Station. It is powered by a '48 Ford motor and has a '34 Ford body and chassis. Joe has 2 sisters and one brother, Bobby, who is also a racing driver. Joe has had 1 turn-over but wasn't injured. And that is the story of our featured driver for today, Joe Harrod.

This is a Beech Bend Park racing program broadside featuring the youngest driver that raced at Beech Bend Park in 1951, Joe Harrod, who was 16 years old. (Courtesy of Yvonne Guy.)

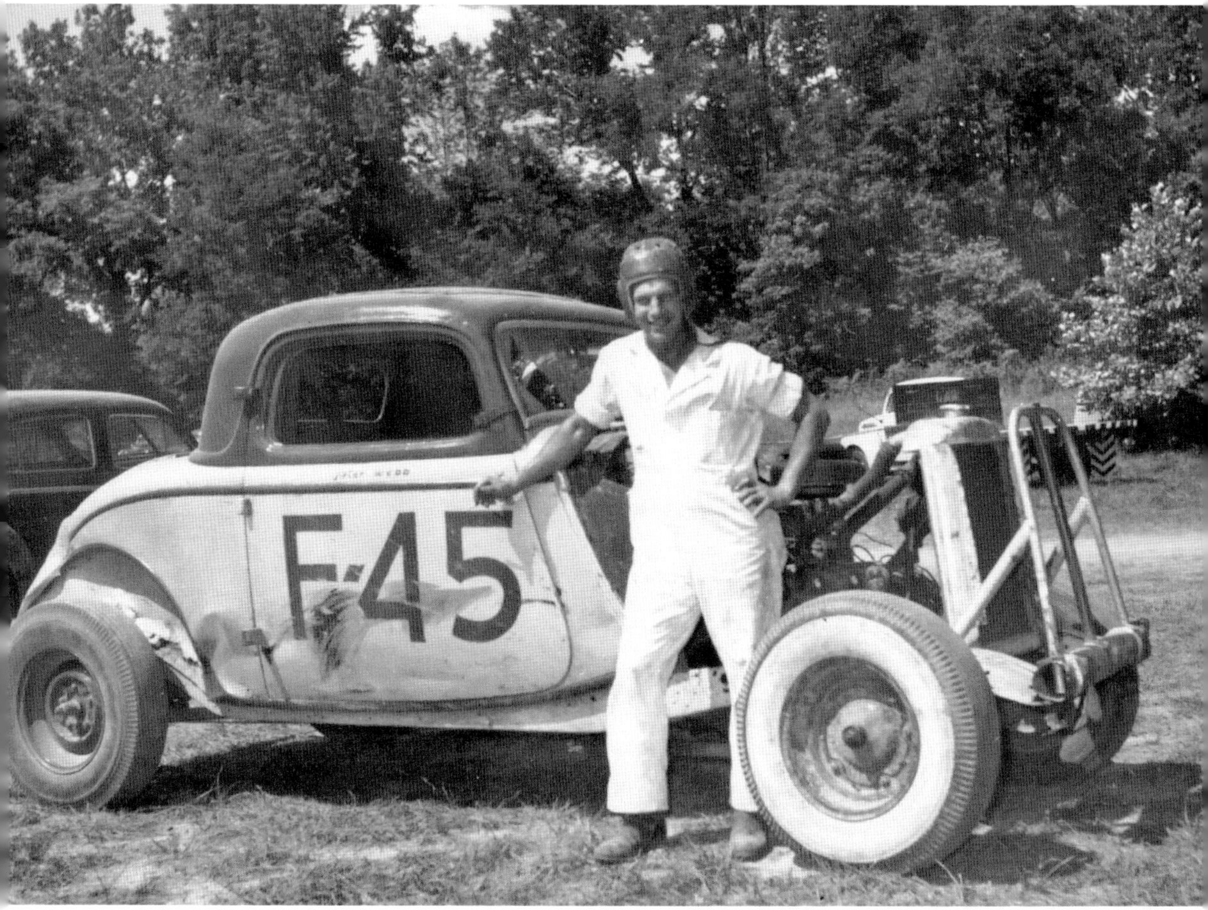

William "Bill" Manning, a native of Bowling Green, is pictured with his 1934 Ford powered by a 1945 Ford V-8. The car was owned by Tater Webb. Stock car drivers are always asked, "What's under the hood?" Manning always replied, "Just a Ford." It is a rare driver who will reveal what has been done to "soup up" the engine. (Courtesy of Marshall Love Jr.)

Marshall Love Jr.'s Soapbox Derby helmet was worn during his 1940 quest for the Bowling Green championship. The Soapbox Derby was held annually on College Street hill. This helmet is now in the possession of the Kentucky Library and Museum, WKU.

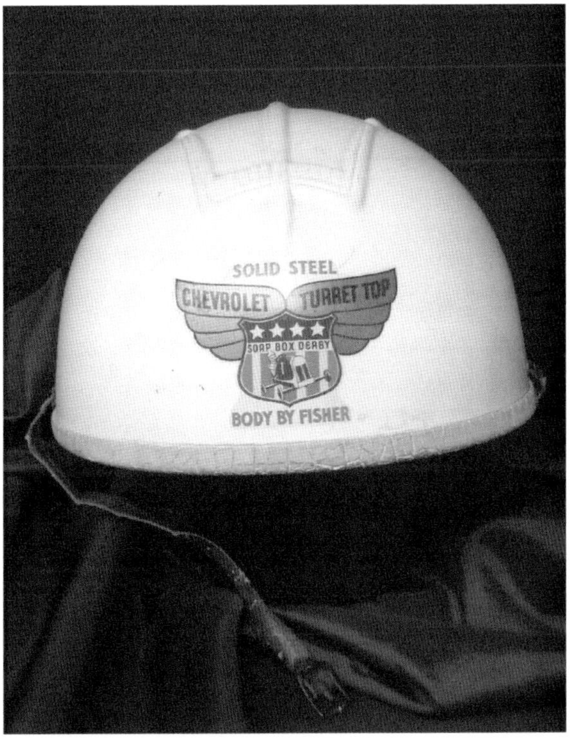

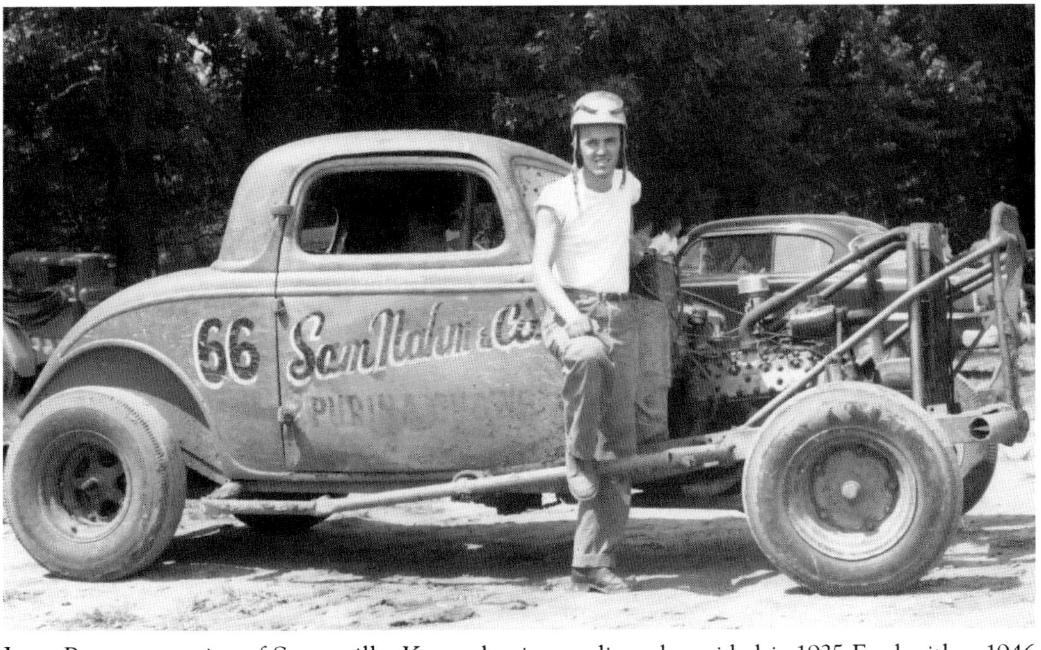

Jerry Patton, a native of Scottsville, Kentucky, is standing alongside his 1935 Ford with a 1946 Ford V-8 motor, owned by Sterling Owens and Ernest Jones and sponsored by Sam Nahm and Company. Patton raced at Russellville, Greensburg, and Bowling Green, Kentucky. (Courtesy of Marshall Love Jr.)

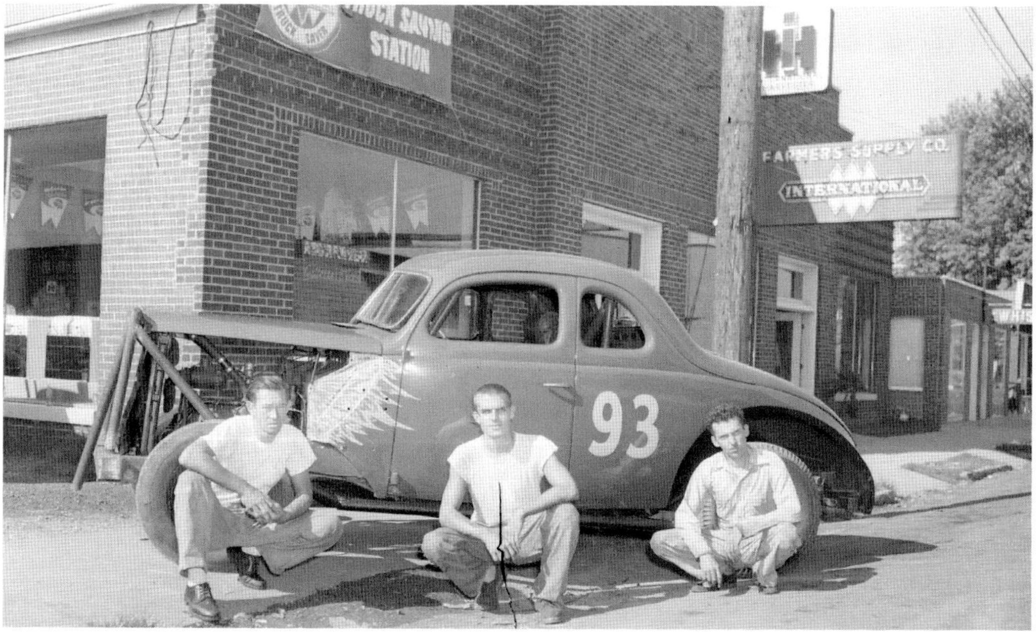

The best time to show off a new race car is before the first race, after which the old cliché, "rubbin' is racin'," also known as "door banging," takes the sheen off the car. Here is car No. 93, a 1937 Ford coupe sponsored by the Farmer's Supply Company, an International Harvester dealership. The men in the pictures are unidentified. (Both, courtesy of Marshall Love Jr.)

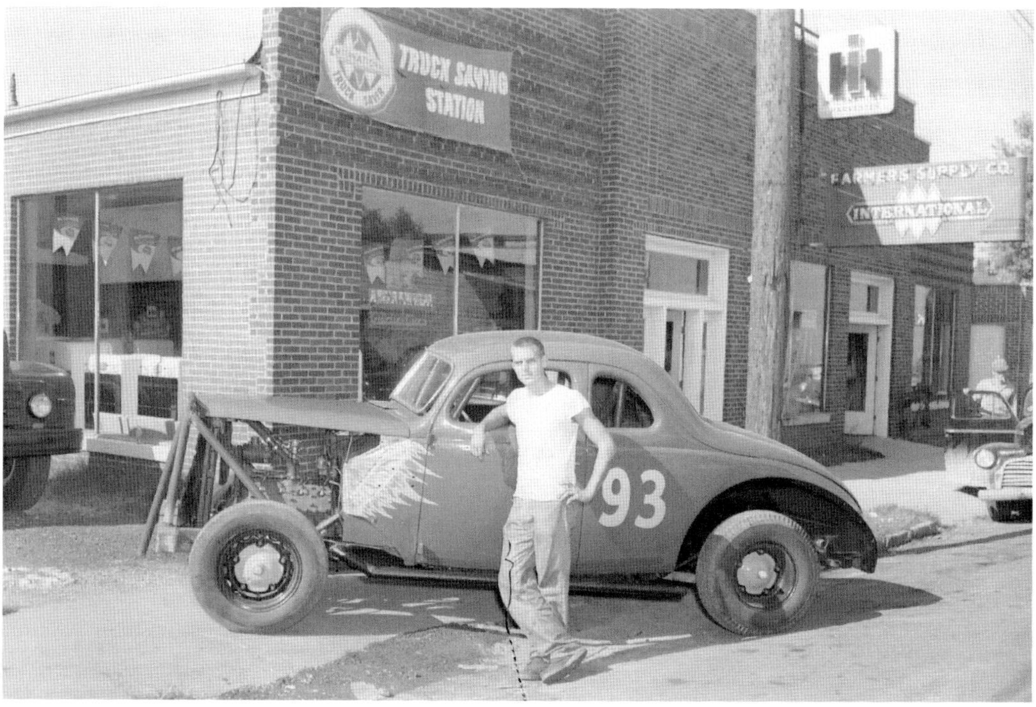

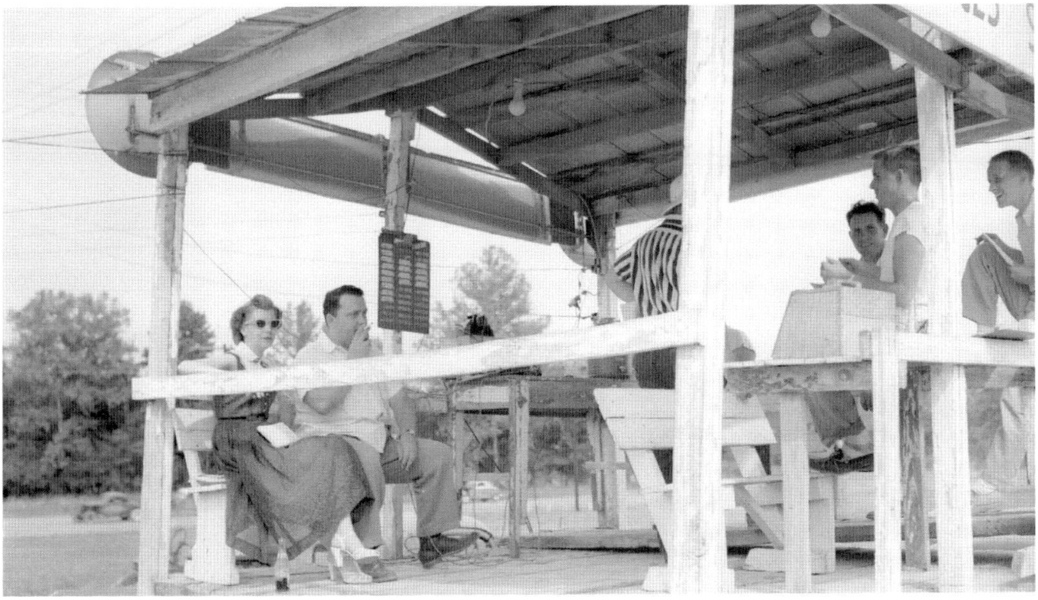

This is the judges' stand, which is located in the middle of the front straightaway and facing the grandstands at Beech Bend Park. Notice the woman (left), apparently one of the scorekeepers, is wearing a dress and high-heeled shoes. One never sees that at a modern-era racetrack. (Courtesy of Marshall Love Jr.)

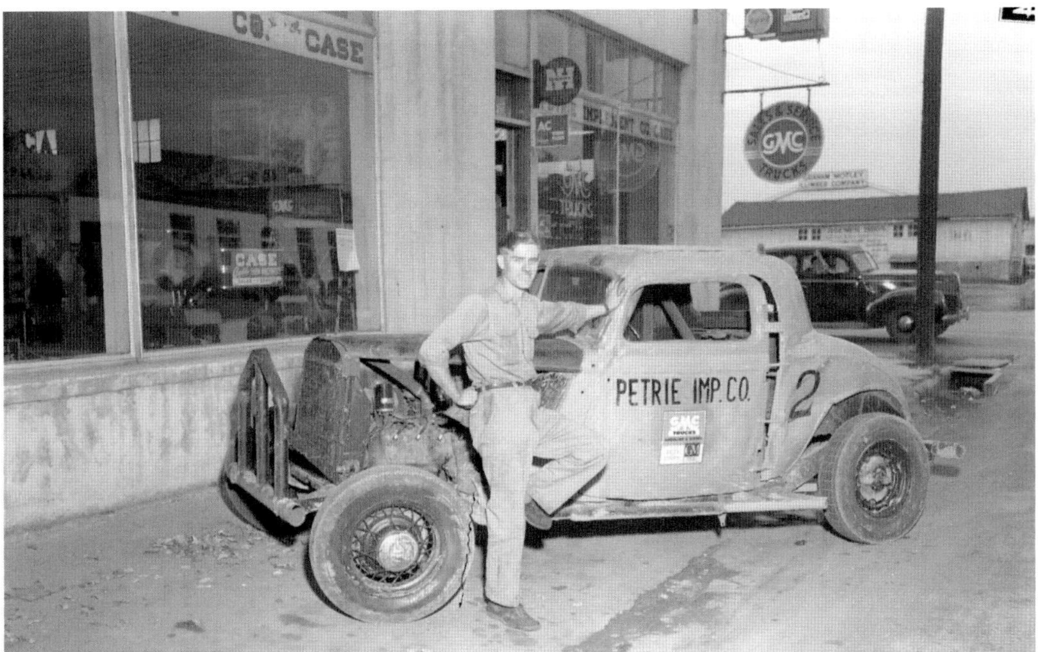

This photograph features the Petrie Implement Company's first entry in stock car racing at Beech Bend Park. The man with the car is unidentified. Petrie Implement Company sold and serviced Case farm equipment and GMC trucks. (Courtesy of Marshall Love Jr.)

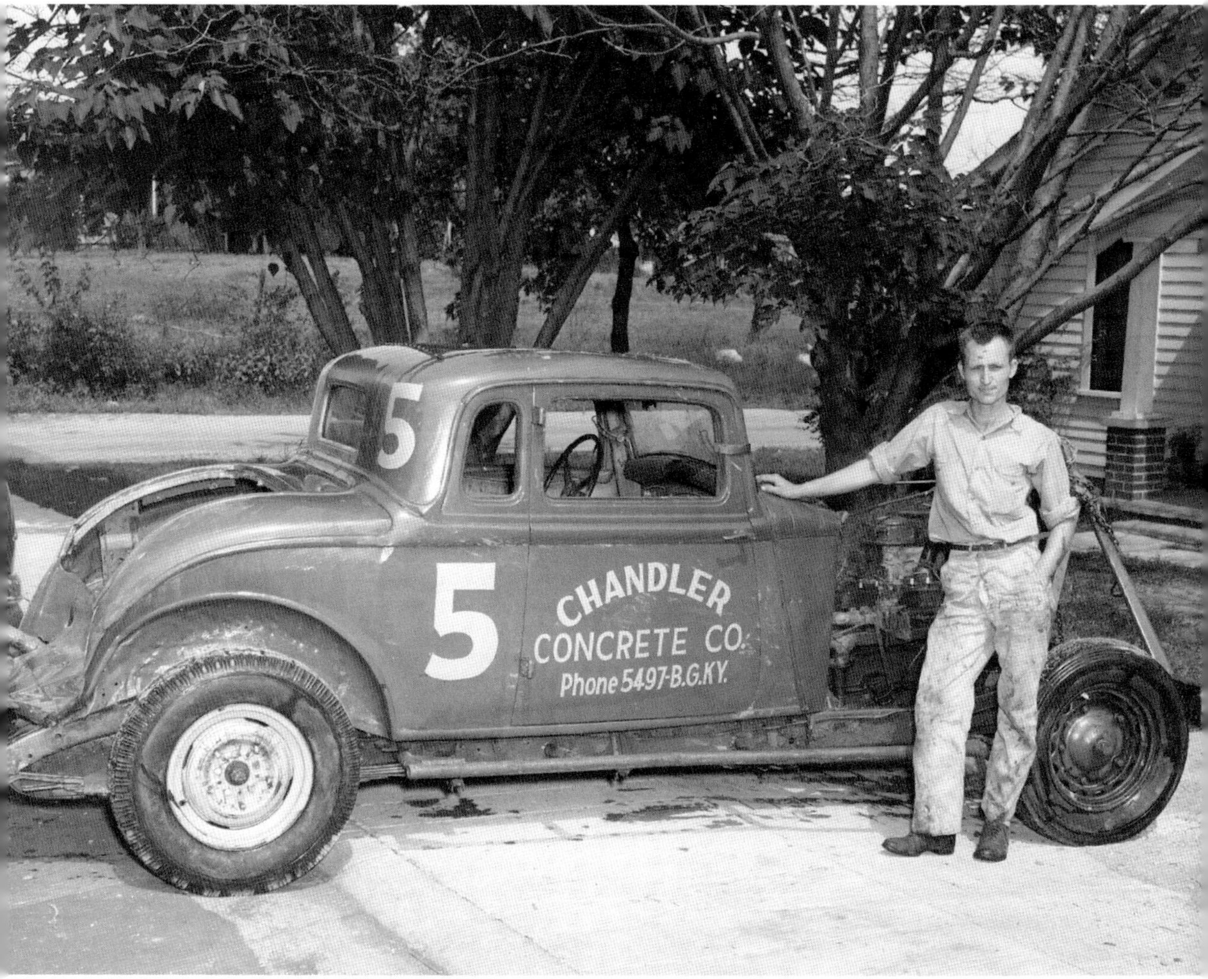

Ralph Martin stands with his 1934 Chevrolet. At one race, Martin bragged that with his new engine he was going to "clean everyone's plow." During time trials, the car was fast but emitted a strange smell from the exhaust, and as he opened it up for lap two, there was smoke and a loud explosion. The car coasted to a stop. Later Martin admitted that he had put lacquer thinner in his gas tank.

3

Beech Bend Park Stock Car Racing

At all levels, stock car racing is full of small dramas that build into somewhat colorful stories and enhance the overall spectacle of the sport. NASCAR also thrives on the publicity of these behind-the-scenes stories. Beech Bend Park drivers, then and now, experience the same issues with ethics and attitudes.

In 1952, Larry Graham and his twin-carbed Hudson Hornet were hot commodities, and Graham had developed a big fan base. A new half-mile track at Hopkinsville, Kentucky, was getting underway, and the promoter offered Graham "show" money to race at a special event. The local celebrity driver of Hopkinsville was a young man small in stature but large in ego. His short-fused temperament earned him the nickname "Little Smitty." He drove a 1934 Chevrolet Coupe with a GMC engine that hummed like a mad bee.

After the warm-up laps, a large contingent of drivers led by Little Smitty came into Graham's pit and announced that he would not be racing that day, as the twin carbs were illegal. When word of the altercation reached the promoter, he came to the pits and informed the drivers that Graham was racing at his invitation. Little Smitty replied to the promoter, "You run the show, but the Hornet won't get through the first turn." Graham thought it over and finally said, "I can't fight all of you, and I don't want my car torn up, so I'm leaving. But Smitty, don't you ever show up in Bowling Green."

Shortly thereafter, Little Smitty did show up at Beech Bend Park. As it turned out, Smitty started on the front row of the heat race in front of Graham. As the cars raced through turns three and four on the second lap, the fans watched the Hornet move to the inside and slide its nose inside Smitty's left rear fender as they charged down the front straight. As the two cars raced side by side into turn one, the Hornet drifted towards the outside, forcing Smitty's Chevrolet over the track's edge, where it bounced and bucked down near the Barren River with a broken tie-rod. The car was loaded on a trailer and hauled back to Tennessee.

Graham says, "I was never proud of that particular event . . . but there are some things on the racetrack and in life that simply cannot be overlooked."

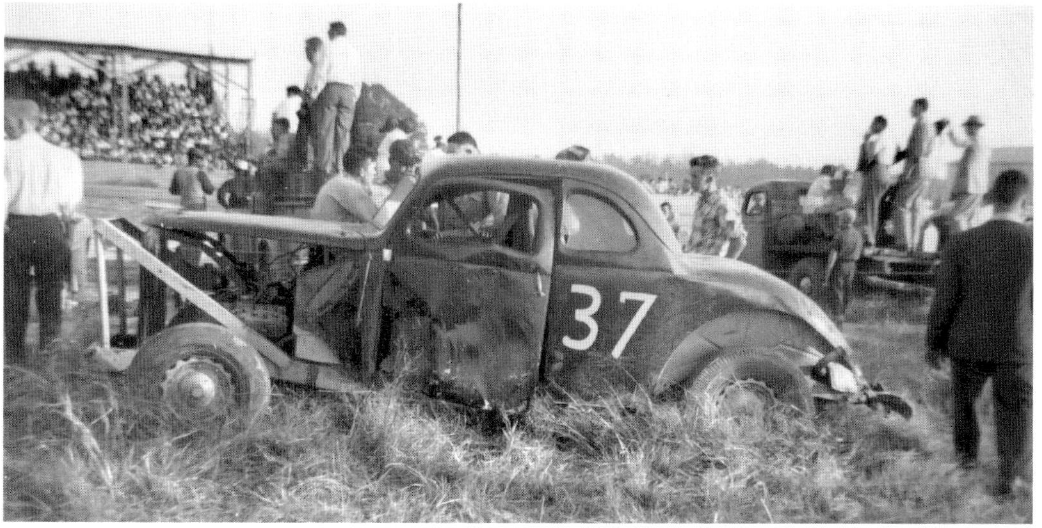

This crashed No. 37, a 1939 or 1940 Ford coupe, sits forlorn and ignored in the infield of the Beech Bend Park track. Notice the man to the right of the car and another standing on the bed of the truck dressed in business suits. Also, note the other fans wearing white shirts and slacks. One rarely sees this type of dress today at any racetrack.

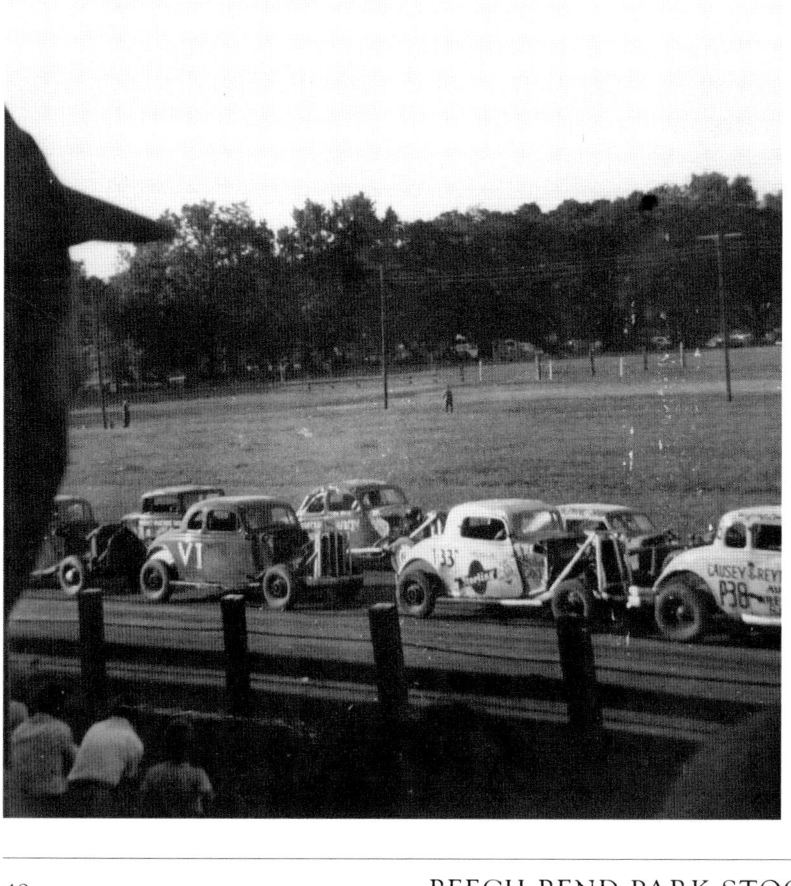

The cars are in line for the beginning of a race in 1951 at Beech Bend Park. On the outside row is Terre York Jr. at the wheel of No. P-38, followed by Bill Manning in No. T-33, and No. V1. York was a salesman for York and Son Wholesale Company and often joked that he sold "everything from soup to nuts." P-38 was a 1934 Ford with a 1948 Ford motor. York's track name was "Terrible Terre, the Termite."

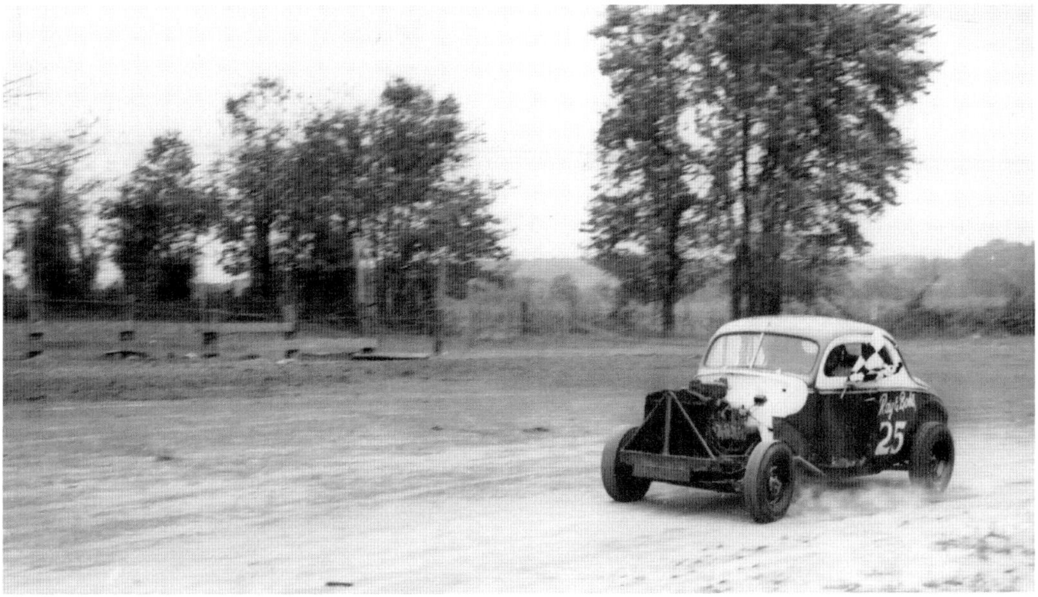

Wayne Guy takes another victory lap in his Ray Mercer–built car. What most people do not realize is that a stripped down race car at slow speeds shakes, rattles, and wobbles around a racetrack. It drives like an ornery pig; however, when the driver drops the hammer and races at high speed, a good race car glides around the track like it is on ice.

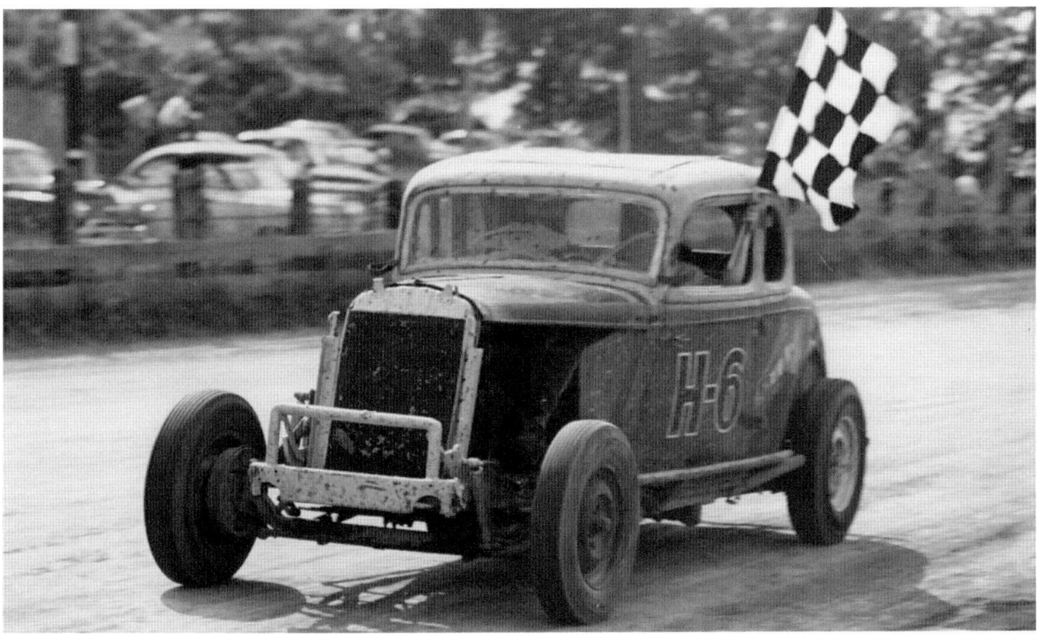

Owned and driven by Cliff "Pappy" Goad, the H-6 is a Ford chassis with a strictly stock 1952 Hudson Hornet straight six-cylinder engine. The car was sponsored by B&G Sign Company, which was owned by Goad's brother, Estil. Cliff Goad, a mechanic, loved motorcycles, cars, and airplanes. He was an early Bowling Green airplane enthusiast, owning and piloting his own airplane.

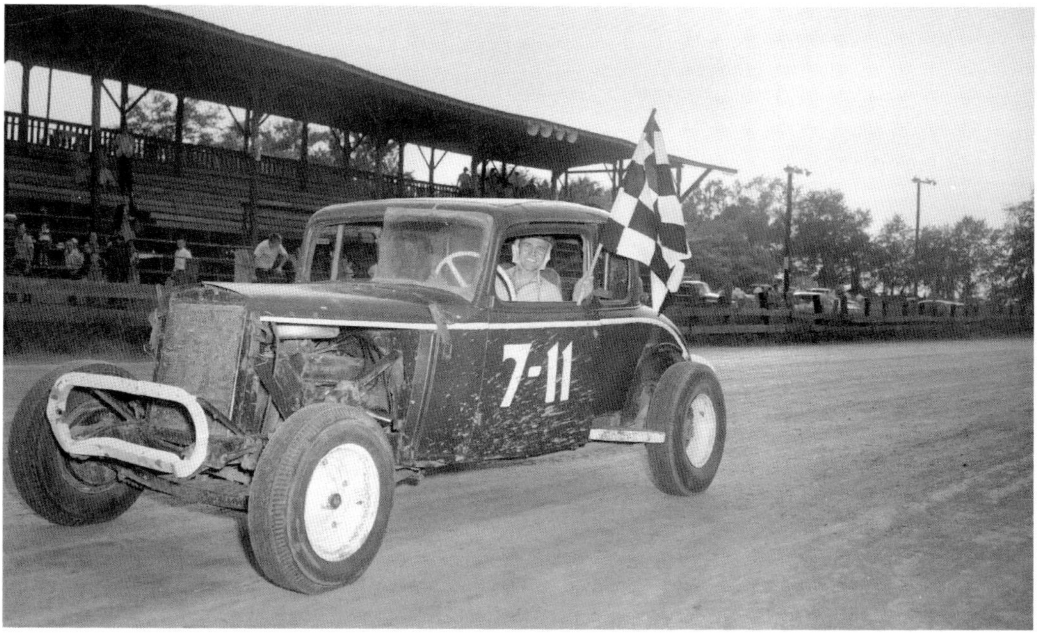

Elmo Guy in the No. 7-11 car takes another win. He was without a doubt one of the most intense competitive drivers in Bowling Green. Elmo was a top motorcycle racer until he switched to stock cars. During an interview at age 80, Elmo said, "I still like to go fast," and revealed that he recently had taken his Suzuki motorcycle out on the road toward Morgantown, Kentucky, and hit 135 miles per hour.

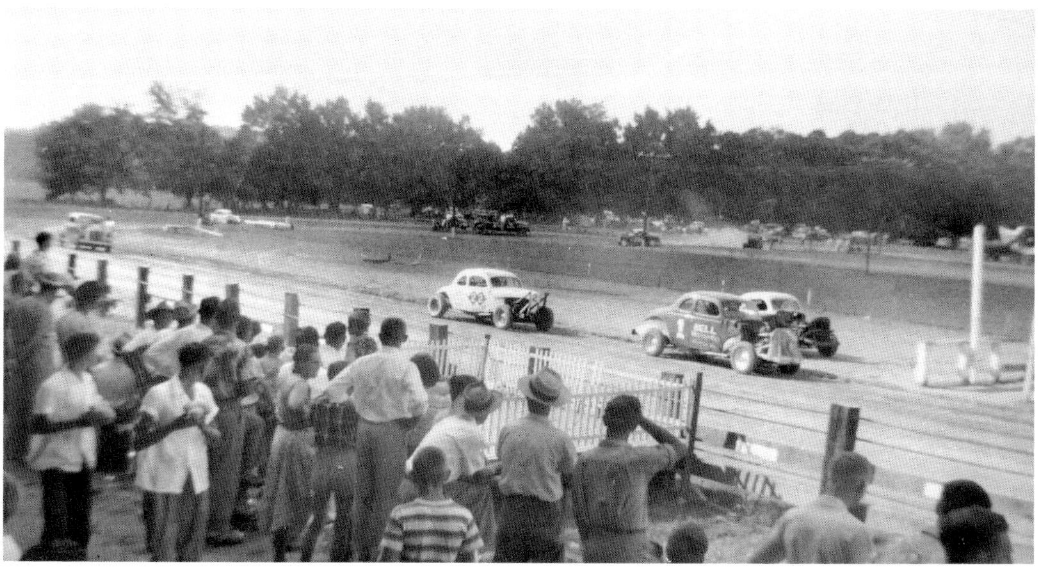

This race in 1951 appears to be stopped, waiting for the wrecker in the center background to remove a car from the track. Wayne Guy is sitting in his No. 25 on the infield near the judges' stand on the front straightaway. On the outside of Guy is Bill Manning in Bell 1 and behind them is the Lindsey Gulf Service No. 22.

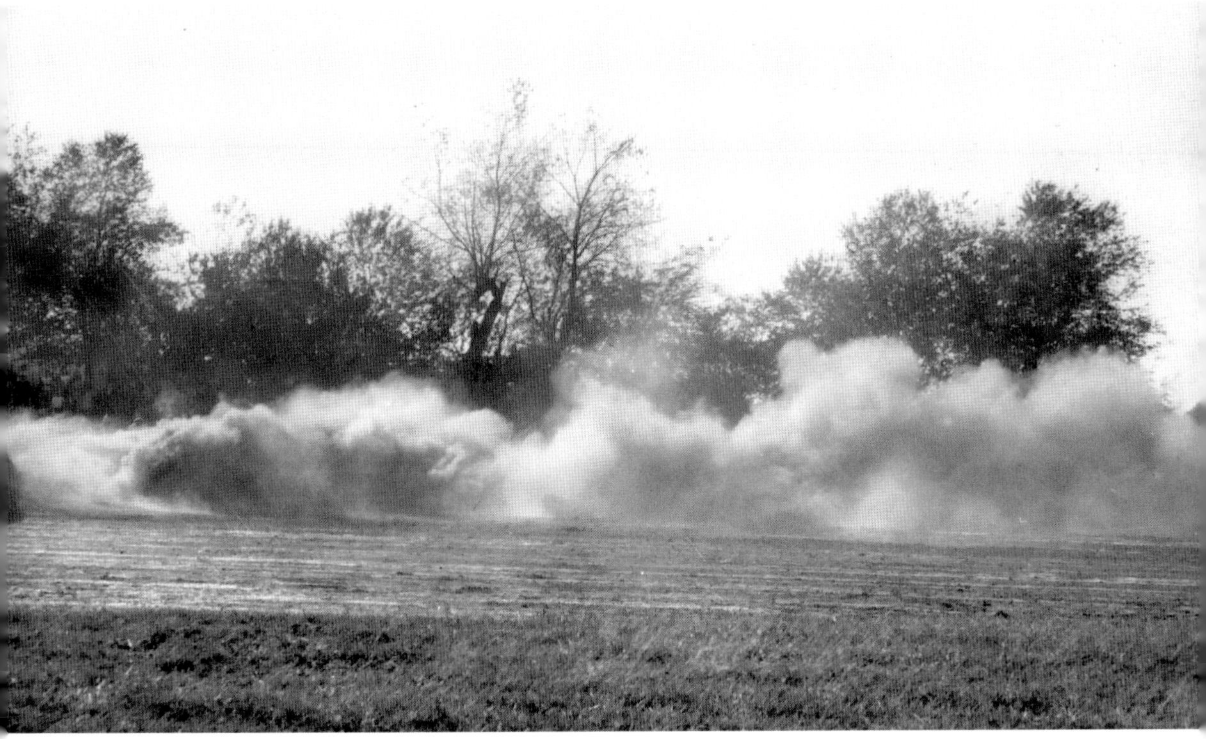

These clouds of dust were the scourge of drivers and fans alike. Stock car drivers coughed up dirt for days after a Sunday of racing. Their only protection against the menacing dust was to wear goggles and a handkerchief over the nose and mouth but with minimal effect. Although Big Bill France of NASCAR vowed that stock cars would always race on dirt because it was more exciting, putting down asphalt probably has had more of an effect on the growing popularity of stock car racing than any other single improvement.

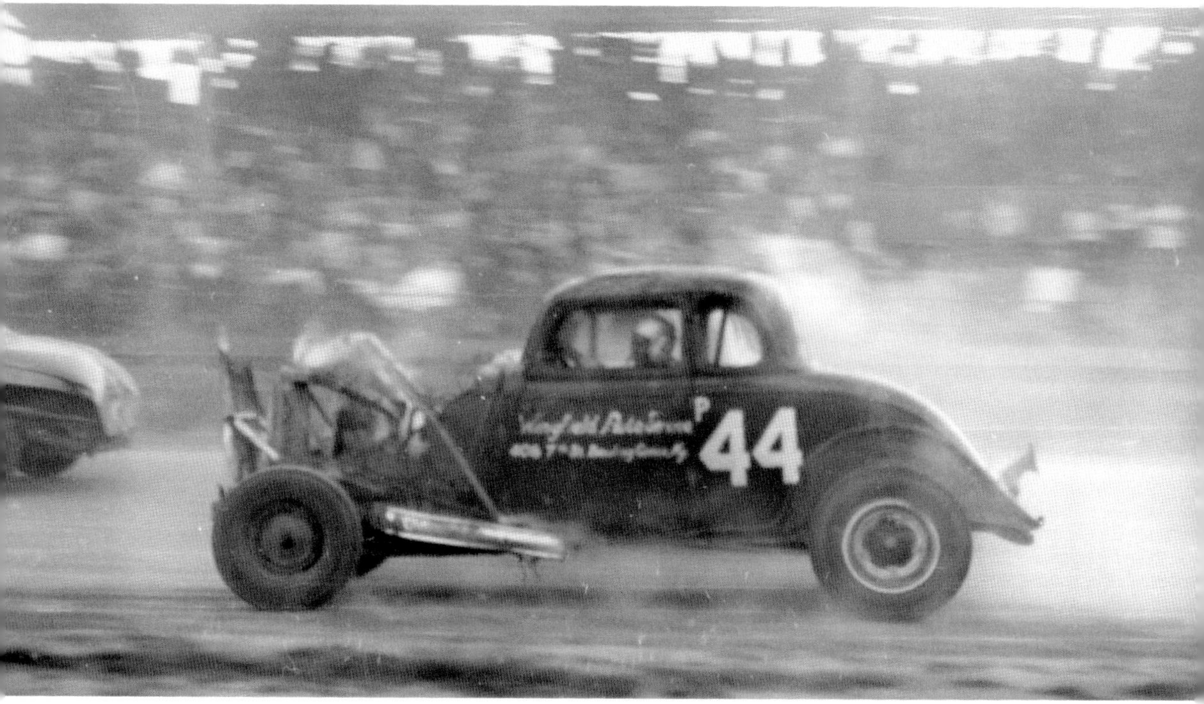

Marshall Love Jr. drove his first stock car race in Wingfield Automotive's 1934 Ford. Love's work as a photographer at Beech Bend Park is the foundation of all recorded stock car history in Bowling Green. Love was and remains a high-energy man, who has been devoted to numerous projects in Bowling Green through the years. Love chased all over Bowling Green, prior to the 1951 season, capturing to film the stock cars before they were banged-up in competition. On race days, Love would race, jump out to set up his camera to record the action on the track, and then climb back into his race car for the next event. Love's racing days ended upon his engagement to Irene Sparks. She gave him the ultimatum: love me or love the stock car. Irene said in a 2004 interview that she had to make him pick one or the other because he was addicted to racing and speed. Love does admit that he sneaked in another race or two.

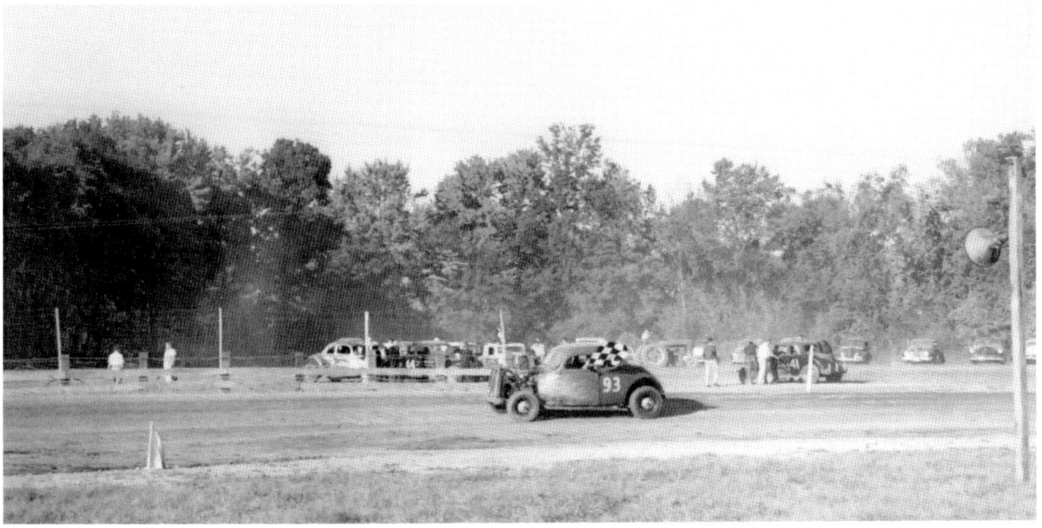

Car No. 93, a 1937 Ford coupe sponsored by Farmer's Supply Company, has just won a heat race and is taking the traditional victory lap. This driver drove the car hard, felt the track, and used the accelerator as part of the steering mechanism. Stock cars are designed to power through the turns, which brings the rear-end around so that the car is pointed in the right direction coming out of the turn.

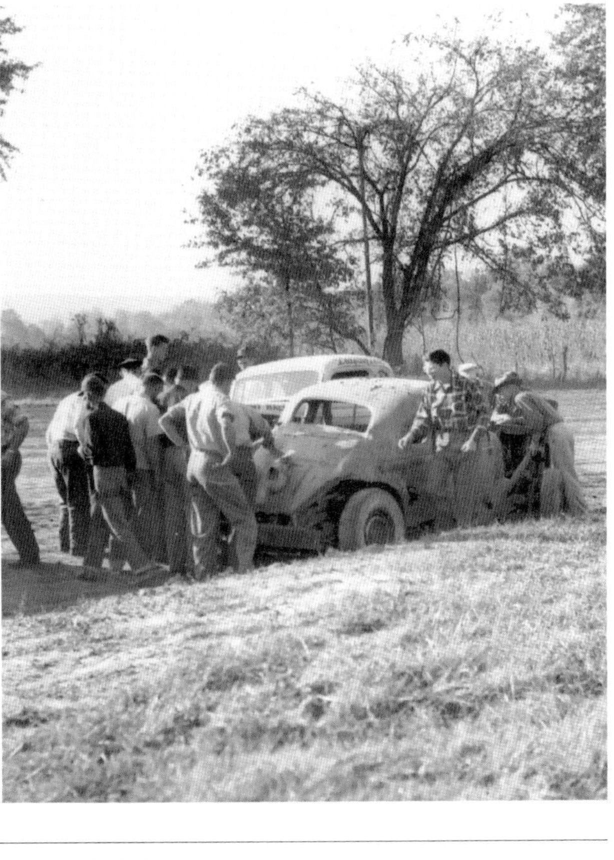

These cars are not surrounded by track officials. In 1951, it was typical—before hard and fast rules were established regarding track behavior—that a spin or crash drew most, if not all, of the men in the pit crews to the scene. Today this would not happen; only officials appointed by the race promoter would be permitted on the track.

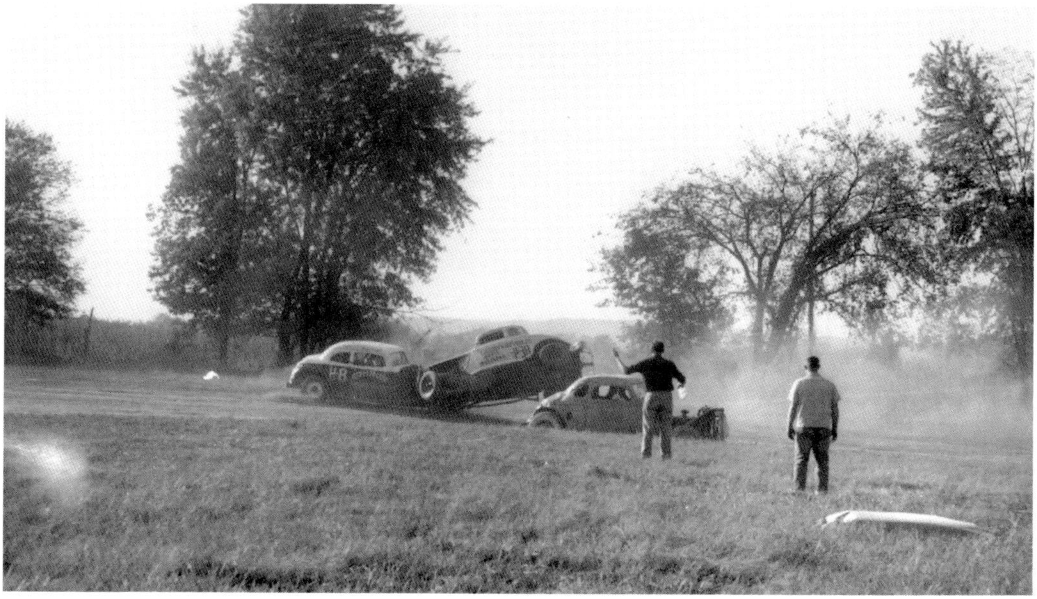

Jimmy Neighbors in P-51 and Cohron Motors' H-8 are facing the wrong direction after spinning out going into turn two at Beech Bend Park. Marshall Love Jr., driving the Causey-Reynolds P-38, does not have time to react and goes airborne after smashing into Cohron's H-8. This type of excitement was a major factor in bringing fans to the track.

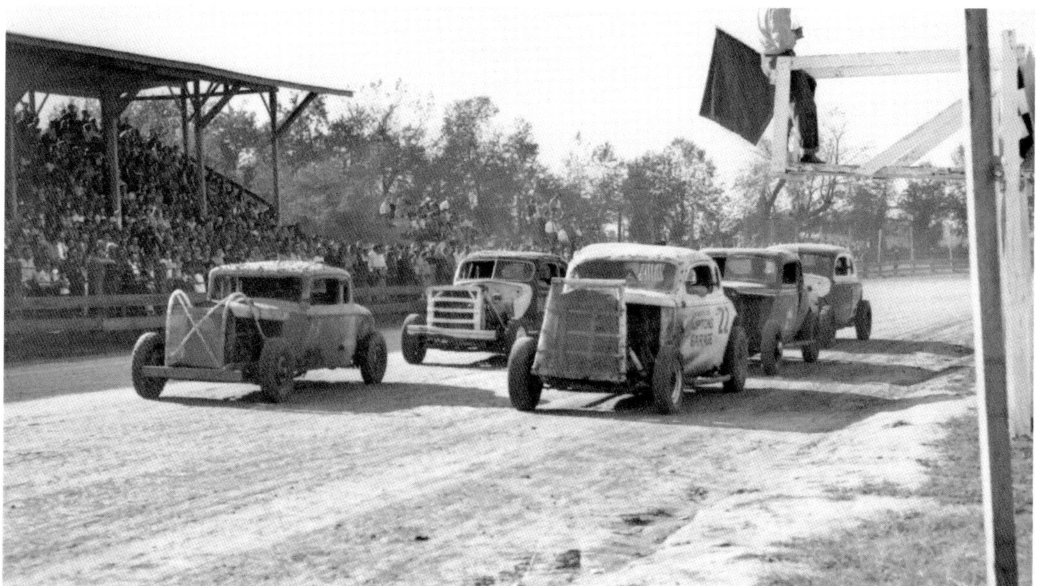

The cars are lined up two-by-two for the beginning of a heat race in 1951. Larry Graham sits on the pole in the Upton's Garage No. 22 while Wayne Guy in No. 25 is lined up on the inside in the third row.

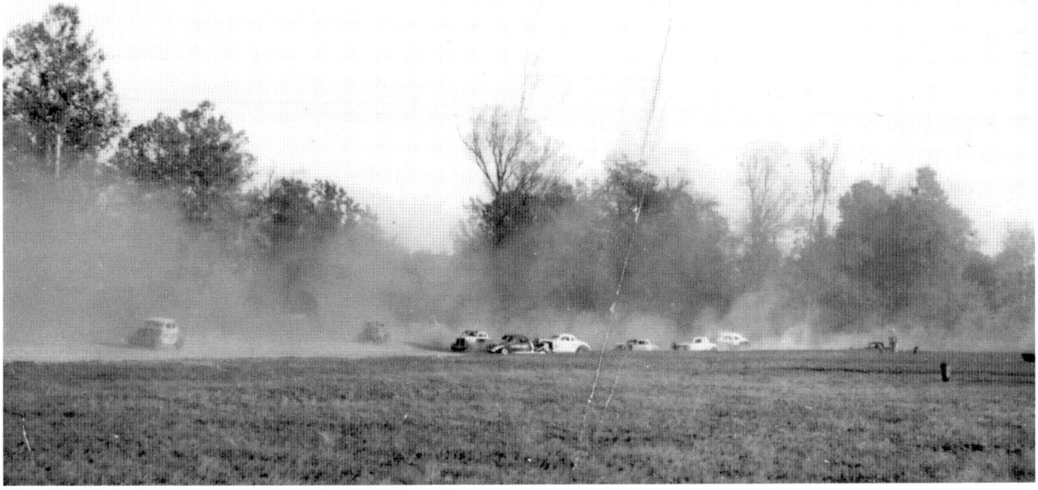

The most dangerous part of a race is immediately after the green flag waves and 20 cars race as fast as they can into turn one. At this point of the race, the cars are tightly bunched, and from the cockpit of a stock car, it seems like a moving wall of metal going through the turn. In this picture, it appears that the cars have just come out of turn two and were running too close together when someone lost control. Elmo Guy is safe as he is far in front of the pack.

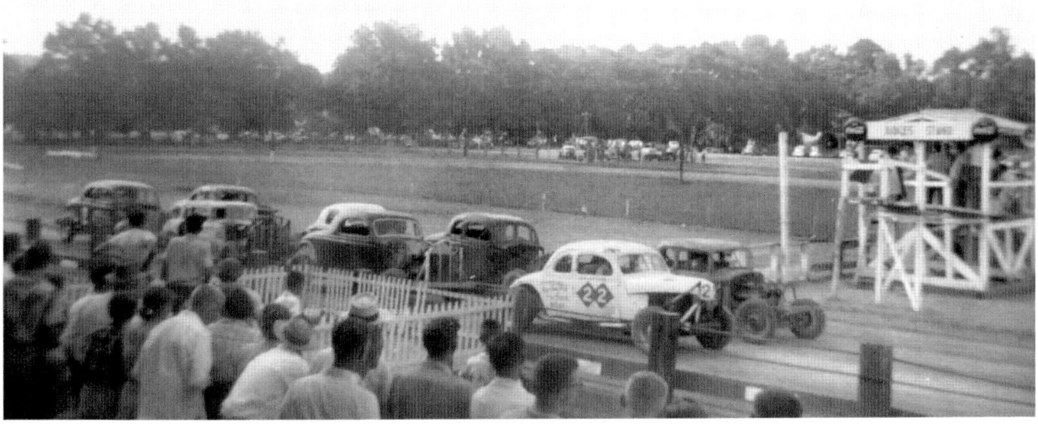

Eight cars are in line for a heat race at Beech Bend Park in 1951. Lattney Upton's No. 22, a 1938 Dodge with a LaSalle V-12 engine, driven by Jimmy Neighbors, is on the outside front row. Neighbors was a steam-fitter worker at Fort Knox and had to commute to the racetrack. Bill Manning driving Bell 1 sits on the back row outside.

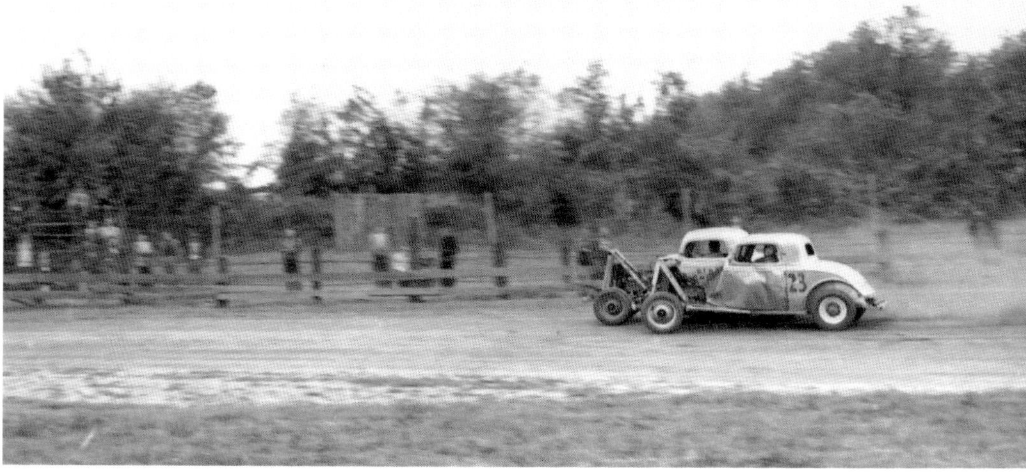

Cliff Goad in his No. 23 is just a nose out of first place as he takes the inside line into turn three at Beech Bend Park in 1951. The pit crews watch from behind the wooden guard rails, which do not appear to offer much protection from an out-of-control stock car.

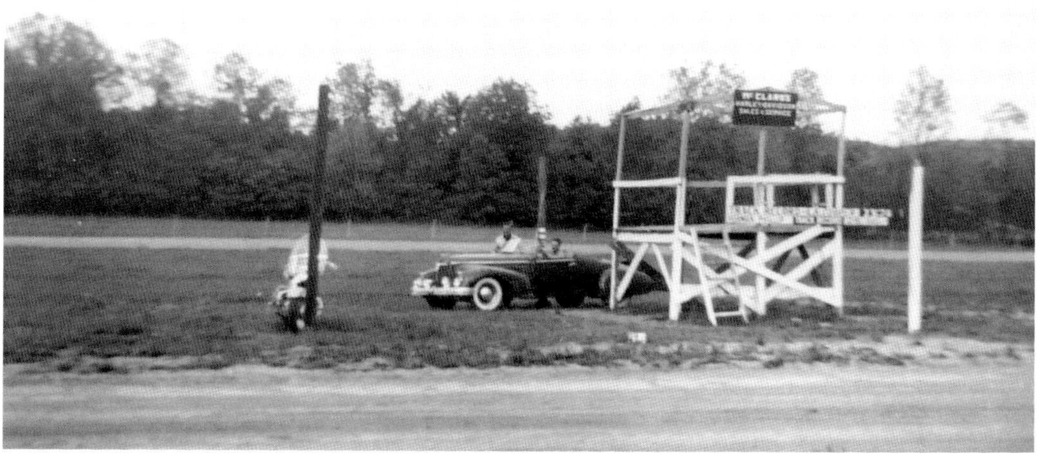

On off days at Beech Bend Park, car owners and drivers often brought their cars to the track to test and practice. Lattney Upton (standing) and his young helper, Billy Louis Young (seated in the car), from Richardsville, Kentucky, are parked behind the judges' stand. The convertible, built by Upton, is a modified 1936 Cadillac chassis with a GMC six-cylinder engine. Notice that the judges' stand has a sponsor sign for McClard's Harley Davidson Sales and Service.

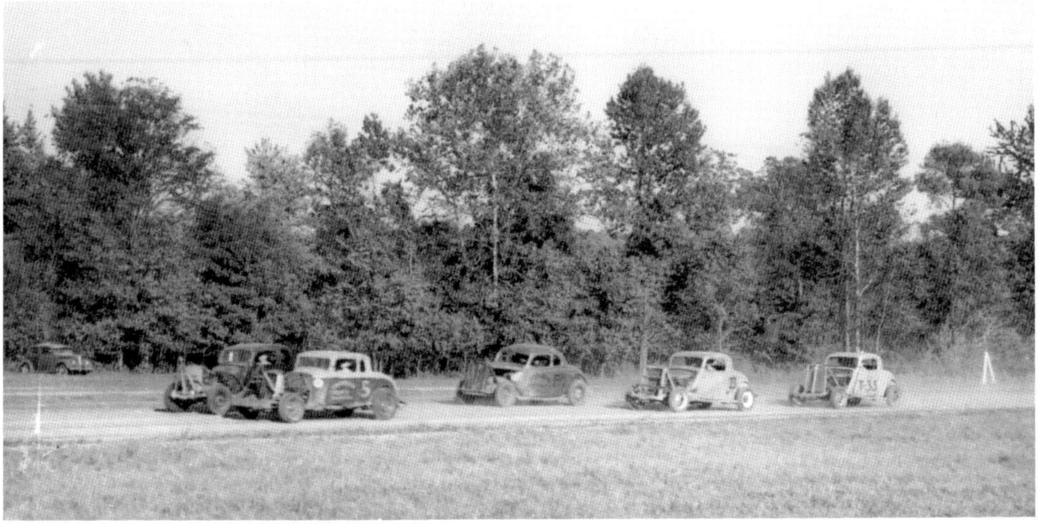

Led by Ralph Martin in No. 5, the cars are coming out of turn two and getting in line for the beginning of a heat race in 1951. Other identified drivers are Cliff Goad in his No. 23 and Bill Manning, a native of Bowling Green, in T-33. In 1951, Manning was 31 years old and worked as a truck driver for Bass and Company. His wife, Evelyn, and his sister, Mary Pebley, were regulars in the "Ladies Races."

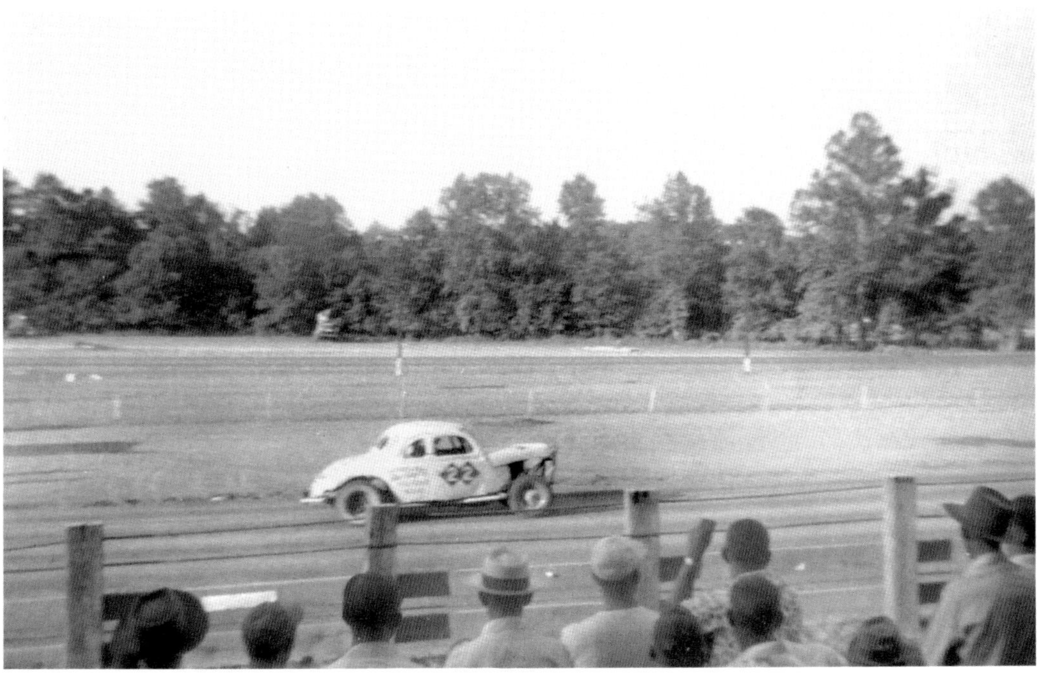

Lattney Upton's No. 22, a 1938 Dodge, was sponsored by Lindsey's Gulf Service in Bowling Green during the early part of the 1951 season. Later in the season, this car was revamped with a 1936 Cadillac V-8 engine. Jimmy Neighbors, of Rockfield, Kentucky, Ralph Martin, and Larry Graham all drove this car during the season.

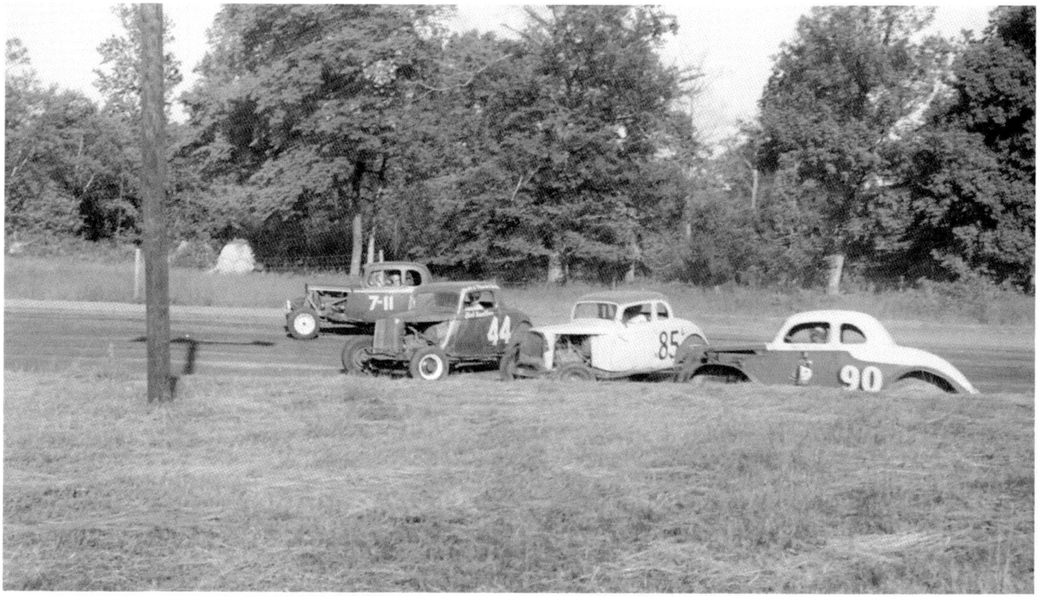

Above, No. 7-11, Elmo Guy, leads No. 44, Nashville's Bob Reuther, and No. 85, Frank Reed, a hard-charger from Murfreesboro, Tennessee. Reed later won the 1955 Nashville Legion Bowl championship over Reuther by two points. According to Steve Cavanah, a Nashville historian, Reed was tragically killed in a race at the Tennessee State Fairgrounds horse track in 1956. He was involved in a wreck along the old wooden fence surrounding the track. Bowling Green drivers Elmo Guy, Anthony "Sluggo" Warden, Ken Reynolds, and Jimmy Belcher participated in this race, with Warden finishing third. From the fans' perspective, this is stock car racing at its best. This type of slam-bang action happens fast, without warning; it appears that No. 41 and the unidentified car on the right are rushing to join the fight!

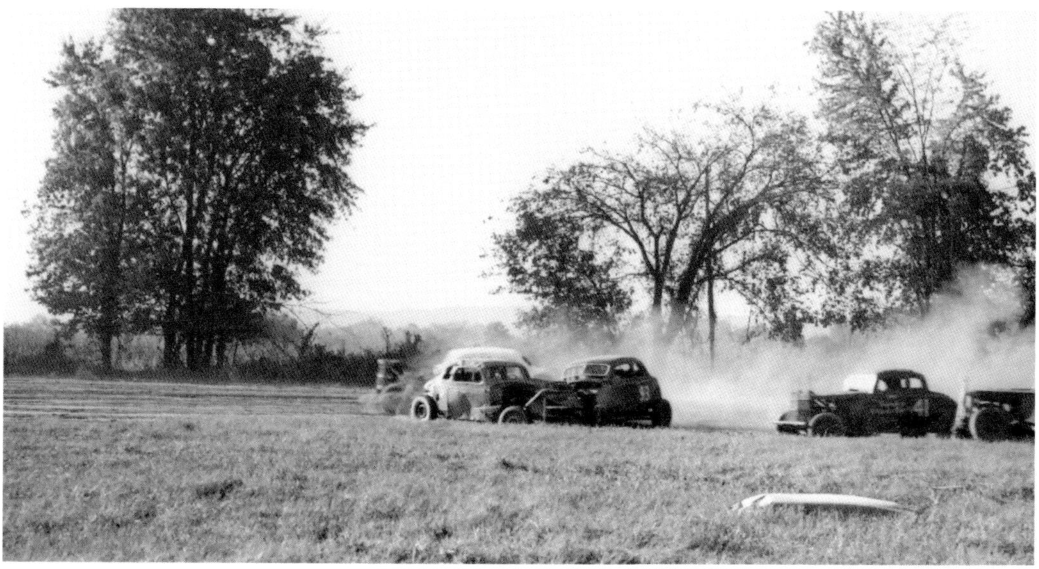

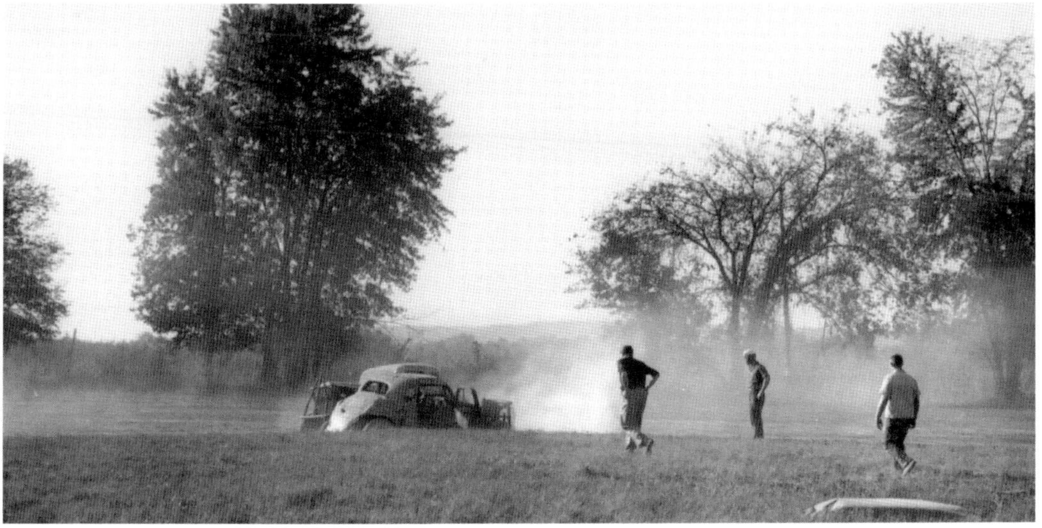

The most common error for stock car drivers is a spin, usually occurring in one of the turns. Driving on dirt at top speed is an art. Success comes from being able to feel the track through the car and knowing how to use the accelerator, not the brakes. If a driver cannot feel the track and tries to push too hard through a turn, a spin is the likely outcome. Sometimes a "love tap" from another driver can cause a spin.

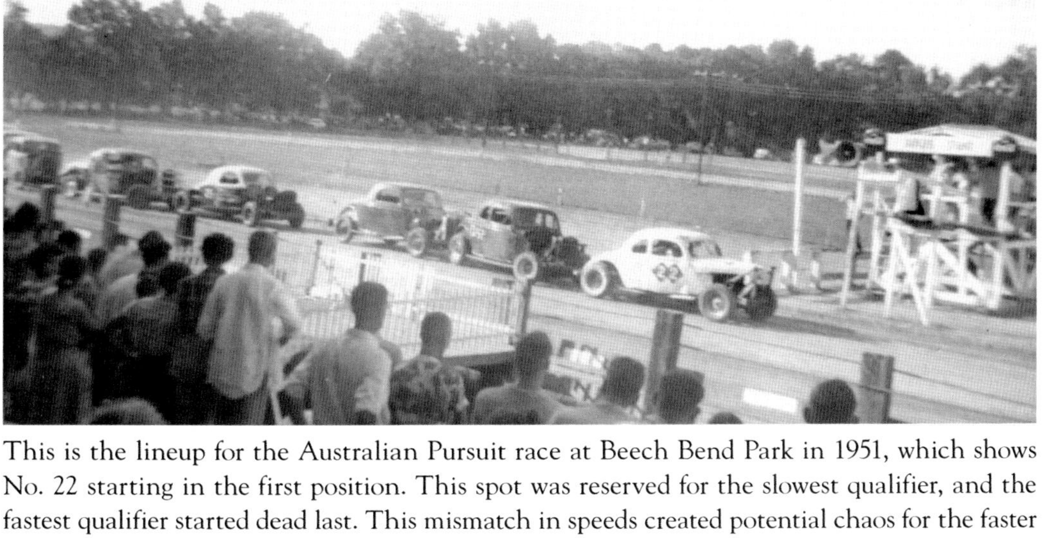

This is the lineup for the Australian Pursuit race at Beech Bend Park in 1951, which shows No. 22 starting in the first position. This spot was reserved for the slowest qualifier, and the fastest qualifier started dead last. This mismatch in speeds created potential chaos for the faster cars trying to move through the field. The top qualifiers hated this race because the likelihood of finishing without blows from fellow competitors was a rare occurrence. This meant that their chances of driving in the "money," or feature race, could have been hindered or halted completely because of the Australian Pursuit. The fans, however, loved it.

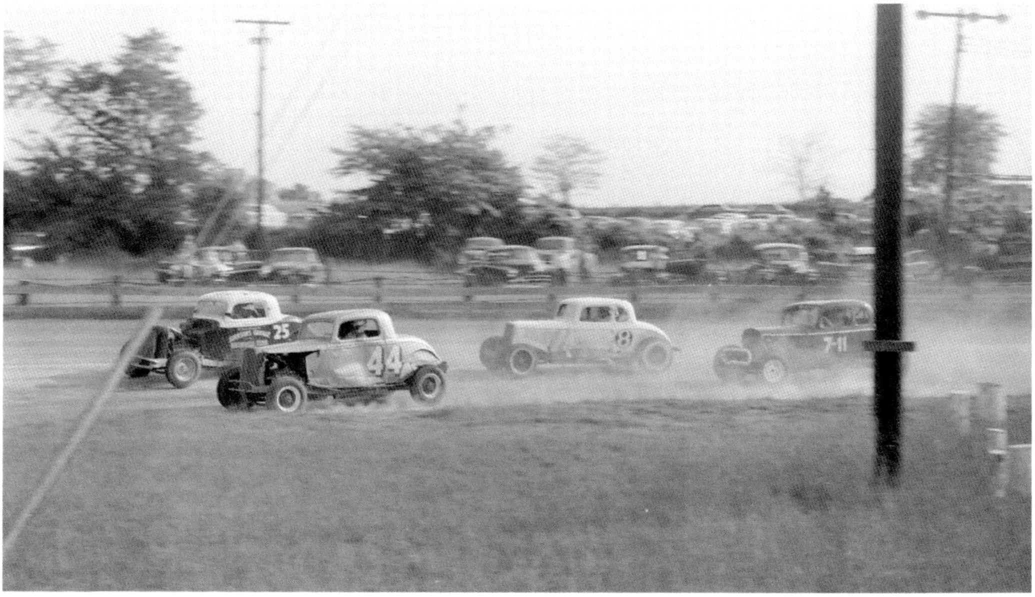

Wayne Guy, No. 25, and Nashville's Bob Reuther, No. 44, race neck and neck through turns three and four. Running in third is 8-Ball followed by Elmo Guy in No. 7-11. Jimmy Belcher, a mechanic for Yellow Cab Company in Bowling Green, was the owner and driver of 8-Ball, which was a 1934 Ford with a 1946 Ford V-8 motor. Car enthusiasts curious about the insides of Belcher's Ford engine always received the same good-natured reply, "It's nobody's business." (Courtesy of Marshall Love Jr.)

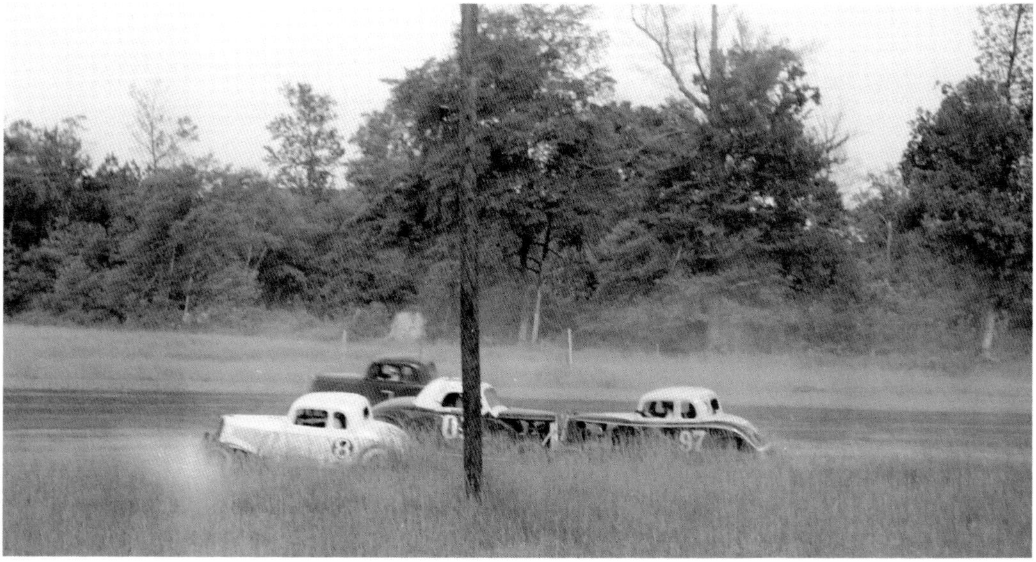

Jimmy Belcher, driving the 8-Ball car, squeezes through an unfolding crash on the back straightaway. Although counterintuitive, patience is a trait of the best drivers, i.e. patience at high speed. Patience allows the driver to take advantage of luck just as Belcher has done by letting the crash play out in front of him and then making the pass. (Courtesy of Marshall Love Jr.)

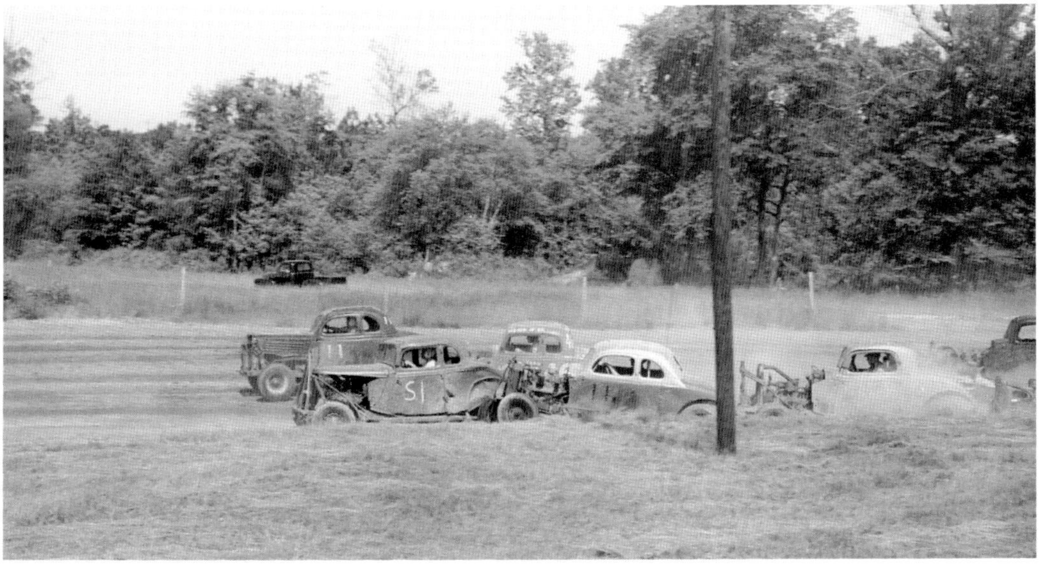

Raymond Finney Richards in S1 pushes through on the inside coming out of turn two. The inside line is always popular as it is simple arithmetic that the shortest distance around the track is low and inside. Furthermore, the car trailing has a challenge getting under the left rear of the car in front than if it is cruising high and outside. However, the laws of physics dictates that if one runs the inside line, the car must have the power to dig out of the turn, as the car has less momentum running that line. (Courtesy of Marshall Love Jr.)

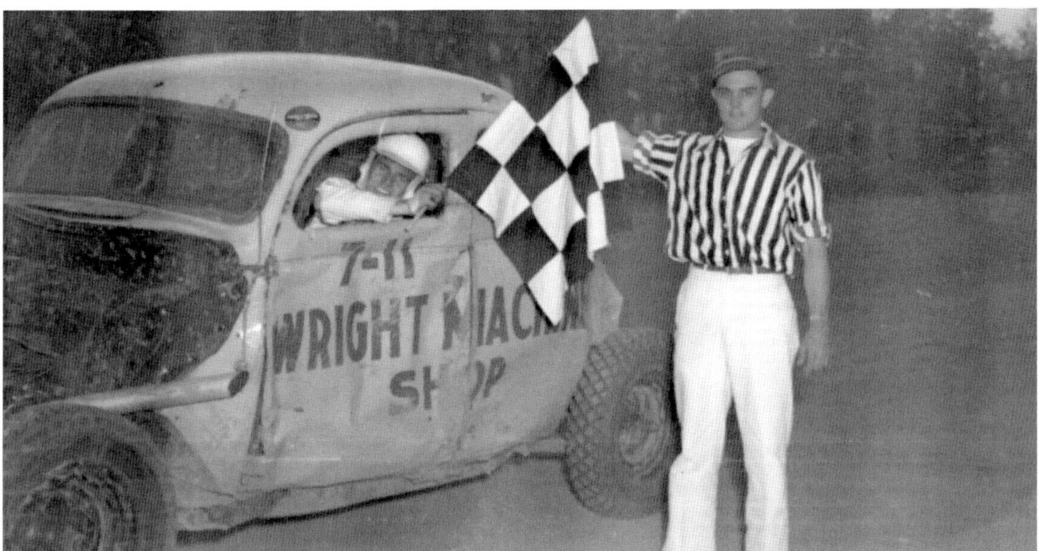

Elmo Guy in his Wright's Machine Shop No. 7-11 takes another checkered flag. Elmo was probably the most prolific winner at Beech Bend Park over the years, including his stint as a drag racer. According to Larry Graham, track rules initially developed because some people thought men like Elmo won too often; these constant winners needed to be reined in. Actually, the winner is typically just an outstanding driver with good equipment and some luck.

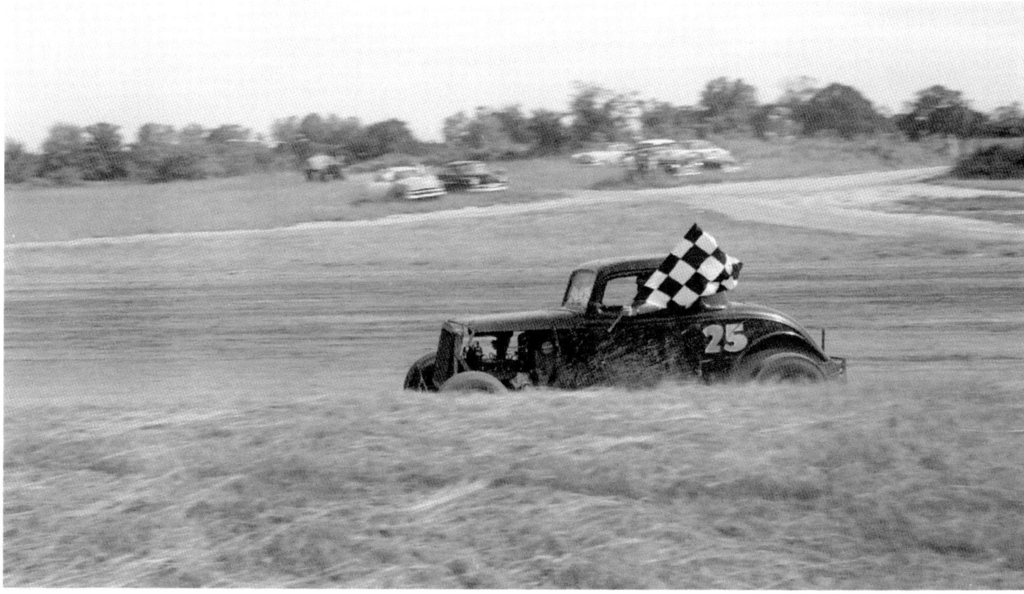

Elmo Guy's younger brother, Wayne, takes a victory lap. Wayne only raced for five years, but he was a regular in the winner's circle. In a 2003 interview, when asked what he had learned from stock car racing, Wayne retorted, "Racing certainly made me a believer in seat belts." (Courtesy of Marshall Love Jr.)

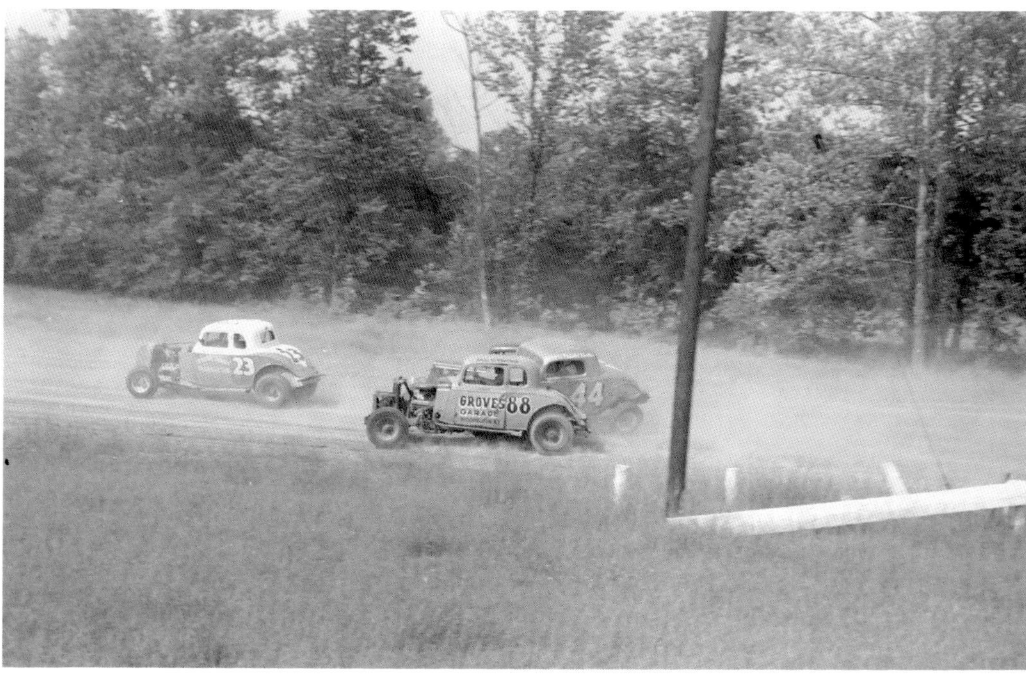

Bob Reuther in No. 44 and Paul Stradtner in the Groves Garage No. 88 chase No. 23. Stradtner's car is a 1936 Ford body on a 1936 LaSalle chassis. The engine is a 1950 Oldsmobile 88. (Courtesy of Marshall Love Jr.)

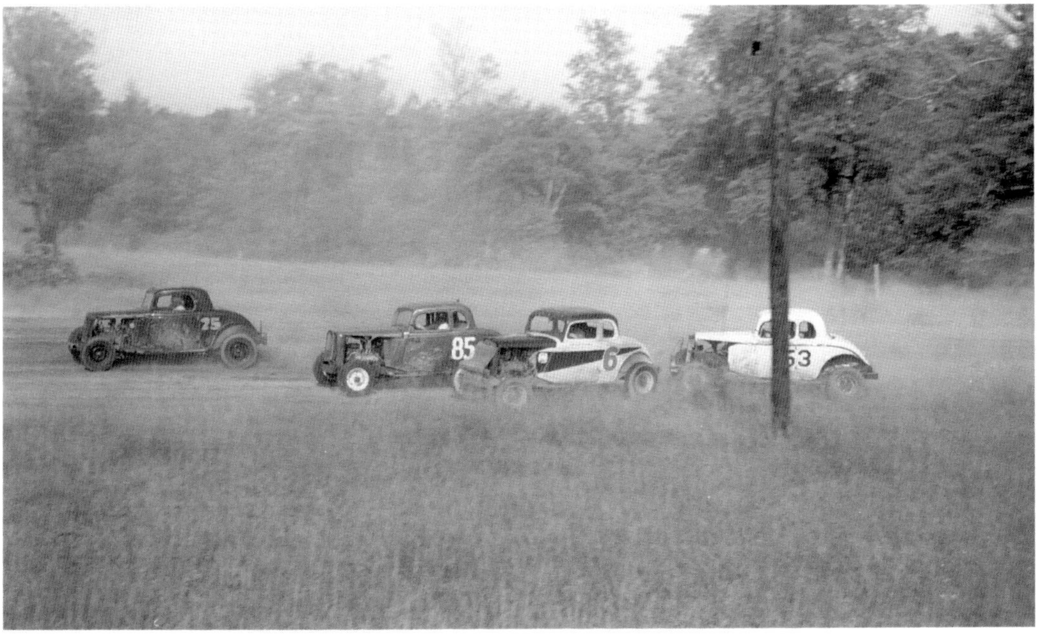

Wayne Guy in No. 25 is out in front of Frank Reed of Murfreesboro, Tennessee, in No. 85. Reed was killed in a racing accident in a 1956 race at the Tennessee State Fairground. (Courtesy of Marshall Love Jr.)

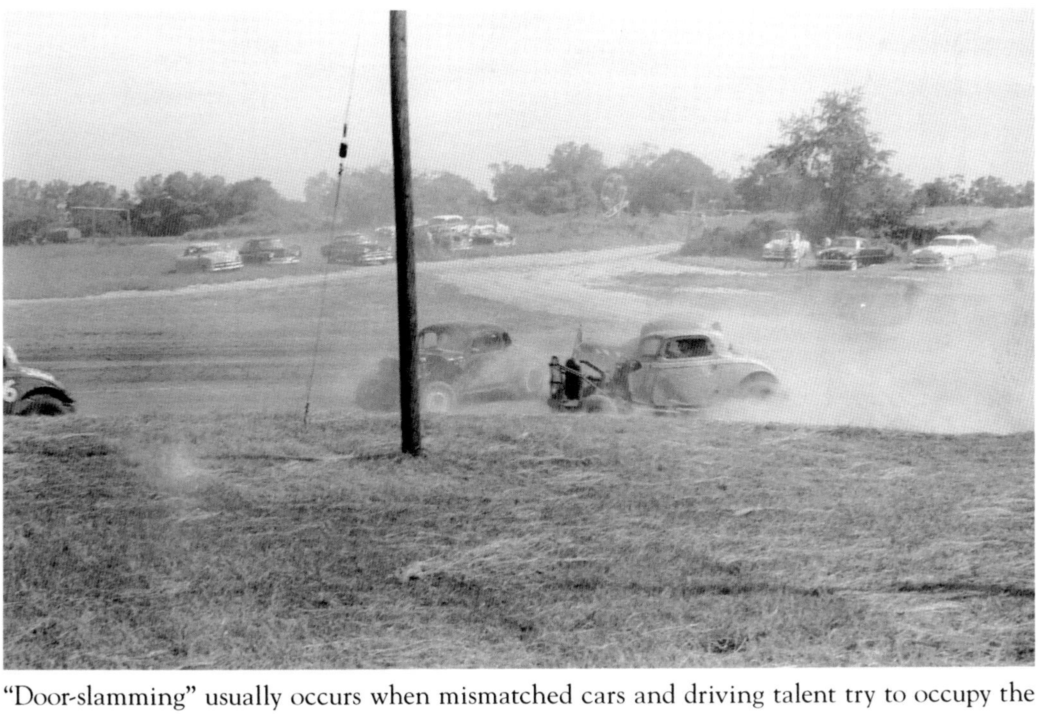

"Door-slamming" usually occurs when mismatched cars and driving talent try to occupy the same space on a small racetrack. Also, aggression may have something to do with it! (Courtesy of Marshall Love Jr.)

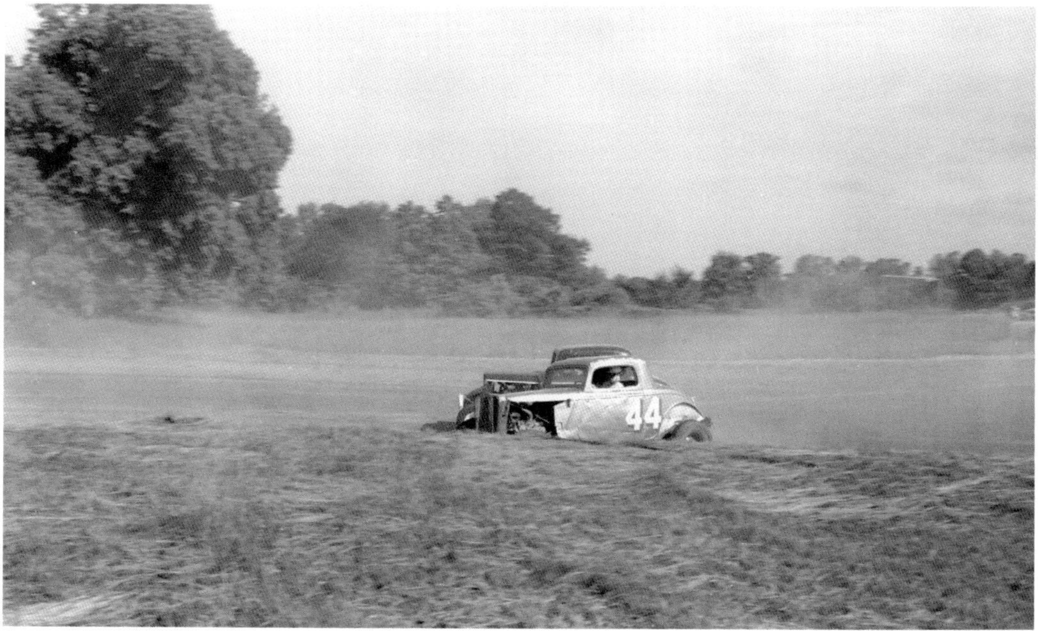

Bob Reuther of Nashville takes to the inside for a pass. In a 2003 interview, Elmo Guy said that Nashville drivers like Frank Reed and Bob Reuther were so talented and drove such hot cars that the Bowling Green drivers complained to Charles Garvin to tighten the rules on the Nashville racers: no more than one carburetor and no alcohol in the gas tank. (Courtesy of Marshall Love Jr.)

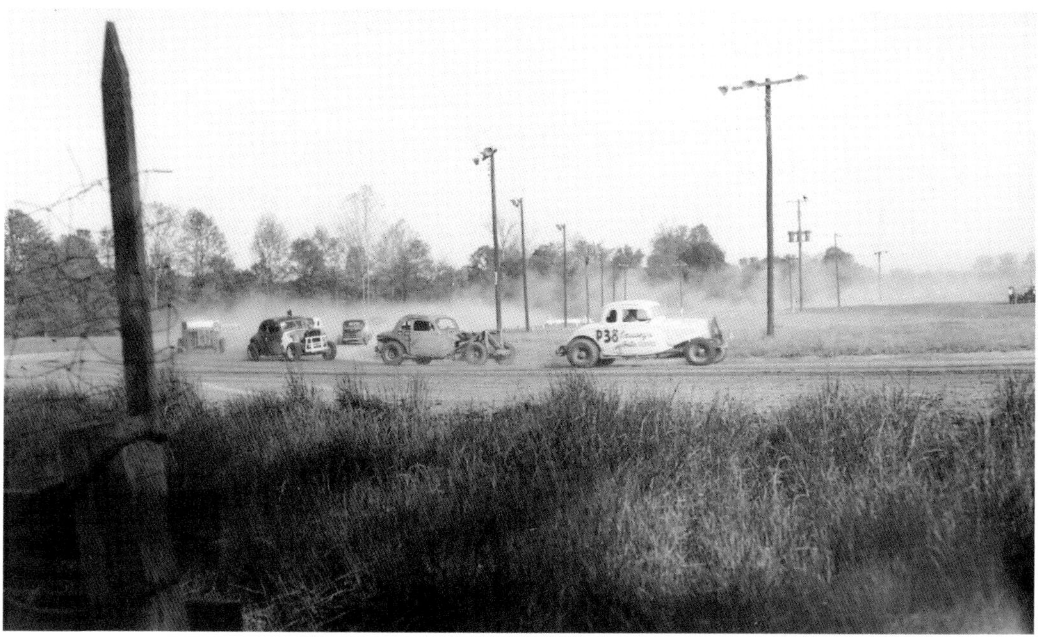

A. W. Nolen, behind the wheel of Hugh Porter Causey's P-38, leads the pack out of turn two and into the back straight at Beech Bend Park. The noise will be deafening as the cars give it full power coming out of the turn. (Marshall Love Jr.)

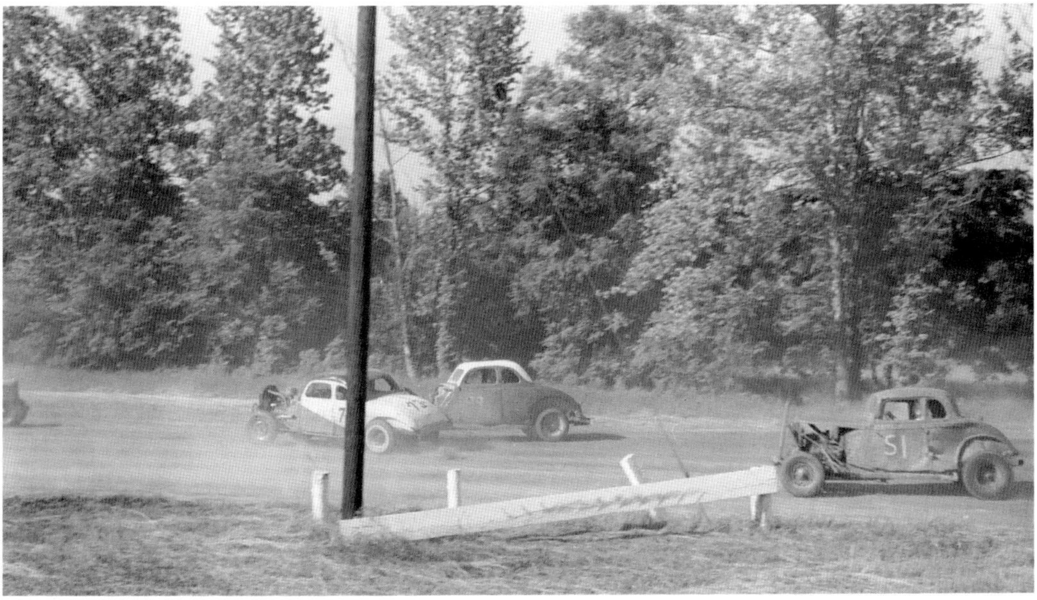

In the far left of this picture, one car is facing the wrong way to the oncoming traffic at top speed. It appears that Ralph Martin's No. 73 is about to cut in front of one car while Raymond Finney Richards in No. S1 is taking the inside and hoping to stay out of the trouble. (Courtesy of Marshall Love Jr.)

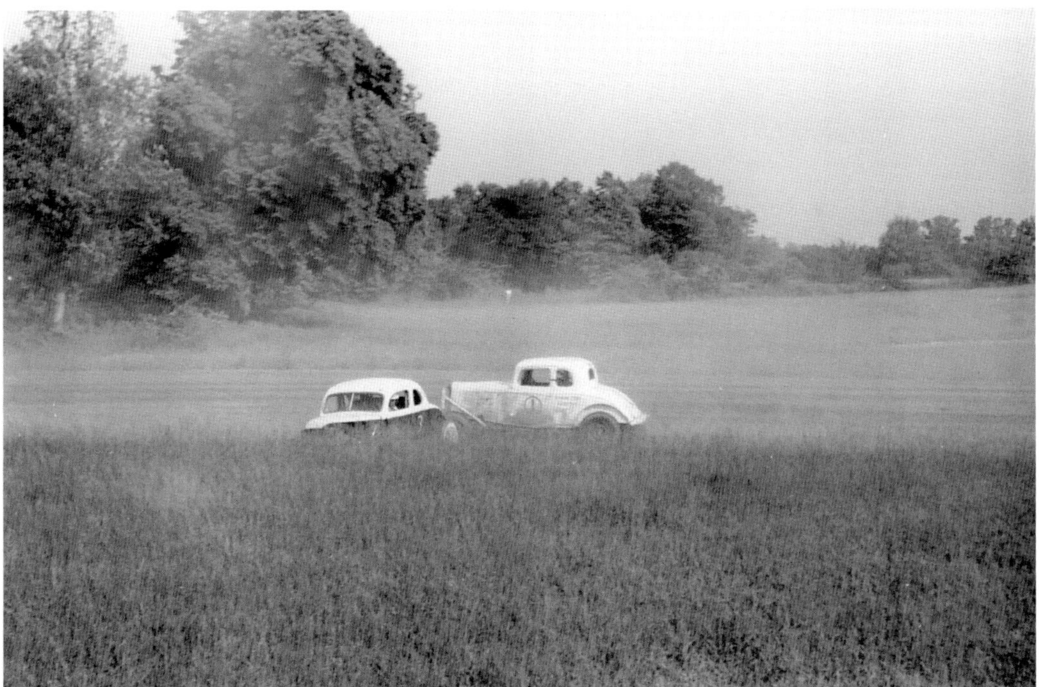

Charles T. Upton Jr. from Nashville, Tennessee, in the No. 1 car is making a pass coming out of turn two at Beech Bend Park in 1951. (Courtesy of Marshall Love Jr.)

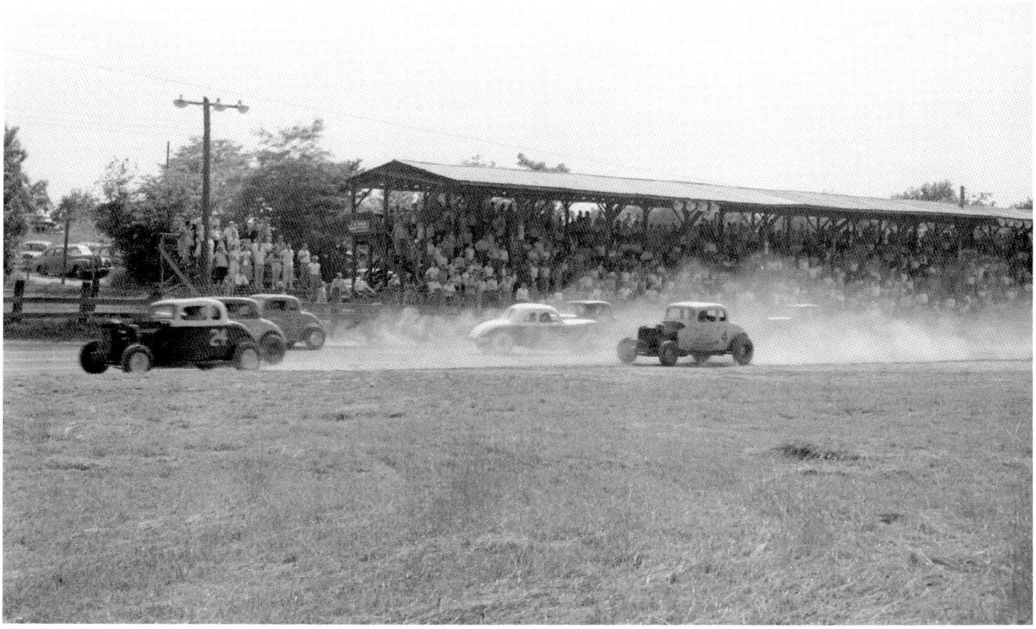

The cars are running close together coming down the front straight about to enter turn one with at least one car going the wrong way. Notice that the grandstands are packed, and everyone is standing to watch the action. (Courtesy of Marshall Love Jr.)

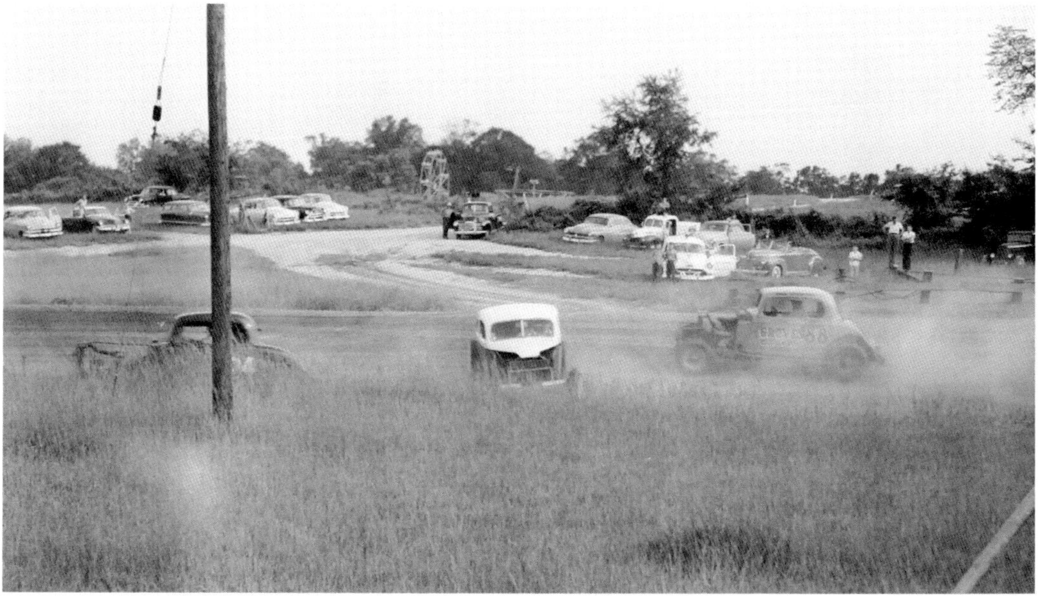

Paul Stradtner in Groves Garage No. 88 is making a pass as one car spins. Stradtner got his start in racing at Hopkinsville, Kentucky, when his boss's driver did not show up for a race. Paul's boss said, "I guess you're it." Stradtner protested, "But I don't even know what the flags mean!" His boss said, "All you need to know is that the checkered flag means the race is over." Notice the Ferris wheel in the center background. (Courtesy of Marshall Love Jr.)

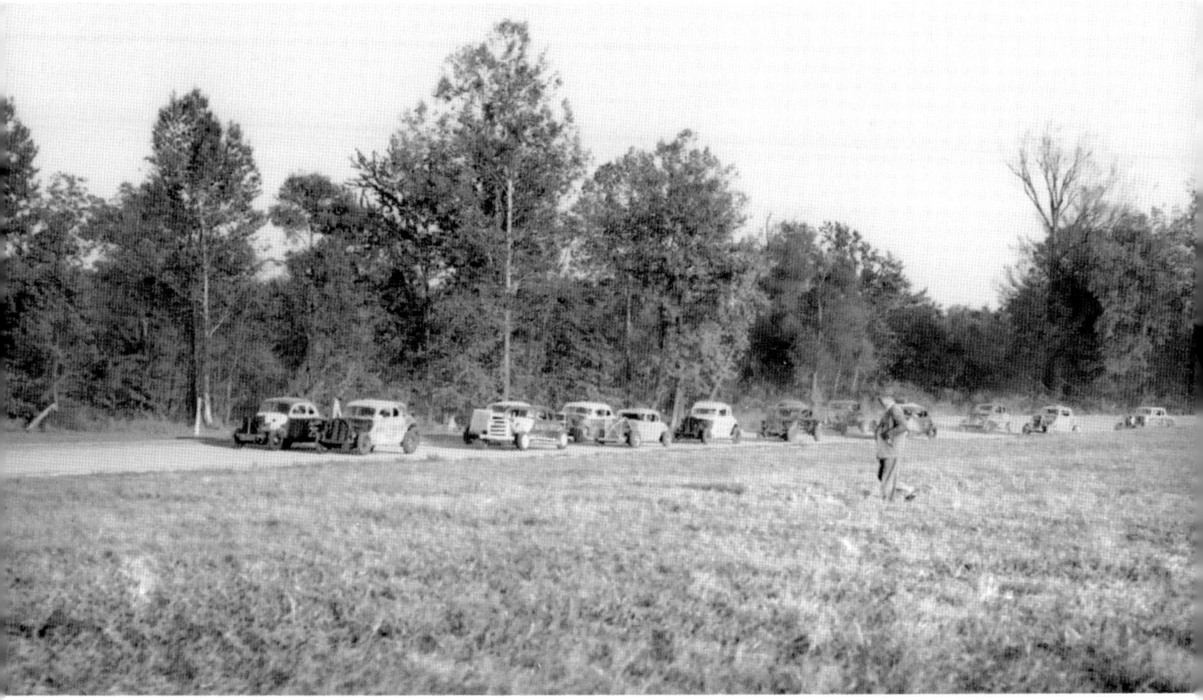

The stock cars are coming out of turn two at Beech Bend Park on their parade lap for the feature race. It appears that Elmo Guy in No. 7-11 is on the front row inside with his brother, Wayne Guy, in No. 25 on the front row outside. This line up indicates that Elmo was the fast qualifier and Wayne was the second fastest qualifier as feature races lined up based on qualifying times. Notice the man in the business suit walking across the infield in the right center of the picture.

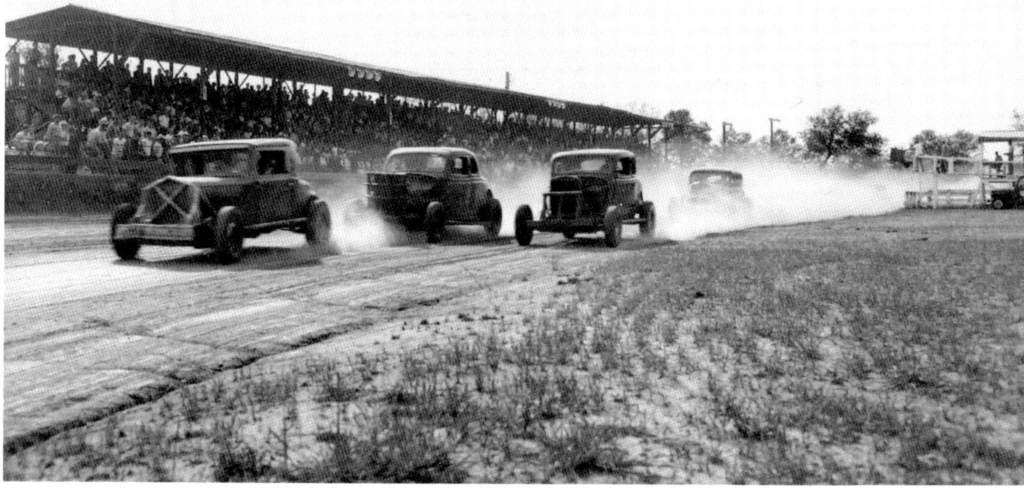

As Neil Cornell in No. 92 leads the pack, dust follows the action. In 1951, the fans always stayed for the conclusion no matter how dusty the air was. This is because all of the dirt and grime was considered part of the fun of stock car racing. From the modern, televised pristine view of stock car racing, it may be difficult to comprehend the passion for live dirt track racing. Today it is all about business and avoiding dirt! (Courtesy of Marshall Love Jr.)

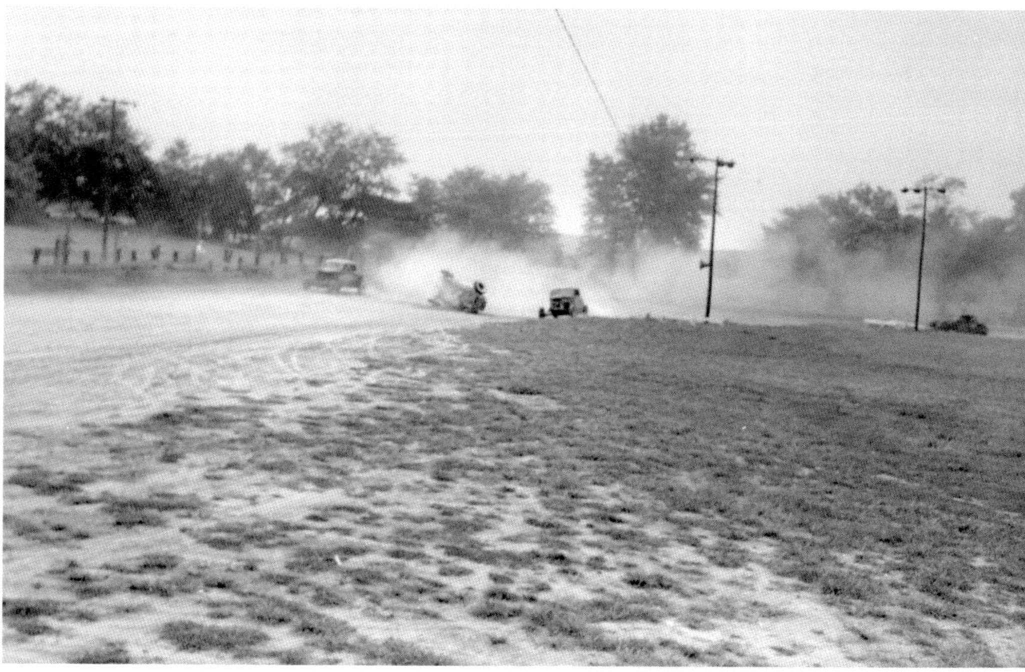

When a driver rolled his car, he joined the infamous "Upside Down Club." Ralph Martin may have held the Beech Bend Park record as he had at least four rollovers, leading to his nickname "Reckless Ralph Martin." (Courtesy of Marshall Love Jr.)

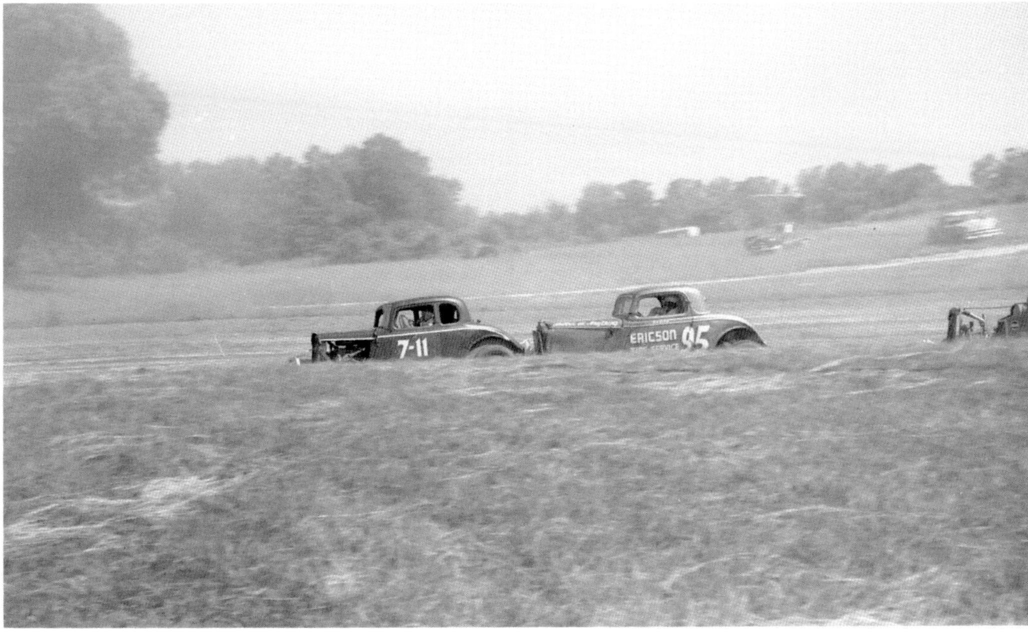

Elmo Guy drives No. 7-11 in a familiar place, i.e. first place. Winning is a lot about luck. During one event, Elmo's army surplus lap belt came loose while he was driving at top speed in traffic, and when he tried to re-hook it, he lost control and rolled the car. (Courtesy of Marshall Love Jr.)

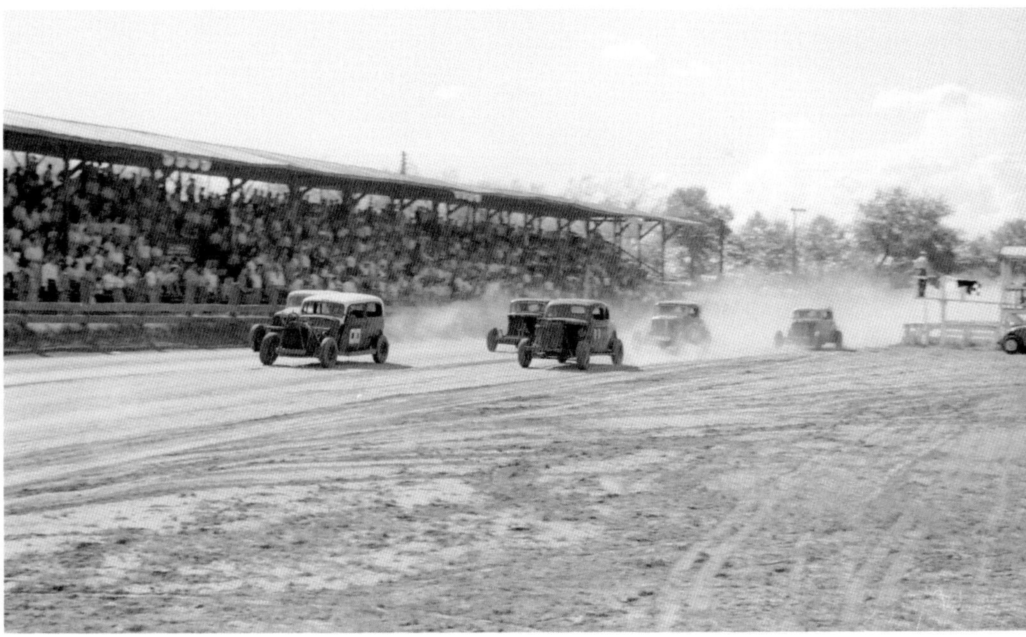

As the cars rumble out of turn four, the dust cloud moves into the grandstands. After a day at the stock car races in the early 1950s, a bath was the first thing the fans wanted upon returning to their homes. What is surprising is the more formal dress that fans wore to the races then compared to the type of informal clothing worn today. (Courtesy of Marshall Love Jr.)

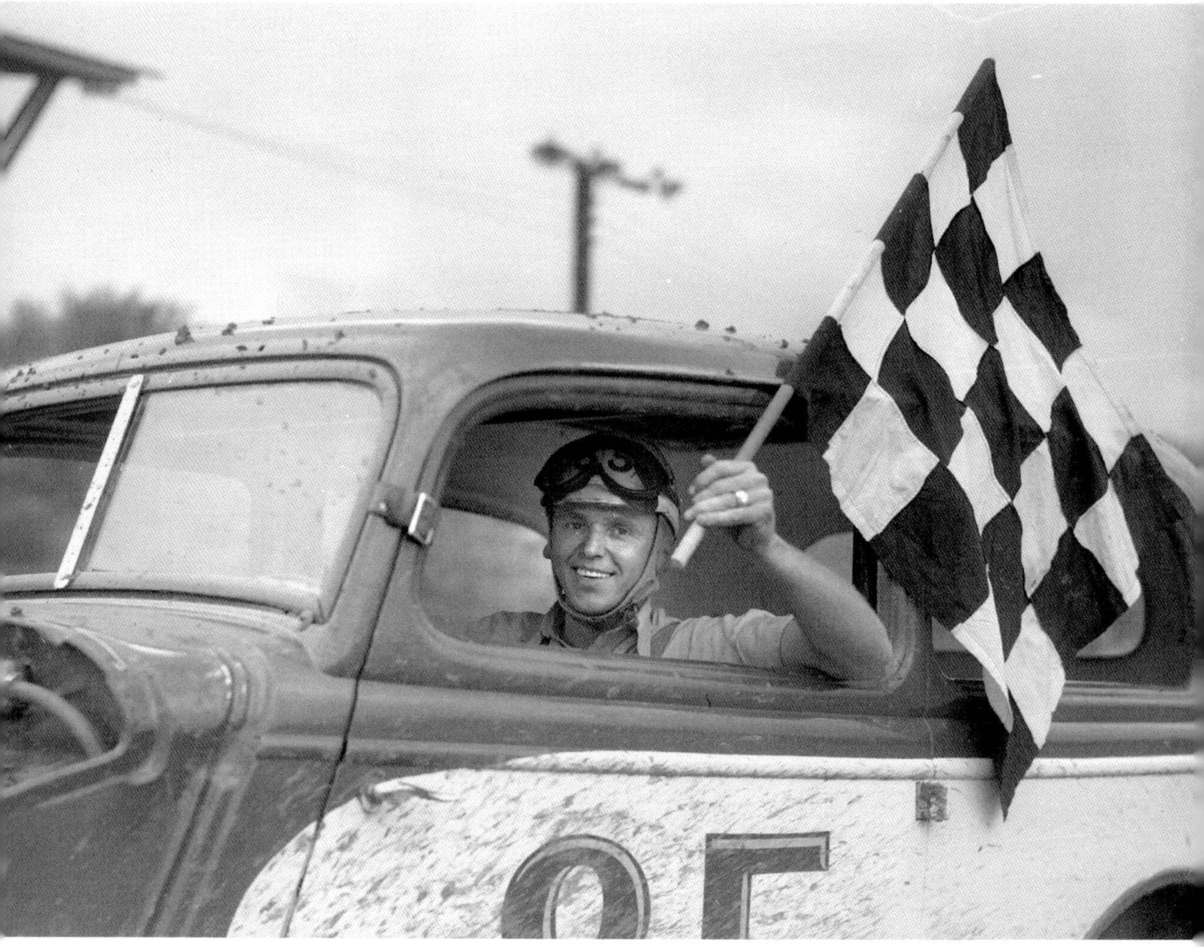

An unidentified driver takes a win. Many deep-thinkers have speculated about what motivates race car drivers and have suggested that it is the adrenaline rush, a desire to reach a state of arousal generally called "the zone," to develop a feeling of invincibility, or simply to have fun. Those who have raced know that it is none of these. The motivation is called winning! (Courtesy of Marshall Love Jr.)

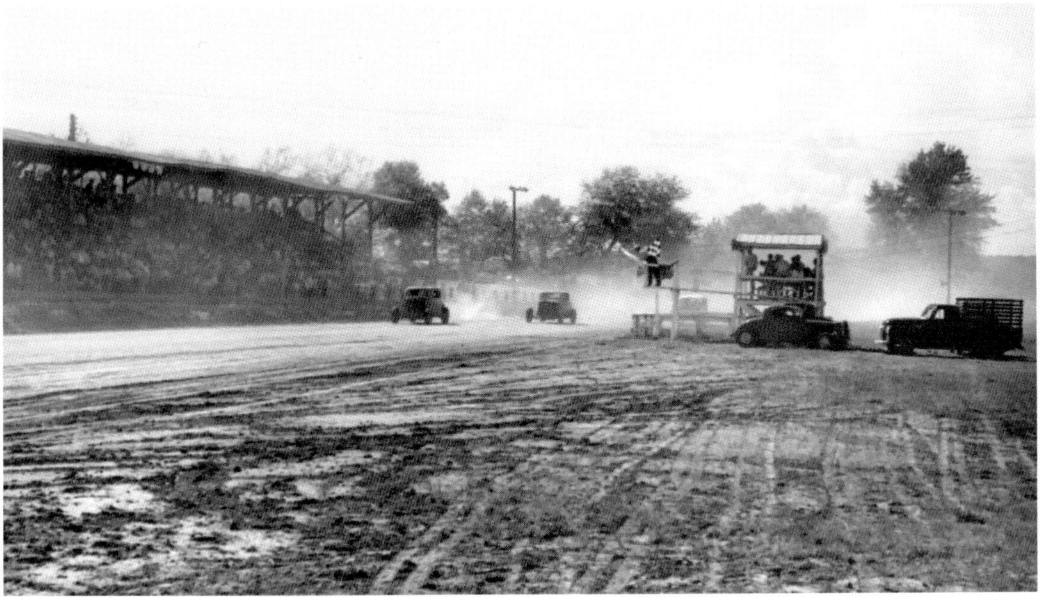

Raymond Finney Richards in No. S1 is heading toward the checkered flag on opening day, April 25, 1954. Raymond was called Ray by many people but was best known by his middle name, Finney. His first stock car the previous year was No. S11, but he took S1 for the 1954 season. Richards's car is a 1934 Ford with a 1946 Ford V-8 motor. (Both, courtesy of Marshall Love Jr.)

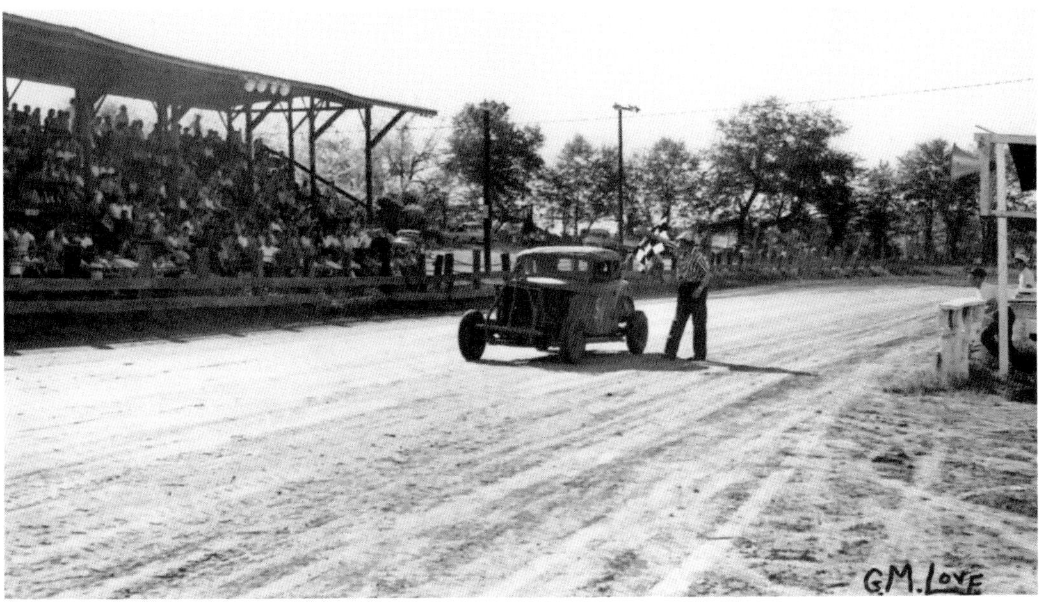

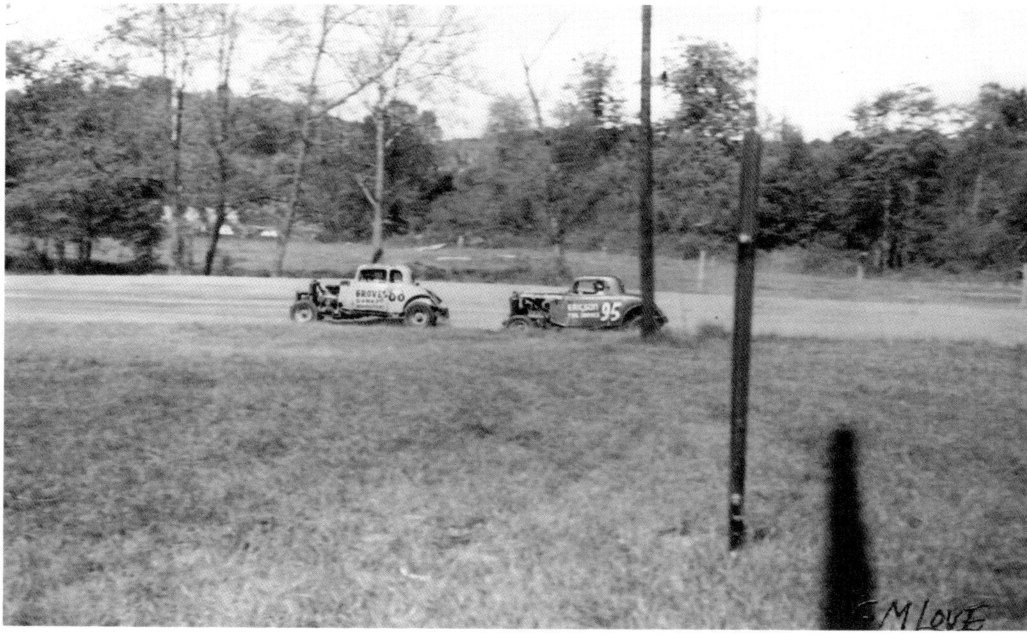

Driving Groves Garage No. 88, Paul Stradtner is on his way to another heat race victory. Stradtner's first race was on a 1-mile horse track in Hopkinsville, Kentucky. After one lap he had the lead, and he maintained that until the last lap. Coming out of the final turn, he could see the checkered flag waving when a wheel spindle broke, costing him the win. (Both, courtesy of Marshall Love Jr.)

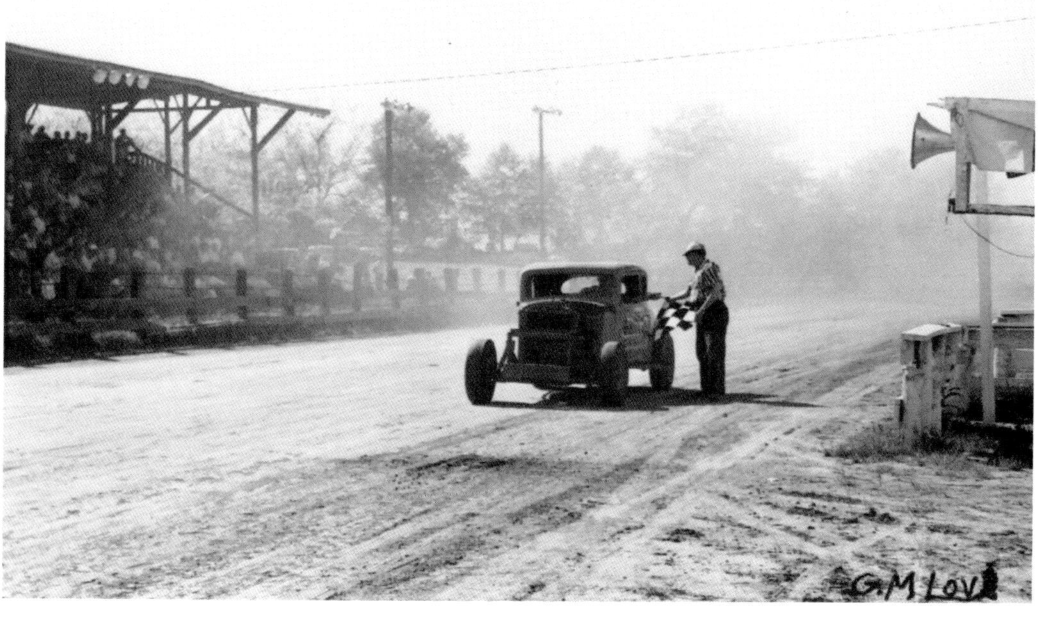

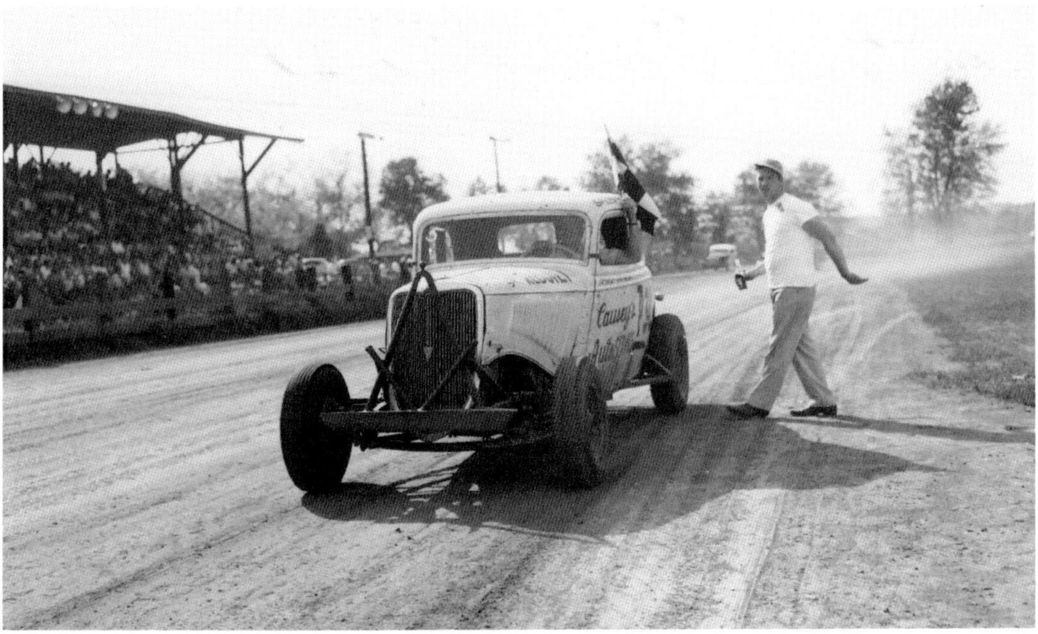

Beech Bend Park's mystery man, A. W. Nolen (above), takes another win. Nobody ever knew what Nolen's initials A. W. represented. Nonetheless, A. W. was a top stock car driver of the era. Below, flagman Roe Murray hands the checkered flag to another winner in the 1953 season. (Both, courtesy of Marshall Love Jr.)

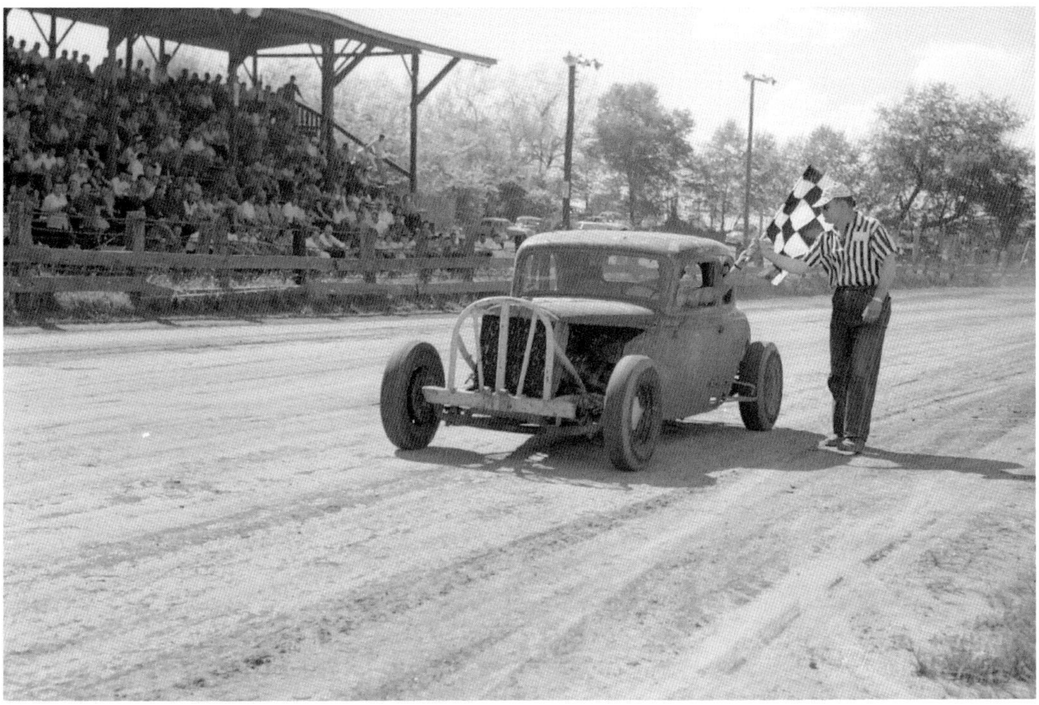

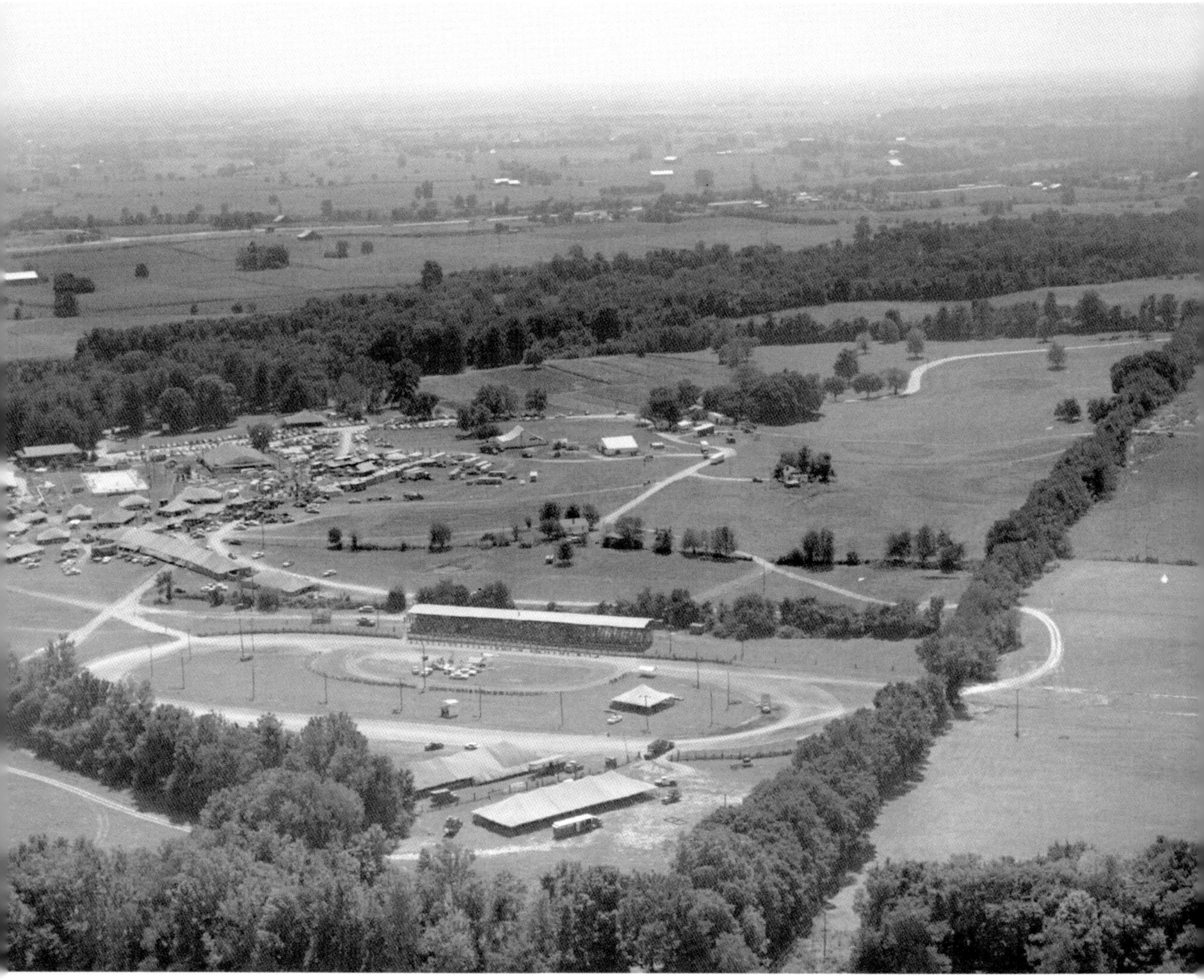

This photograph is an aerial view of the stock car track at Beech Bend Park. The trees at the bottom of the photograph line the Barren River. The buildings at the top left of the racetrack consist of the carnival-type rides and other entertainment found at Beech Bend Park. The white rectangle set amongst the buildings is the swimming pool. (Courtesy of Marshall Love Jr.)

4

The 1951 Regional Championship Race

Few among us are ever part of a movement that changes the way the world works or thinks or plays. Only a handful of people rise to a level on any scale whereby they are recognized for what they have accomplished with their lives. Even those pioneers who have achieved or laid foundations for achievement either fail to recognize what they have done or they minimize their accomplishments.

The men who launched stock car racing at Beech Bend Park in 1951 were part of the great movement that began after World War II. The United States had been impoverished by the Great Depression of the 1930s. The war disrupted and endangered the nation, and hundreds of thousands of Americans lost their lives in the epic struggle. Peace brought prosperity, and the age of the automobile hit full stride. It seems only natural that the automobile would find itself at the center of the thirst for entertainment by Americans. After the experience of a world war, perhaps only the danger and excitement of power and speed in the hands of young daredevils was capable of sating the American appetite for entertainment, and it exploded on the Bowling Green scene. After that initial Sunday with a throng of 2,500 ticket-buying fans, crowds of 5,000 to 7,000 fans were common.

Participants in stock car racing were touched in ways that most of them did not understand. It is a given that racing and an adrenaline rush go hand in hand. Just the anticipation of the race sends the heart racing and overworks the lungs and nervous system. It is absolutely nerve-wracking. The adrenaline rush makes one nervous, jumpy, and prone to errors, which compounds the complexity of dirt-track racing, a sport that is somewhat like driving on ice. The drivers who can control this nervous energy make the fewest mistakes and become winners. But all of these men, without exception, whether they won or lost, remember their moment in the sun when they were part of something new and memorable.

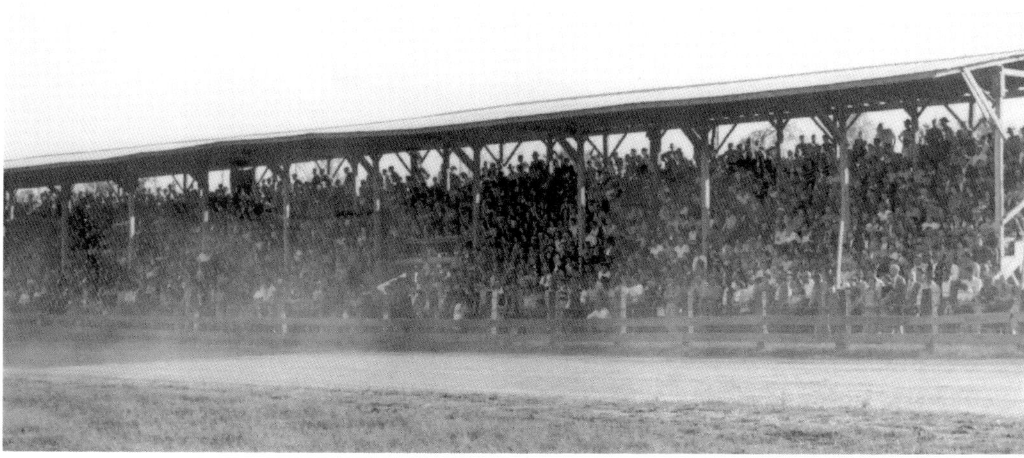

October 21, 1951, was the final stock car race of the inaugural season at Beech Bend Park. The Warren County championship had been run the prior Sunday on October 14, 1951, with Elmo Guy, a perennial favorite, copping the crown. Larry Graham finished second. Charles Garvin announced that he would award trophies for the first time at this final race of the season, which would feature Miss Kentucky 1951, Dottye Nuckols, as the presenter. The crowd was large and enthusiastic.

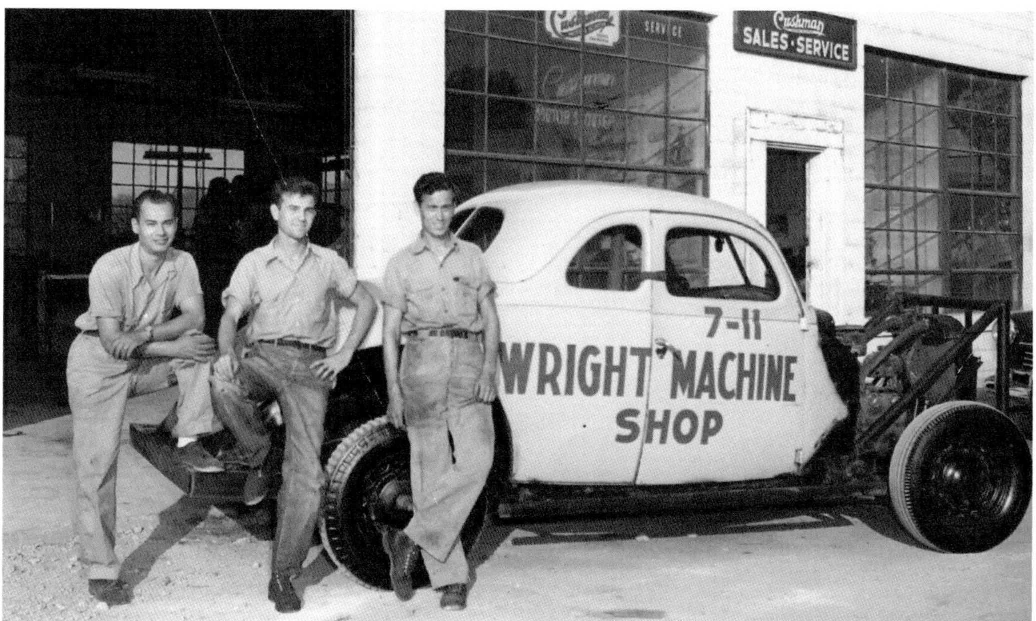

Floyd Wright (left), and his brother, Ernie Wright, the owner of Wright's Machine Shop, flank their stock car driver, Elmo Guy, in front of their 1932 Chevrolet coupe, No. 7-11, in 1951. The car, which was a consistent winner at Beech Bend Park, got its power from a 239 cubic-inch Ford flathead V-8, which was bored and stroked with a roller cam and fired by alcohol. Elmo was a motorcycle man, but he enjoyed the stability of having four wheels under him. In both stock car and drag racing, Elmo Guy set numerous records at Beech Bend Park.

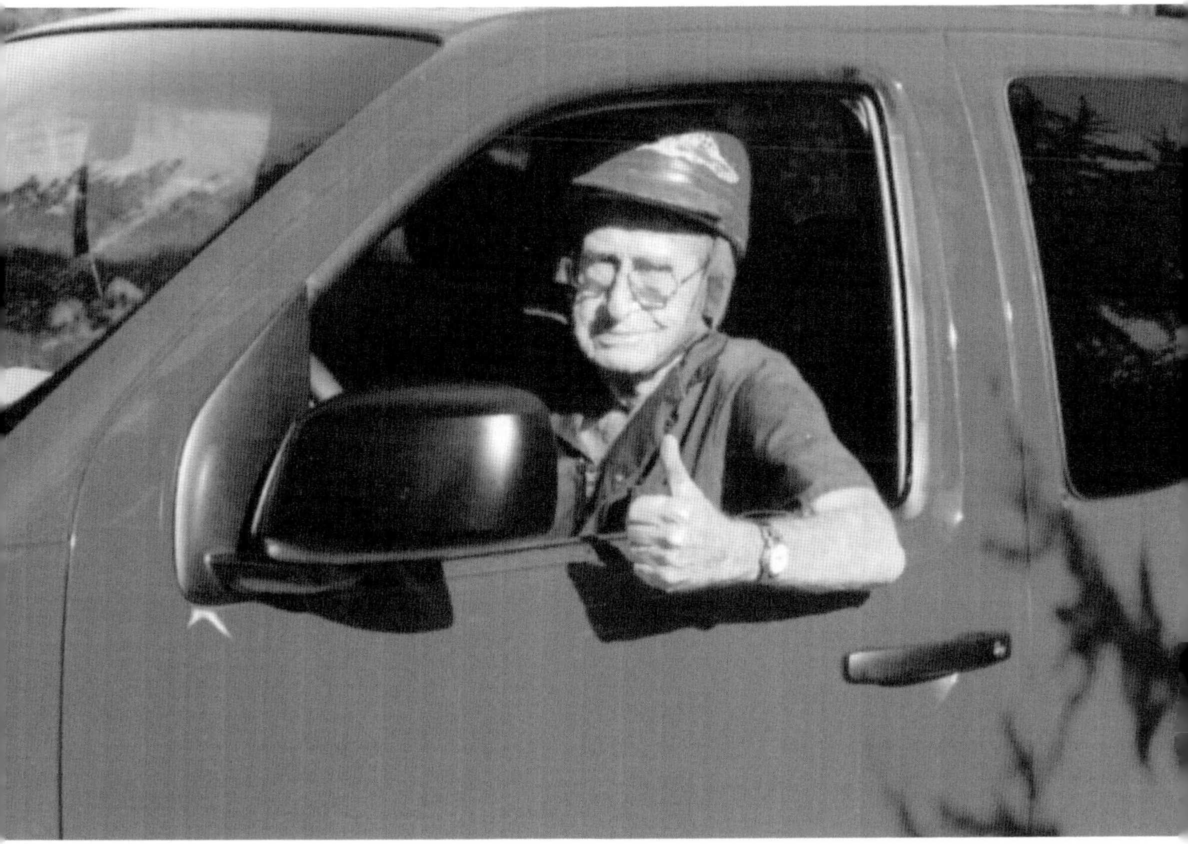

Larry Graham models his 1952 racing helmet, which was made from a World War II tanker's helmet. Graham's genius as a stock car driver was embodied in the methodical way he approached racing. Winning was the goal, but the problem to be solved was getting the necessary horsepower and equipment and using it in a way that winning became possible. Graham always counseled patience as a guiding principle. "Patience will keep you out of trouble so that you are always in a position to capitalize on other factors that will always occur during a race." Graham also believed that racing is 50 percent luck, but the driver with skill and patience will be the one to take advantage of the opportunities that luck provides. He said, "Simply stay out of trouble and let things sort themselves out. If you are in the first four or five cars with a couple of laps to go you can always win unless the leader is half a lap ahead, in which case you keep your car intact and go for second or third. There is always tomorrow!" (Courtesy of Larry Graham.)

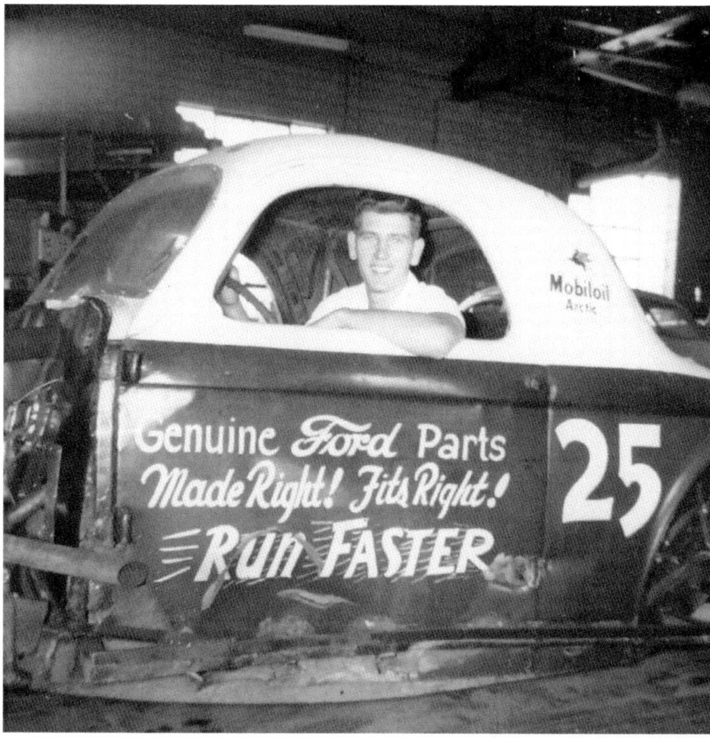

Wayne Guy in his 1934 Ford, which was powered by a 1946 Ford flathead 239 cubic-inch V8 with a 4-inch stroke, 3 7/16-inch bore, with a full racing cam. The car was owned by Ray Mercer, the shop foreman for Wallace Motor Company, the Bowling Green Ford dealership where Wayne also worked as a parts salesman; he retired 42 years later as manager of the parts department. (Courtesy of Yvonne Guy.)

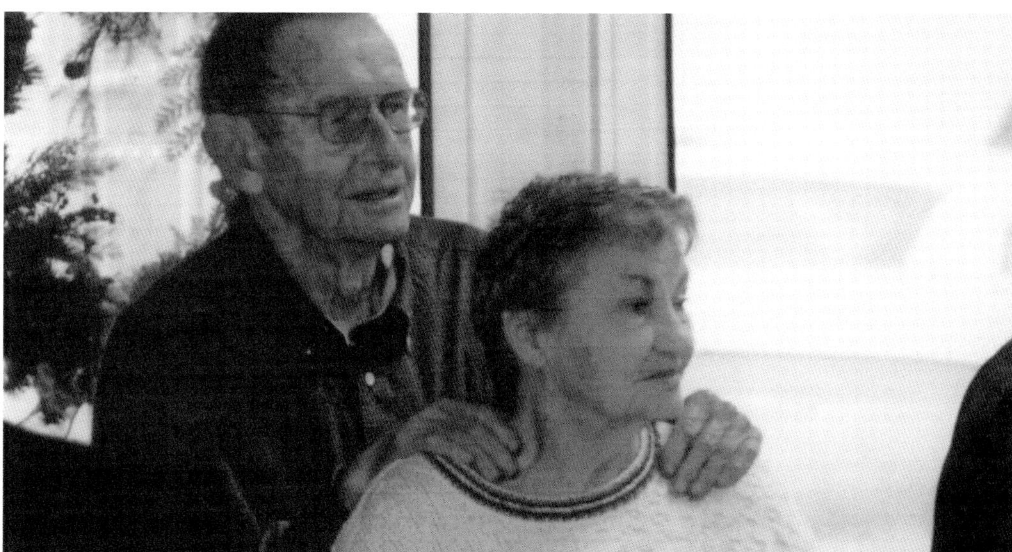

Pictured here is Larry Graham at age 80 with his wife, Beverly. After winning the Regional Championship at Beech Bend Park in 1951, Graham became a very "hot" commodity in 1952, driving a Hudson Hornet with a straight six engine with two carburetors. Graham and Elmo Guy battled it out every weekend at Beech Bend Park until Graham reported for U.S. Air Force duty as a second lieutenant in July 1952. Guy went on to take over the points lead and win the championship. (Courtesy of Larry Graham.)

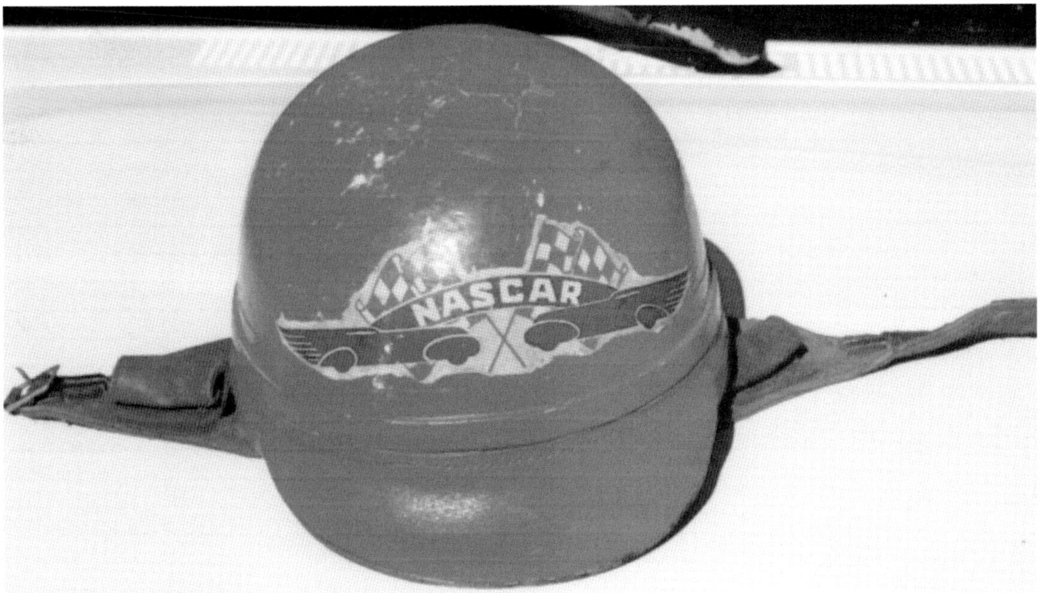

Larry Graham purchased a World War II tanker's helmet from an army surplus store, took it to Harvey's Saddle Shop located on Potter Street in Bowling Green, and had the flaps and bill added to make it look like a racing helmet of the day. Graham painted the helmet red and added the NASCAR logo. (Courtesy of Larry Graham.)

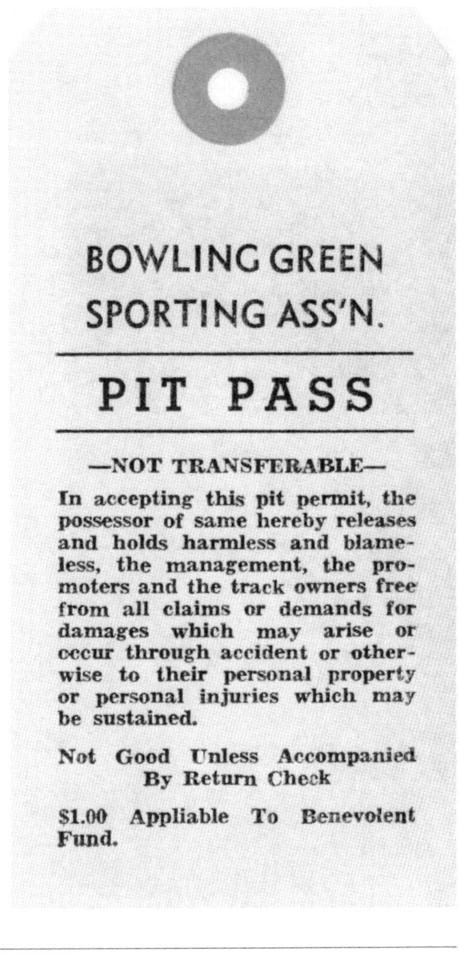

BOWLING GREEN
SPORTING ASS'N.

PIT PASS

—NOT TRANSFERABLE—

In accepting this pit permit, the possessor of same hereby releases and holds harmless and blameless, the management, the promoters and the track owners free from all claims or demands for damages which may arise or occur through accident or otherwise to their personal property or personal injuries which may be sustained.

Not Good Unless Accompanied By Return Check

$1.00 Appliable To Benevolent Fund.

This was Lattney Upton's pit pass for October 21, 1951, which was his 38th birthday. Larry Graham drove his Upton's Garage No. 22 to victory on this date for the Regional Championship race, the last race of the inaugural 1951 season. The pit pass is in the possession of the Kentucky Library and Museum, WKU.

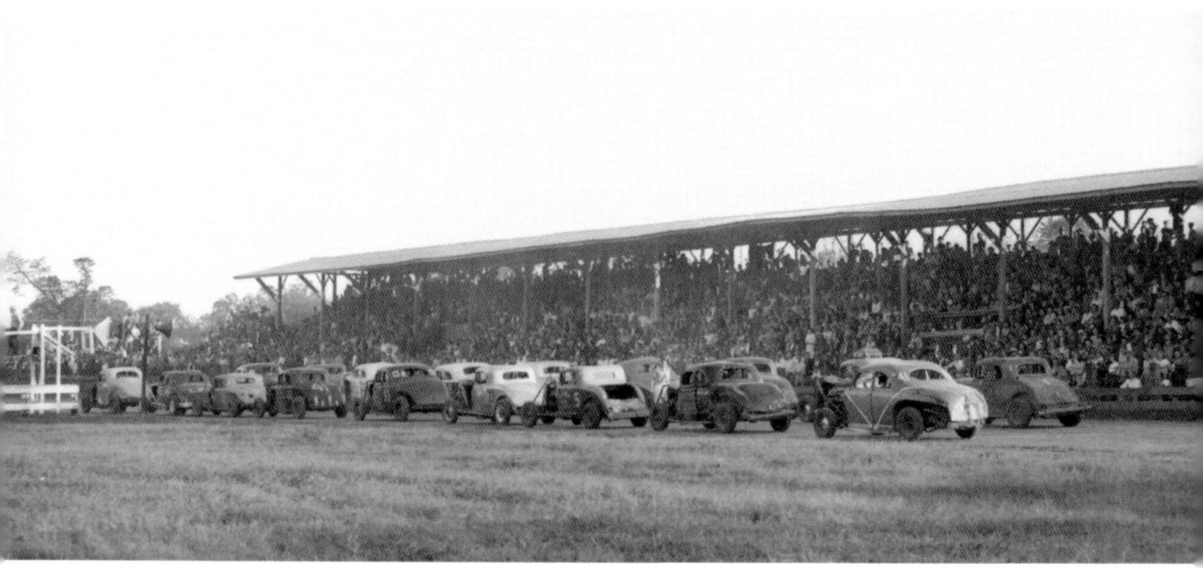

The cars are in line for the Regional Championship race on October 21, 1951, which was open to all comers. The local newspaper, the *Daily News*, tabbed Elmo Guy, the previous week's winner of the Warren County championship, as the favorite, with his brother, Wayne Guy, a close second. Elmo Guy is on the pole. Other identified cars are No. 22, Larry Graham, third row outside; Cliff Goad in No. 23, inside sixth row; and No. 5, Ralph Martin, inside seventh row. Also, for the first time, the race was broadcast live over a local radio station, WLBJ. The Kentucky Library and Museum, WKU, has a recording of the last five minutes of the race, including interviews with the winning driver, Larry Graham, and the car owner, Lattney Upton.

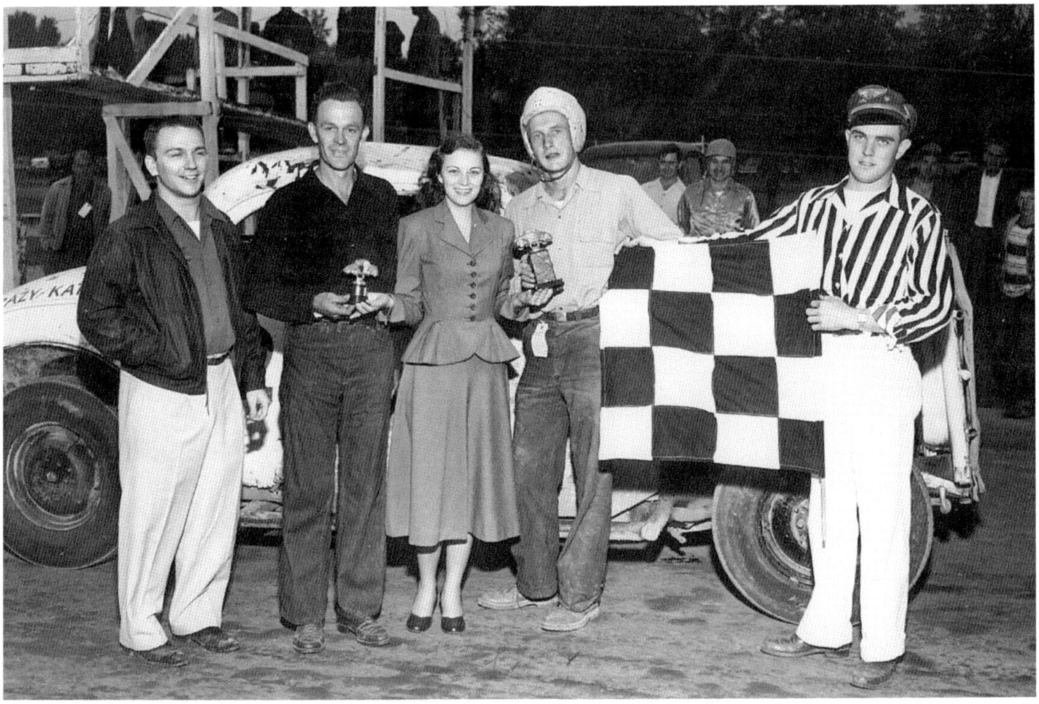

Miss Kentucky 1951, Dottye Nuckols, makes the trophy presentation at the first Regional Championship Stock Car Race at Beech Bend Park on October 21, 1951. From left to right are unidentified; Lattney Upton, car owner; Dottye Nuckols, Miss Kentucky; Larry Graham, driver; and Wayne Norris, flagman. Dottye was a lifelong schoolteacher and advocate of the Miss Kentucky pageant. She passed away at age 79 on November 8, 2008. (Courtesy of Sadie Upton Blind.)

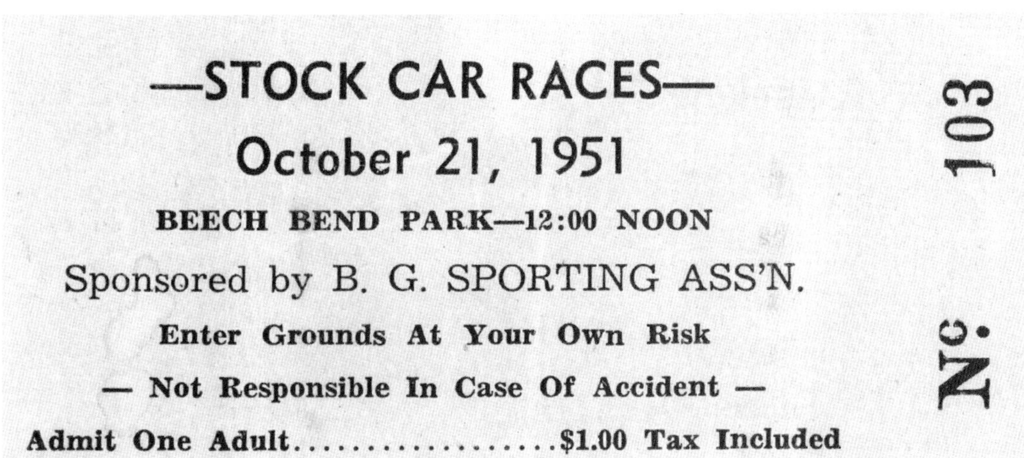

—STOCK CAR RACES—

October 21, 1951

BEECH BEND PARK—12:00 NOON

Sponsored by B. G. SPORTING ASS'N.

Enter Grounds At Your Own Risk

— Not Responsible In Case Of Accident —

Admit One Adult..................$1.00 Tax Included

Nº 103

This is Betty Upton's ticket to the final race of the 1951 season at Beech Bend Park. Notice that Betty's ticket is No. 103; she was one of the first in line along with her 10-year-old son, Larry, who got in free, to watch her husband, Lattney, and his driver, Larry Graham. Graham won the race. This ticket is part of the Kentucky Library and Museum, WKU's Bowling Green stock car collection.

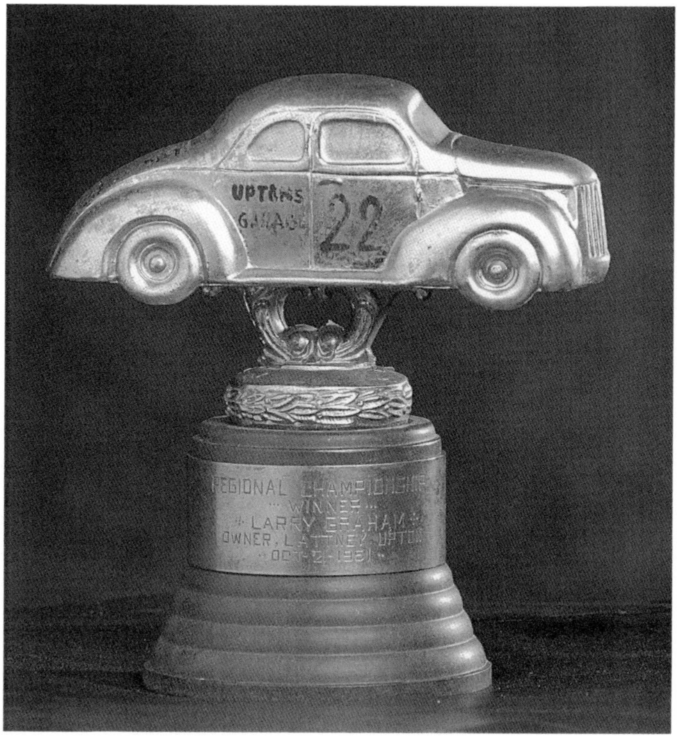

This is the car owner's trophy presented to Lattney Upton on October 21, 1951, when Larry Graham drove the Upton's Garage No. 22 to the win in the Regional Championship race. The inscription on the trophy reads, "Regional Championship Winner, Larry Graham; Owner, Lattney Upton, October 21, 1951." The Regional Championship trophies were the first trophies ever presented at Beech Bend Park. (Courtesy of Sadie Upton Blind.)

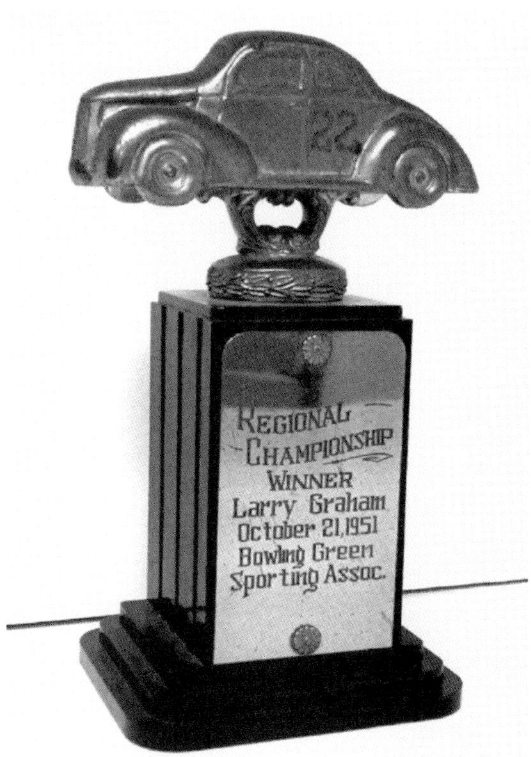

This is the driver's trophy presented to Larry Graham on October 21, 1951, after winning the Regional Championship race at Beech Bend Park. The inscription on the trophy reads, "Regional Championship Winner, Larry Graham, October 21, 1951, Bowling Green Sporting Assoc." This trophy is in the possession of the Kentucky Library and Museum, WKU.

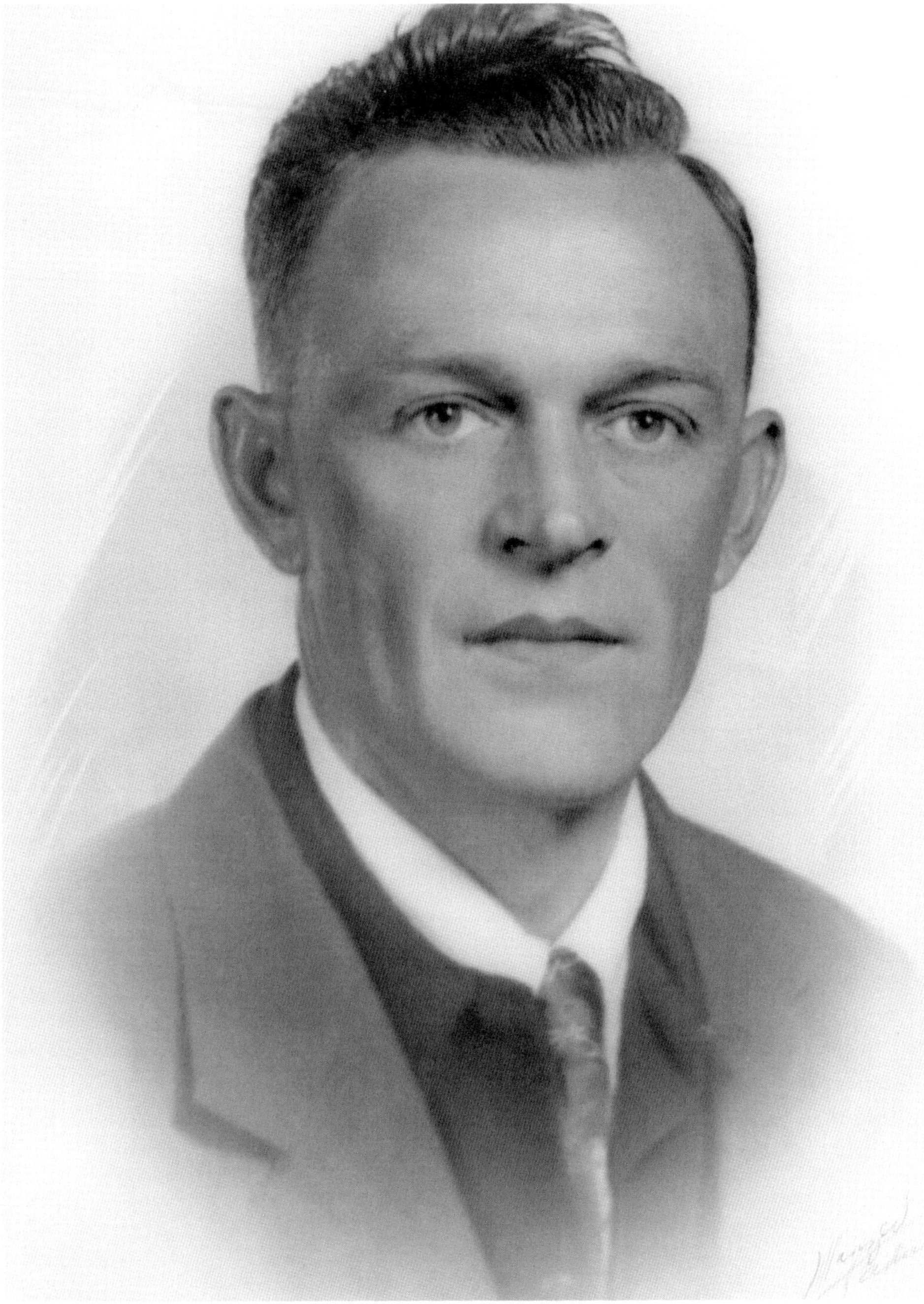

This is a portrait of Lattney Upton in 1946. He was the owner of Upton's Garage located at College and Sixth Streets in Bowling Green. Upton was born on the family farm in Richardsville, Kentucky, to Eli and Sadie Upton. His forebears had moved from Charleston, West Virginia, to Richardsville in 1801 to farm. The farm was substantial and, with the addition of land grants awarded to Elijah Upton for his service in the War of 1812, supported several generations of the Upton family. Upton fell in love with cars at age 21 when he bought his first car, a 1926 Star.

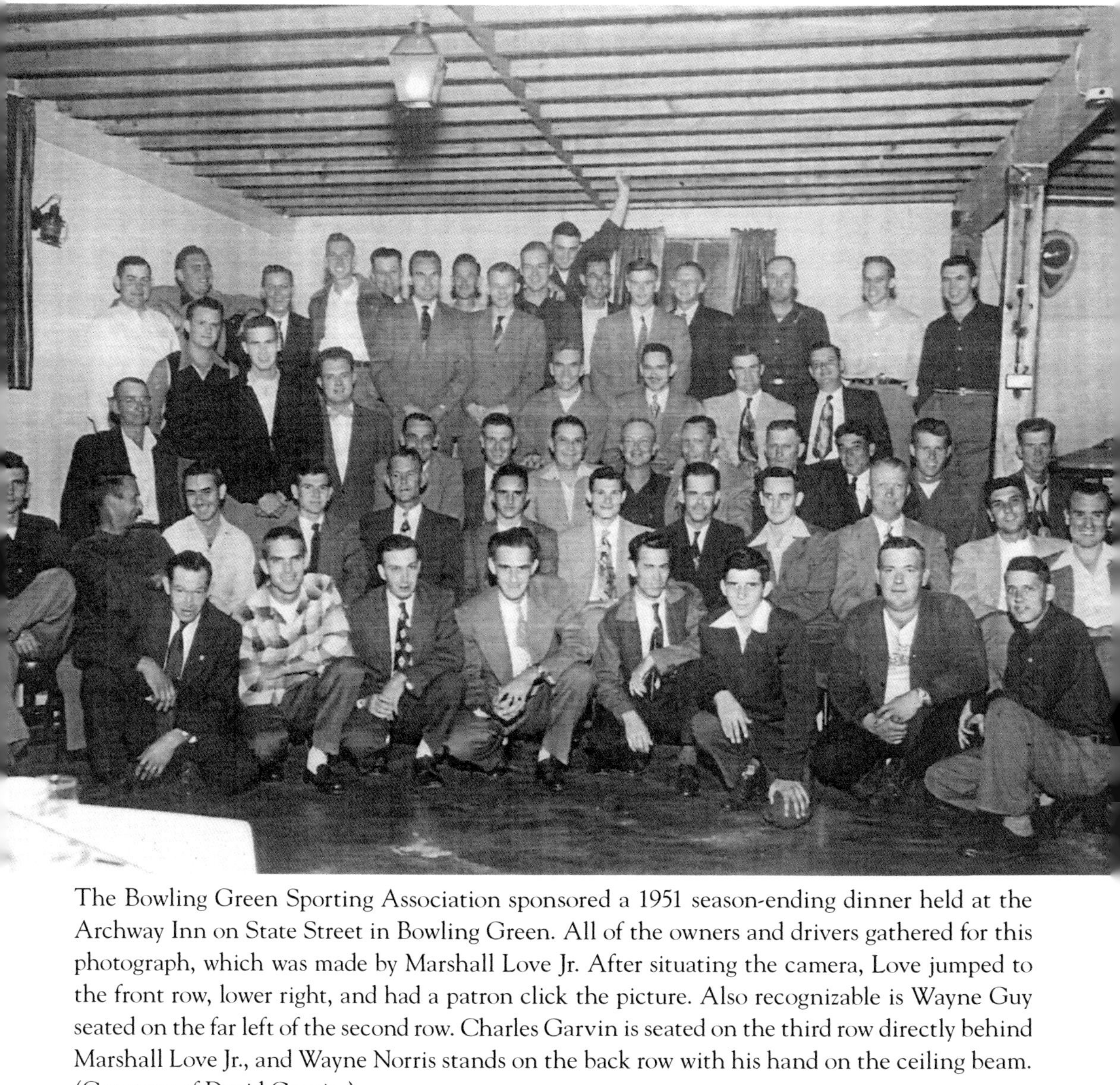

The Bowling Green Sporting Association sponsored a 1951 season-ending dinner held at the Archway Inn on State Street in Bowling Green. All of the owners and drivers gathered for this photograph, which was made by Marshall Love Jr. After situating the camera, Love jumped to the front row, lower right, and had a patron click the picture. Also recognizable is Wayne Guy seated on the far left of the second row. Charles Garvin is seated on the third row directly behind Marshall Love Jr., and Wayne Norris stands on the back row with his hand on the ceiling beam. (Courtesy of David Garvin.)

5

Charles Garvin, Promoter

Charles Garvin may not have been as grand a promoter as P. T. Barnum, but he was good! Garvin came up with "special events" week after week; one of the best was the "Mule Derby" held on Memorial Day 1952.

Garvin's call for farmers to race their mules at Beech Bend Park was overwhelming. Expecting to attract 10 to 15 entries, Garvin was surprised when more than 40 showed up. The stock car drivers were astonished when they arrived at the pit area to find it full of mules. The mules had already consumed the water that was kept in open barrels to cool the race cars. At any given moment, 10 or more mules were galloping around the track looking for a row of corn. But the ruckus started when the stock cars cranked up for the qualifying runs. The racket from the cars turned the pits into a pre-race comedy.

The opening parade of mules was led by a long-legged man astride a little pony, feet almost dragging the ground. A huge American flag was carried on the pony's withers. "My Old Kentucky Home" blared from the loudspeakers as the parade leader led the mules around the racetrack. One could almost imagine that one was at Churchill Downs awaiting the beginning of the Kentucky Derby!

One mule called "Big Red" was ridden by an elderly white-haired man in overalls. As the race commenced, Big Red lagged the leaders, but began making a move down the back stretch. As the mules rounded the last turn, it looked like too little too late for Big Red; however, at this point the old man on Big Red pulled out a red bandanna and waved it in front of "Big Red's" eyes. Big Red laid his ears back and was on his way to a win when Raymond McClard, the flagman, stepped out and began waving the checkered flag. Big Red slammed on the brakes and cut across the infield, never crossing the finish line. The old man was so angry that Charles Garvin gave first place money to two winners!

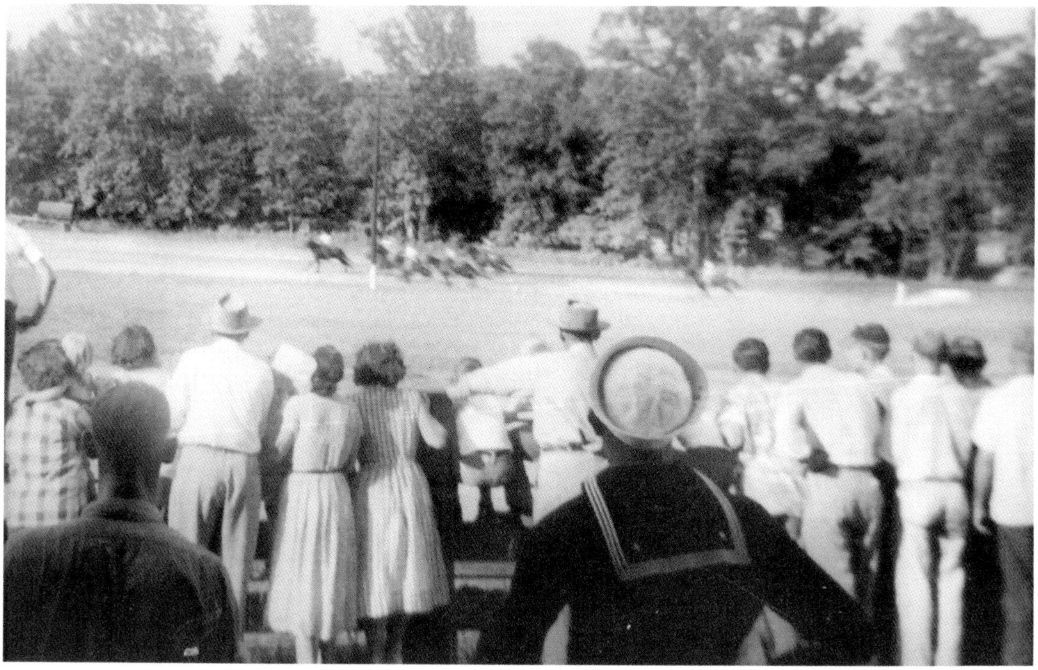

"They're coming down the back stretch with Big Red making his move!" Garvin's Mule Derby was so successful that he ran it two weeks in a row to give all the mules a chance to compete and win. Later Garvin introduced ostrich racing at intermissions, using birds that stood 8 feet tall and weighed 300 pounds.

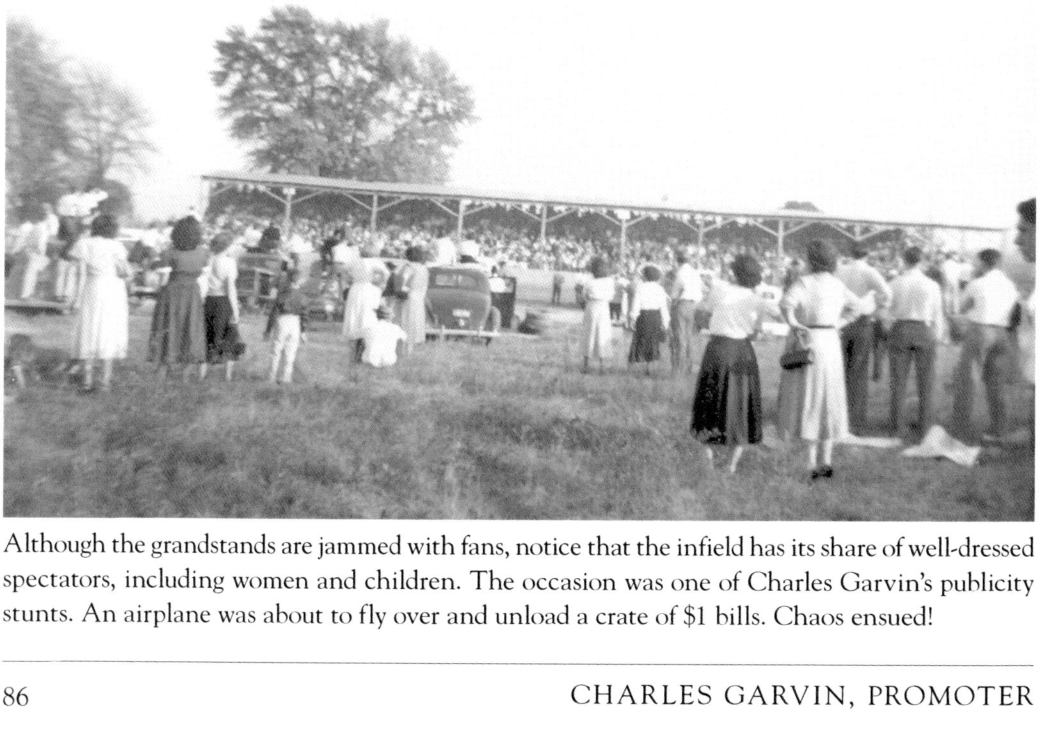

Although the grandstands are jammed with fans, notice that the infield has its share of well-dressed spectators, including women and children. The occasion was one of Charles Garvin's publicity stunts. An airplane was about to fly over and unload a crate of $1 bills. Chaos ensued!

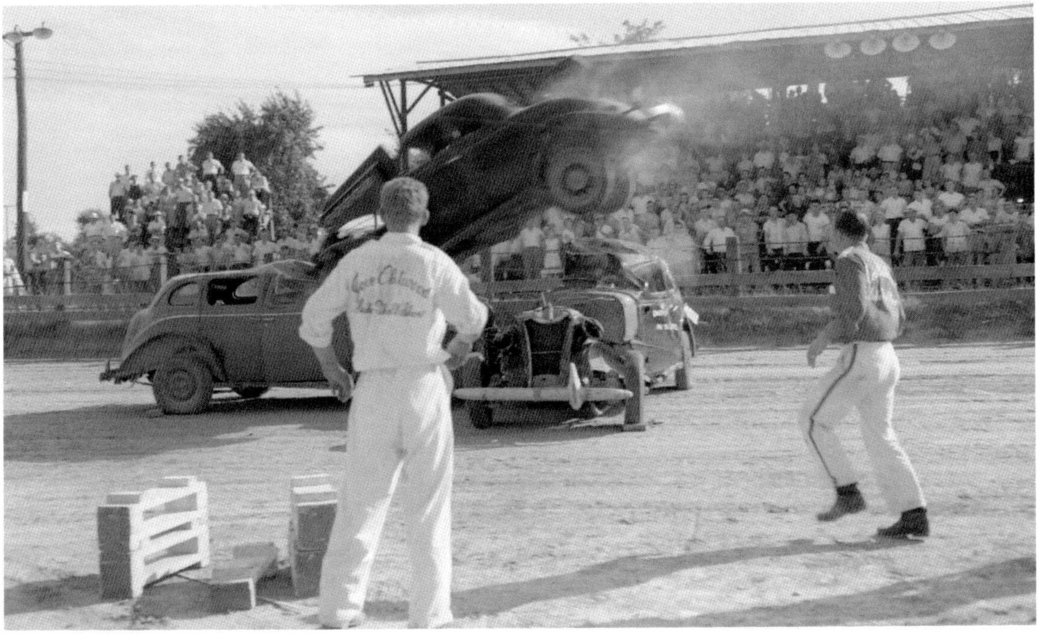

Before there were monster truck shows, Charles Garvin was having stunt drivers drive old cars up a ramp, jump another car, and smash into the top of another. Most people today think that the monster trucks developed these stunts, but it was people like Charles Garvin who were coming up with exciting spectacles to keep fans coming to their racetracks. (Courtesy of Marshall Love Jr.)

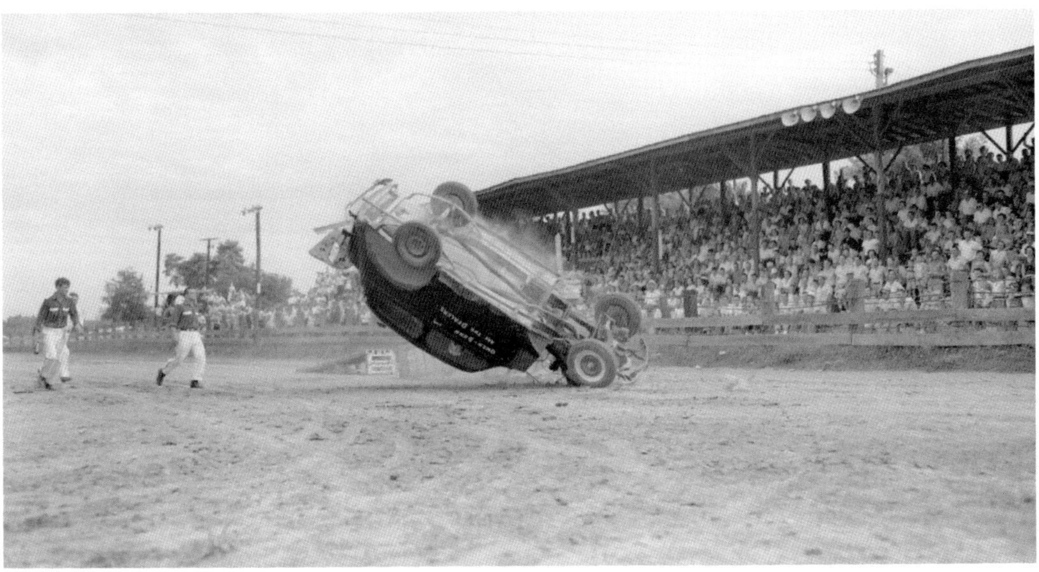

There is nothing like a crash or a rollover to bring the fans to their feet as they collectively gasp in anticipation of an exciting spectacle but with fear of a calamity. Charles Garvin decided to capitalize on the fans' collective emotion for these events and staged his own crashes and rollovers with professional stunt drivers. They were very popular. (Courtesy of Marshall Love Jr.)

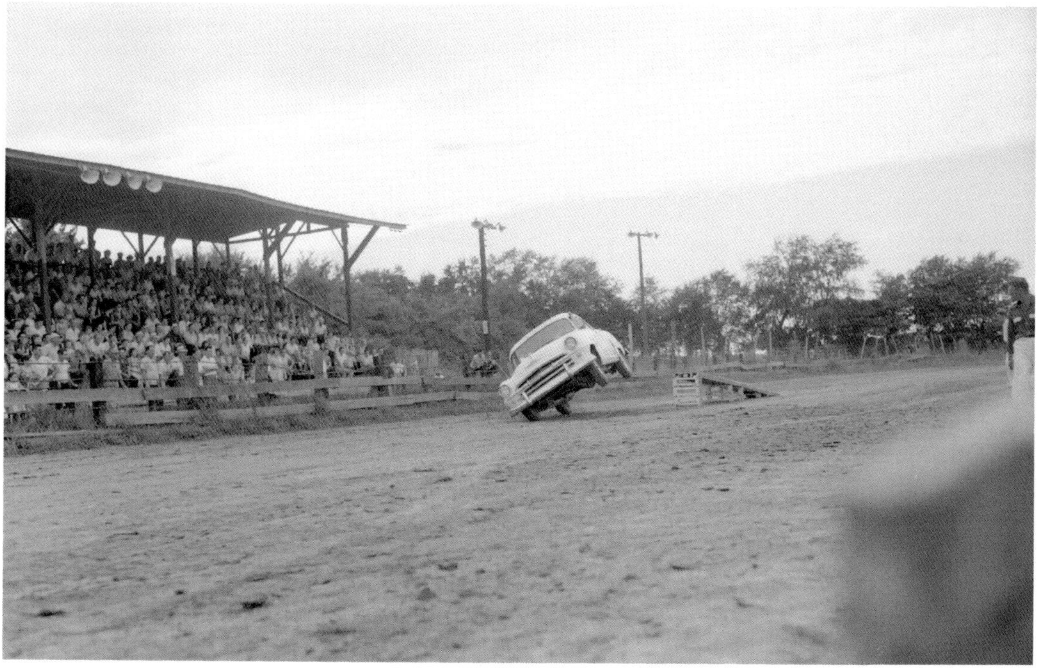

On several occasions, Charles Garvin hired stunt drivers to wow the crowds at intermission. This car runs the driver-side wheels up a ramp and then maintains momentum while driving the car down the straightaway on two wheels. (Both, courtesy of Marshall Love Jr.)

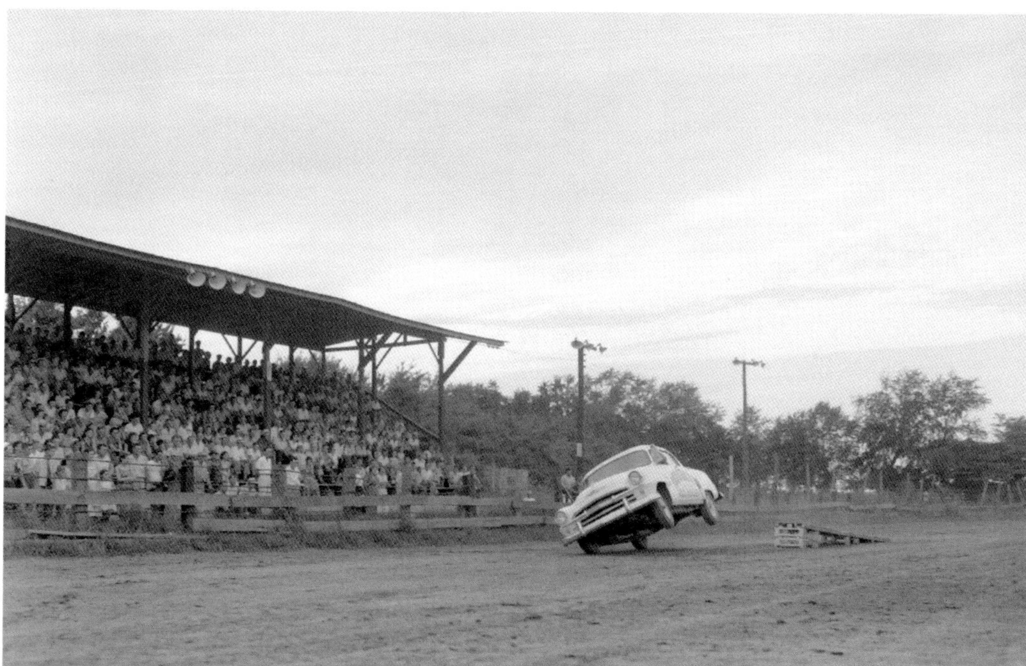

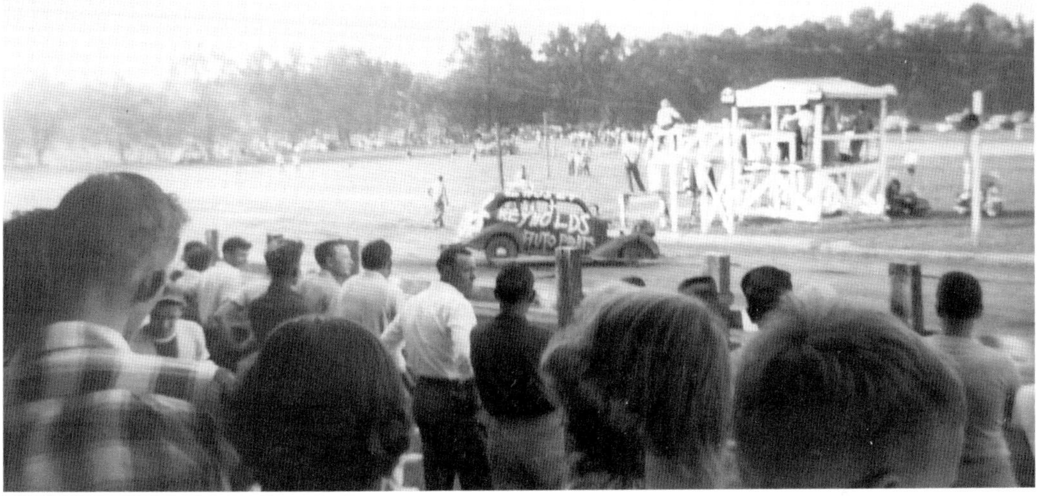

Reynolds Auto Parts is the winner of the "Demolition Derby!" In this bash-fest, the objective of each entry was to deliberately cause crashes. The cars raced around the track looking to smash into another car and disable it. Demolition drivers looked to smash the weak points in the opponents' cars, which were the radiators. The last car that was still moving under its own power was the winner.

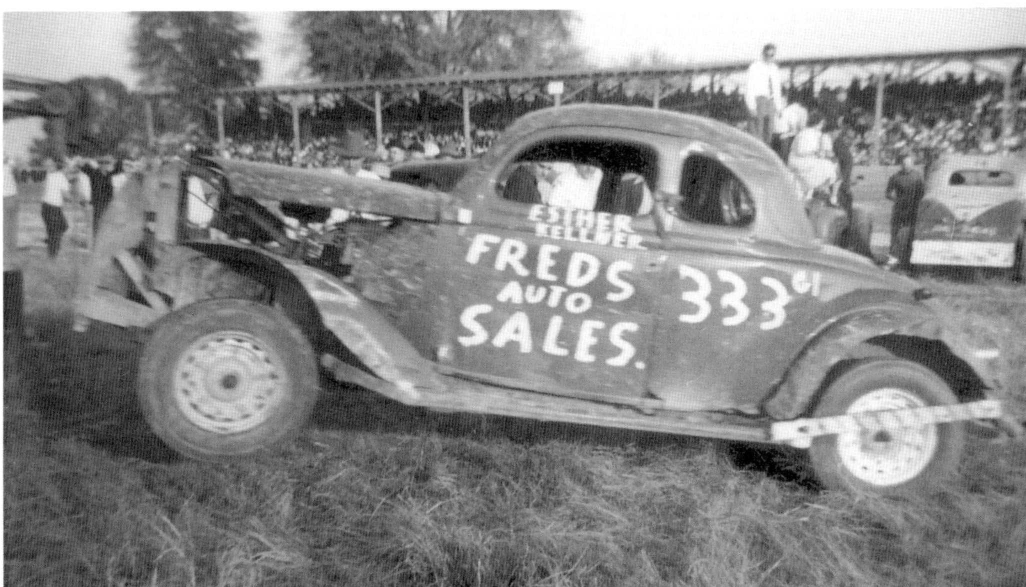

Fred's Auto Sales' No. 333, driven by Esther Kellner, was a casualty in the Powder Puff Derby. In 1951, not a single woman raced at Beech Bend Park; however, beginning in 1952, Charles Garvin occasionally held a special race for the ladies, which was commonly called the Powder Puff Derby. In today's racing, women compete with men; no man has the guts to talk about Powder Puffs.

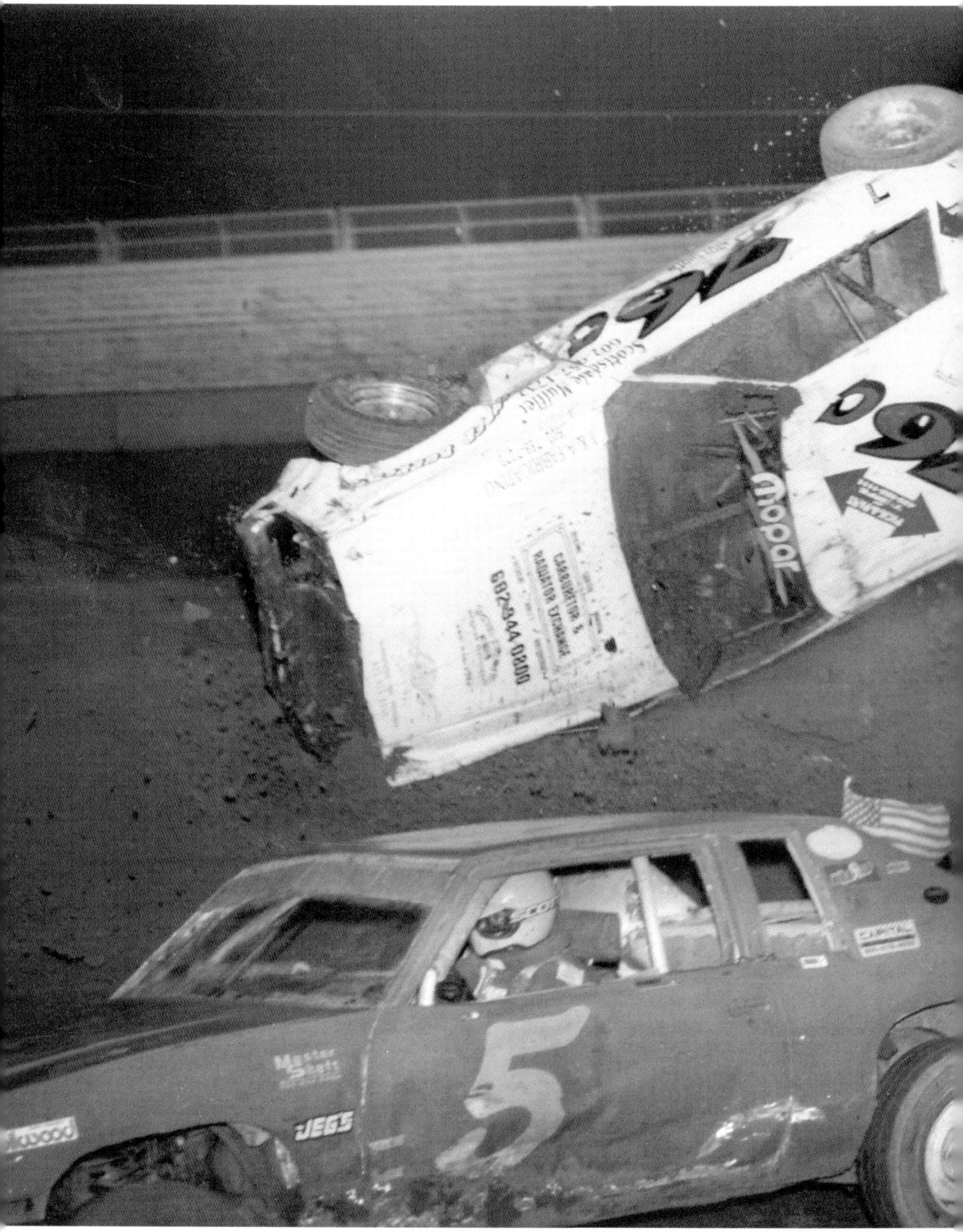
5
JEGS

Some days everything is upside down. This photograph is not one of Charles Garvin's stunts; this is the real thing. This type of action brought the fans back to the track week after week. This "sky walker" came to earth with a jolting crash after going end over end; nevertheless, the driver walked away unscathed. (Courtesy of Jim Fargo, JAF Photo.)

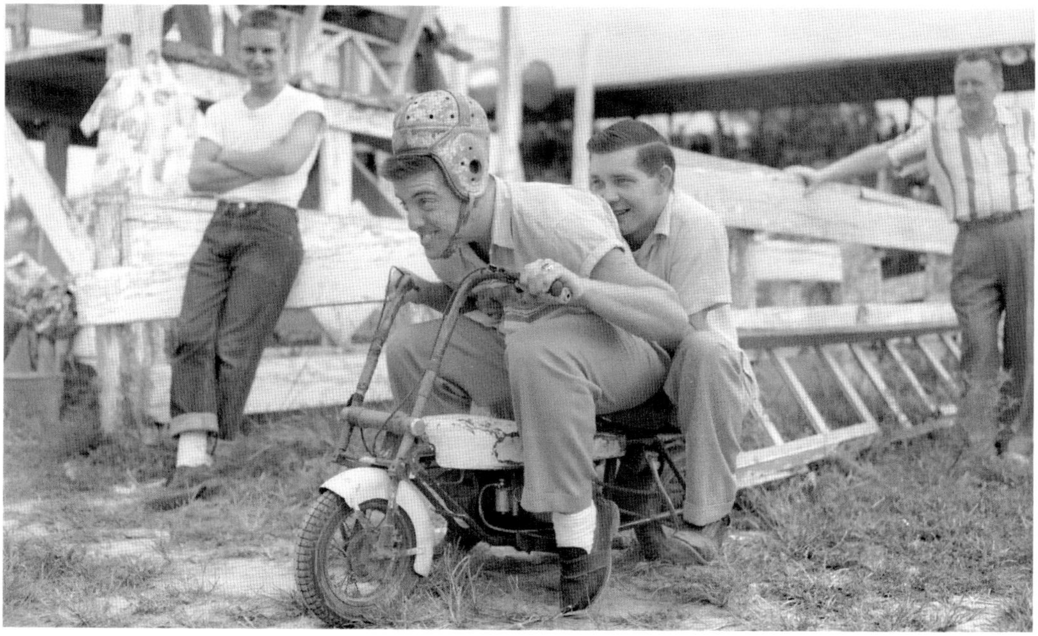

Charles Garvin's stunts knew almost no bounds. This photograph shows two young men riding a child's size motorcycle. Garvin later went a step further, coaxing Elsie Hamilton with a lot of cash to let him bury her alive for two weeks. That stunt ranked right up there with the Mule Derby. (Courtesy of Marshall Love Jr.)

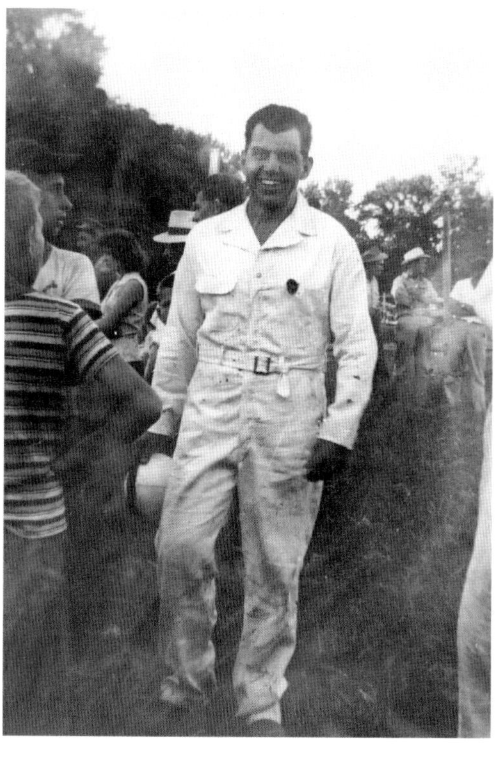

On a Sunday in 1952, Charles Garvin hired parachutist Ken Clough, also known as "Crash Carson," to jump from an airplane at 2,200 feet with the intention of landing on the racetrack. The winds were not favorable that day as Crash fell several hundred feet before his main and reserve chutes opened. He became entangled in the shroud lines and landed on a rocky ledge about 50 feet from the Barren River. Crash had to be rescued by the race car drivers. (Courtesy of Yvonne Guy.)

6

"He Was an Early-Day Dale Earnhardt"

With the dominance of NASCAR on the stock car racing scene today, few people remember the small-town roots of the sport or that NASCAR was organized in 1948, which was the same year stock car racing began to crop up at Beech Bend Park. One never considers that it was stock car drivers like Wayne and Elmo Guy, Jimmy Belcher, Larry Graham, Anthony "Sluggo" Warden, Bob Reuther, and many others who had the ability to compete with the early NASCAR crew.

In particular, Bob Reuther stands out because he was the first stock car driver who raced in Bowling Green to make it to the big time. He raced everywhere in the South where there was a racetrack. He raced at Beech Bend Park as often as he could get his car there. Racing historian Russ Thompson, who contributed to this book, said, "He was an early-day Dale Earnhardt. He was tough and talented and had a flair for making headlines. If he had raced in the modern era, he would have been right up there with the very best." Larry Woody, a sportswriter in Nashville, told a famous episode where another driver wrecked Reuther. Reuther fired up his crumpled car, charged across the infield, and waited in ambush. He T-boned the offending driver as he came down the backstretch. Reuther commented that, "Back then we enforced our own rules. If somebody hit you, you hit them back." That was also the rule at Beech Bend Park.

"Bullet" Bob Reuther made his NASCAR debut at Atlanta, Georgia, in 1951. He set the qualifying speed record for NASCAR's Daytona Beach course in 1957, which will never be broken because the course was abandoned after the 1958 race. He won the inaugural championship at the old Nashville Fairgrounds Speedway in 1958. Bullet Bob was a member of the first class of inductees into the Tennessee Motorsports Hall of Fame in 1987. Reuther, Bowling Green's most famous stock car driver and NASCAR connection, passed away at age 80 on July 3, 2008.

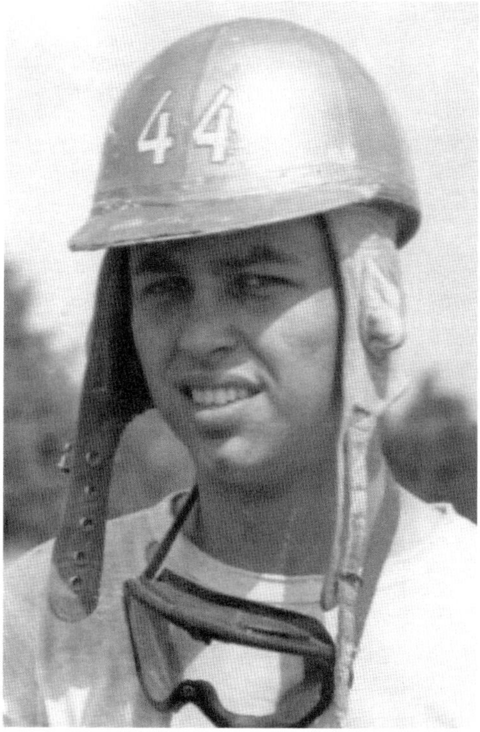

This is a young Bob Reuther of Nashville, Tennessee, as he looked in his early visits to Bowling Green. Reuther was one of the early group of out-of-town drivers that Charles Garvin invited to race at Beech Bend Park to ensure that he had a full field of cars on hand for race day. Initially, the drivers from Nashville, who had much more experience than the Bowling Green drivers, dominated racing at Beech Bend Park. (Courtesy of Russ Thompson.)

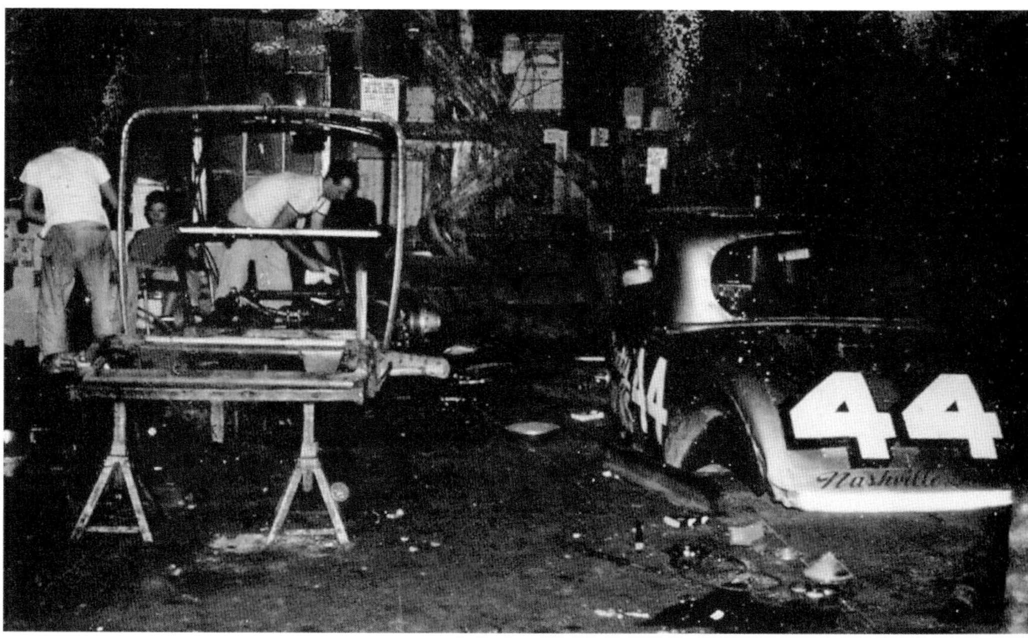

Reuther's stock cars were built in his Reuther Electric Company business in Nashville, Tennessee. Reuther's stock cars were taken apart and rebuilt from the ground up. In this photograph, the chassis is sitting on jack stands in preparation for remounting the body of No. 44. The best stock cars were meticulously built and maintained. (Courtesy of Russ Thompson.)

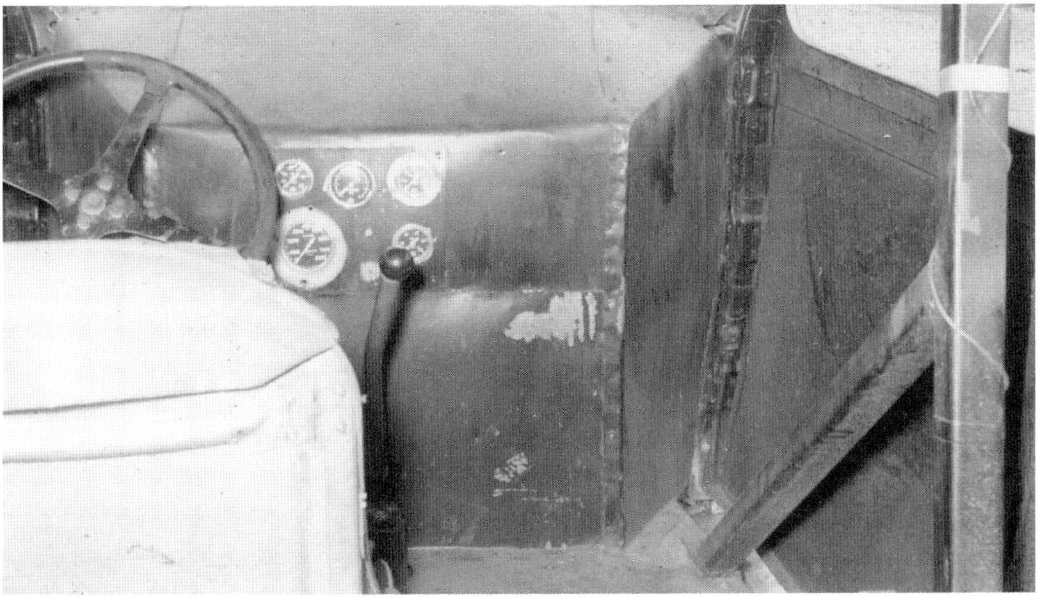

This is the inside of Bob Reuther's cockpit. The dash has been stripped out and replaced with a firewall that holds five instruments, most likely gauges measuring oil pressure, engine temperature, gas, speedometer, and RPMs. The seats have been removed, leaving only the driver's seat; although unseen in this photograph, the back of the interior has been sealed off from the trunk area where the gas tank is stored. (Courtesy of Russ Thompson.)

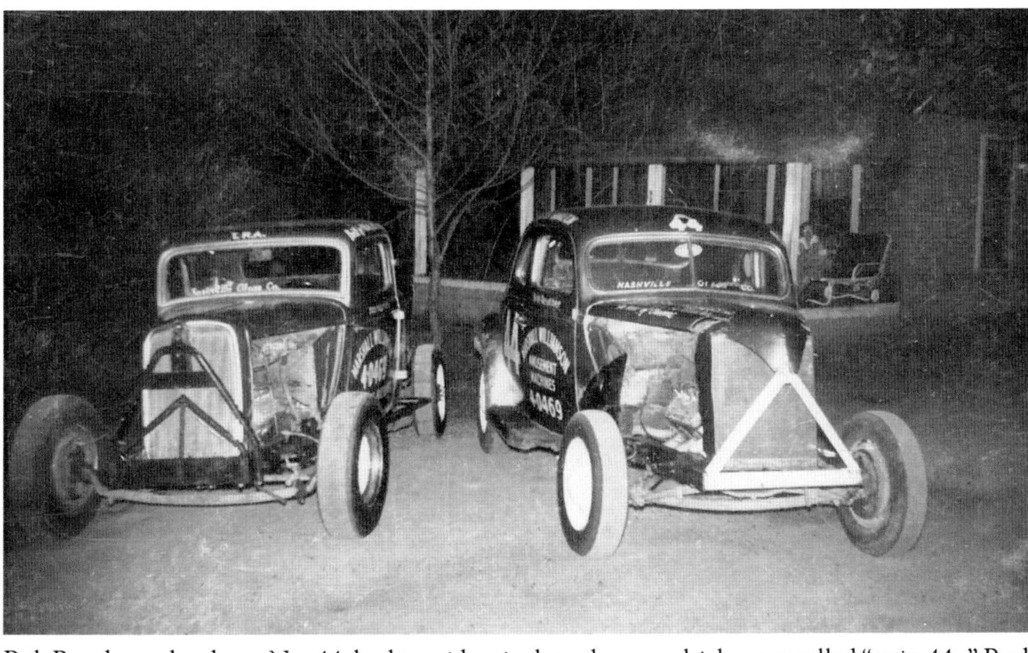

Bob Reuther, who drove No. 44, had two identical stock cars, which were called "twin 44s." Both cars were "hot," meaning they had dual carburetors and ran an alcohol fuel mixture. (Courtesy of Russ Thompson.)

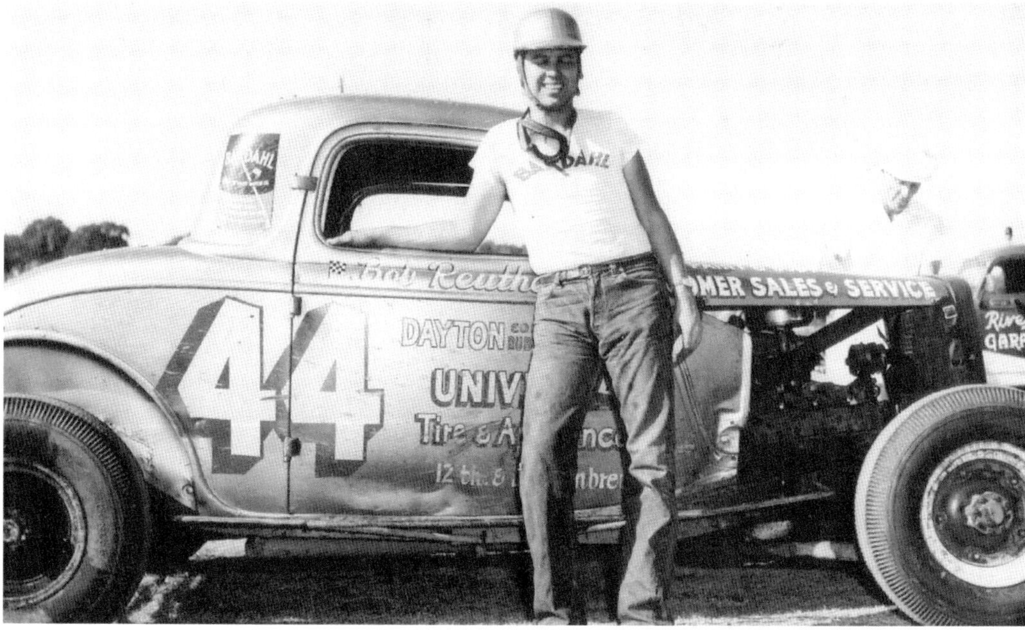

Bob Reuther is dressed in early-day full racing gear, i.e. helmet, goggles, white T-shirt, Levi's, and work shoes. Wearing double-layered fire suits, fireproof gloves and shoes, and specially designed helmets, today's drivers look like astronauts. (Courtesy of Russ Thompson.)

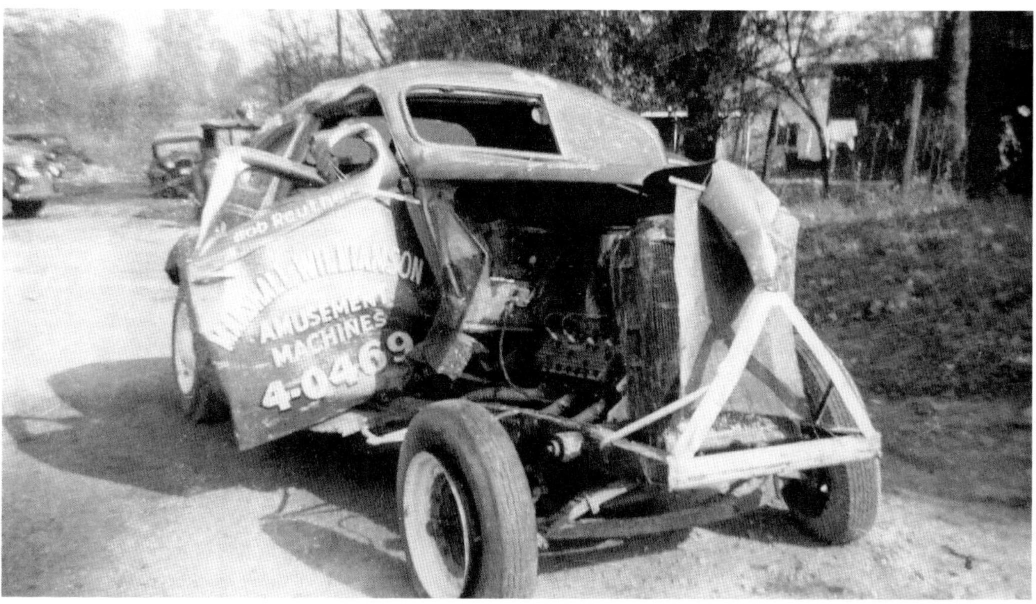

Bob Reuther's big smash up in Owensboro, Kentucky, is a good example of why a serious stock car driver needs a backup race car. Regardless of the skill of a particular stock car driver, it is inevitable that a driver will experience a crash, some worse than others. This car will require numerous new body parts, which will be found by scouring local wrecking yards. Even today, wrecking yards are the typical source of body parts for dirt track stock cars. (Courtesy of Russ Thompson.)

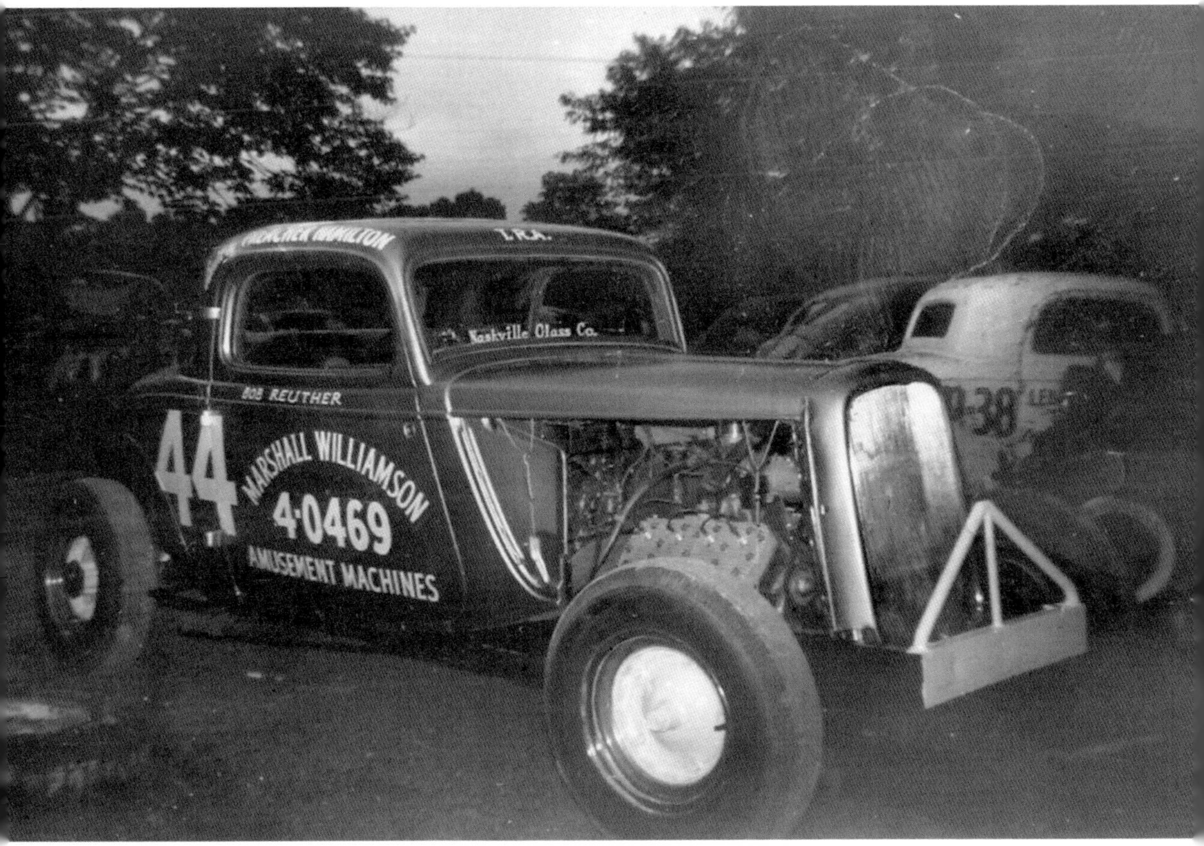

This photograph was taken before the first race of the season. The workmanship and pride of ownership is obvious on this beautiful stock car. Without the racing decals, it could pass for a restored "hobby car." However, it will not look like this at the end of the season because stock car racing is a contact sport. (Courtesy of Russ Thompson.)

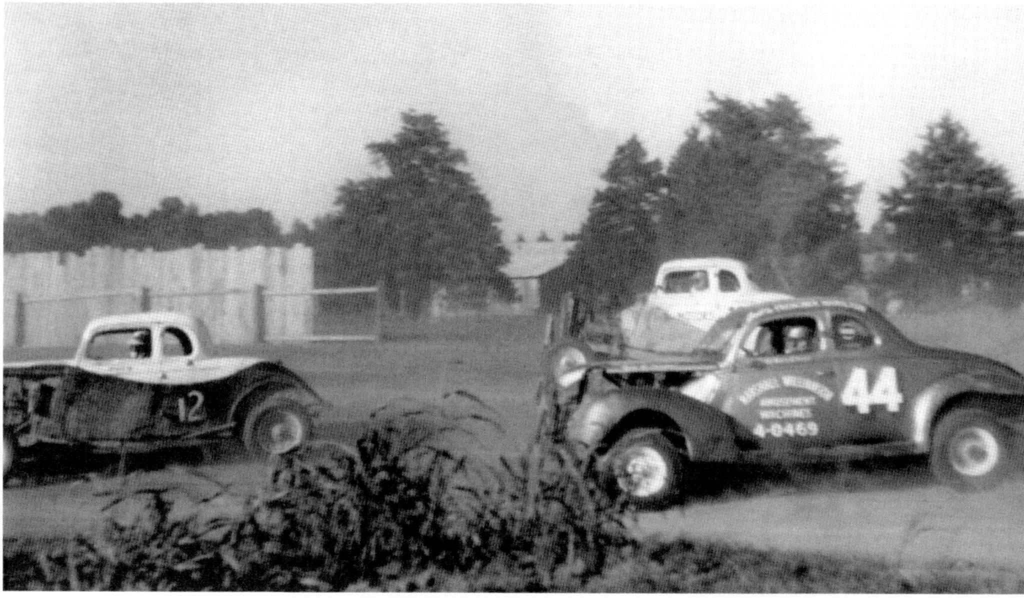

In the early days of stock car racing, racing in converted cornfields was not an uncommon phenomenon. Bob Reuther, No. 44, raced wherever he could find a racetrack, and it was a cornfield in this case. Larry Graham of Bowling Green, Kentucky, raced at the first Hart County track near Mammoth Cave National Park, which had been carved out of a farmer's cornfield. Graham's car ran like it was made for the track as it roared down the straightaways, which ran up and down the old cornrows. But when the car had to cross these ridges and ruts in the turns, it rattled the car and his teeth until his Dodge lost a rear wheel going over the rough rows. (Both, courtesy of Russ Thompson.)

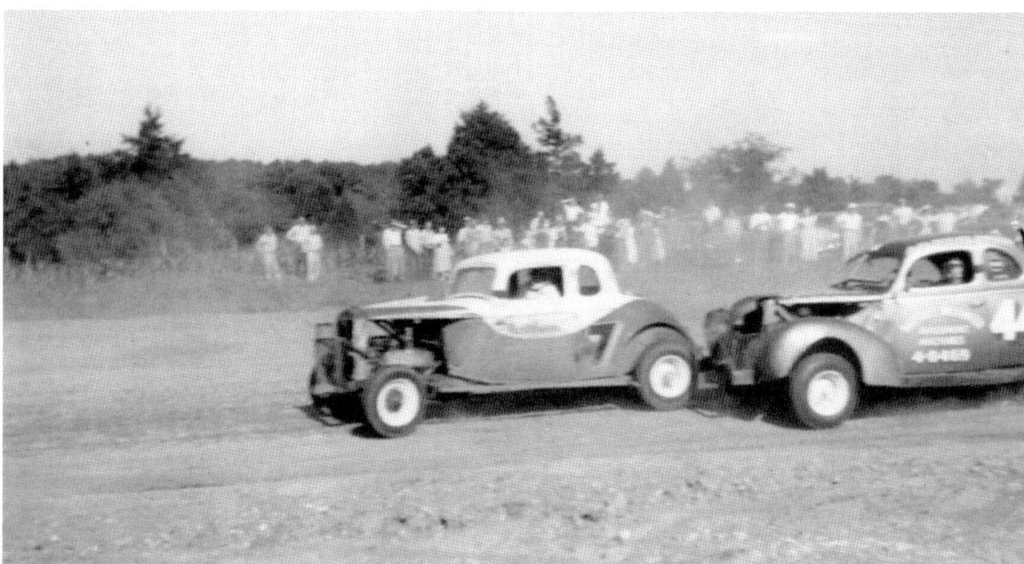

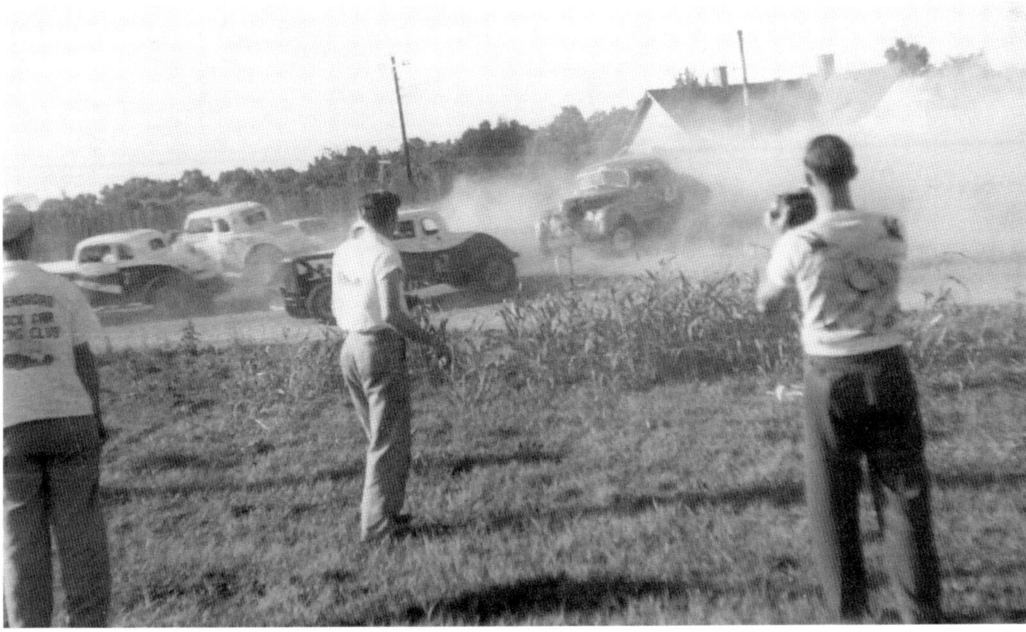

Bob Reuther, No. 44 (far right), coming out of turn four is about to lose his car in the cornfield. Usually, these makeshift racetracks took a toll on both the drivers and the cars. The tracks were rough and dusty, and sometimes the promoter skipped out with the gate, yet dirt track stock car racing fans and drivers remained passionate about the sport. (Courtesy of Russ Thompson.)

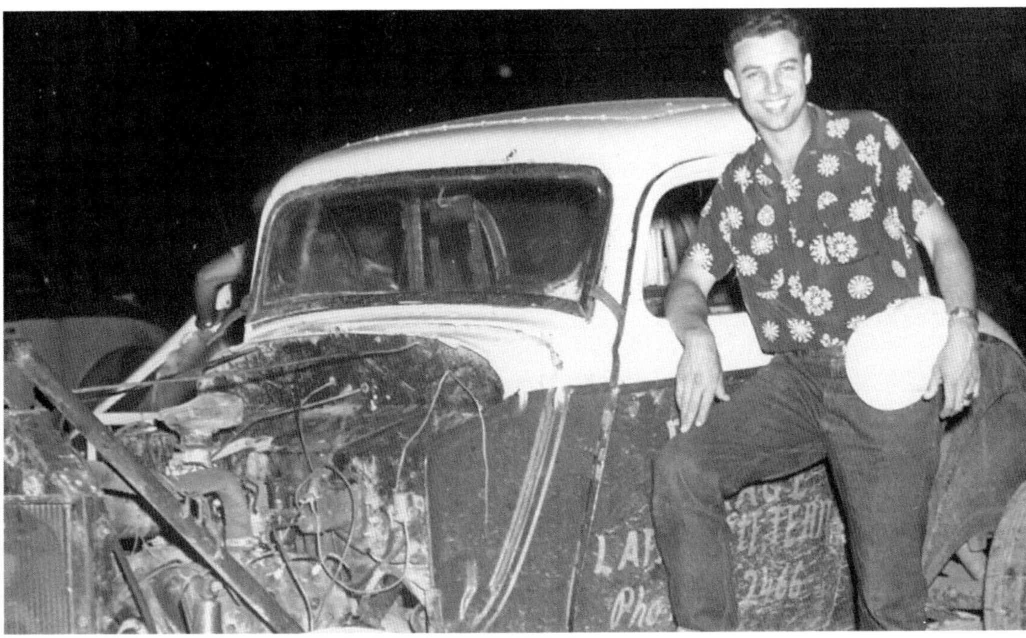

A young Bob Reuther, with a broad smile on his face and his helmet under his arm, is posing with his stock car. He appears happy with his lot in life, chasing the dream of becoming "Bullet" Bob Reuther. (Courtesy of Russ Thompson.)

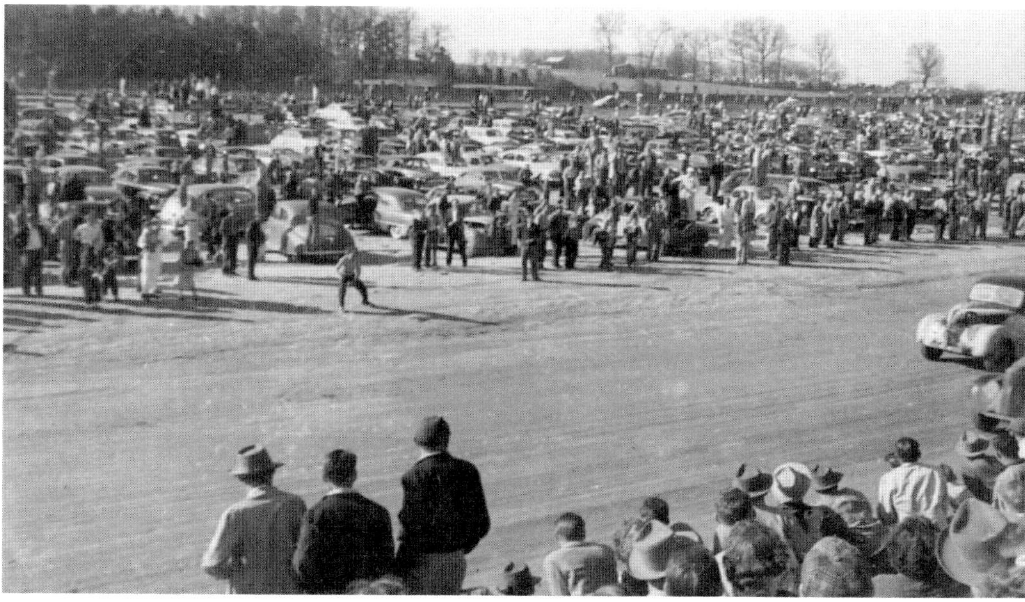

The fans and their cars are lined up along the track during the race with little security or crowd control. The first track in Russellville, Kentucky, had a low barn with a sloping roof supported by wooden posts set in the edge of the track. With no guardrail of any type surrounding the barn, drivers simply had to be careful not to hit it going into turn three. The roof of the barn was a natural spot for young fellows who would sneak in, come over the roof of the barn, and dangle their legs over the edge as they watched the race from the best and most dangerous seat in the house. (Courtesy of Russ Thompson.)

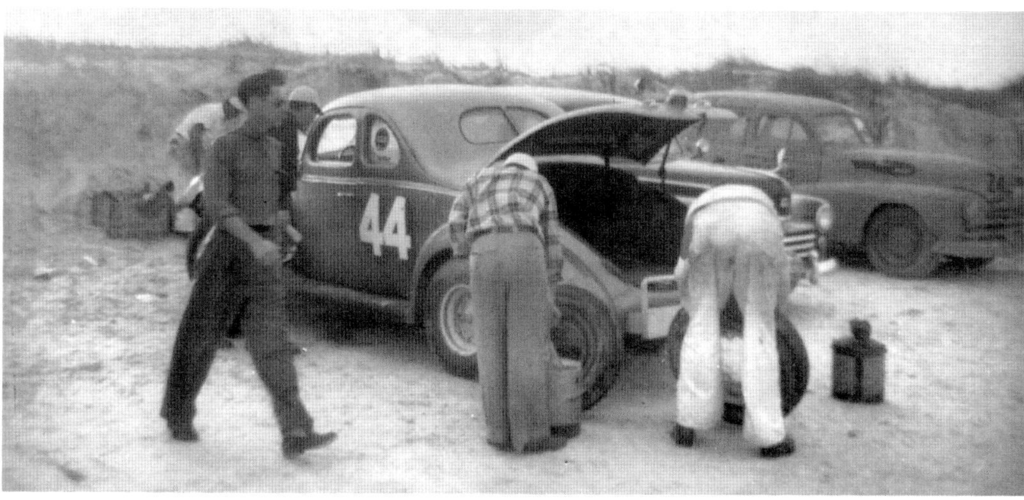

The pit crew prepares Bob Reuther's No. 44 for a NASCAR race. Pit crews usually get little recognition. Regardless, they are essential as it is impossible for the driver to do much of anything except drive on race day. Reuther has several men in his crew, but most dirt-track racers are lucky, if they can con a buddy into working in their pits. Everything a crew member touches is usually dirty, heavy, and extremely hot. (Courtesy of Russ Thompson.)

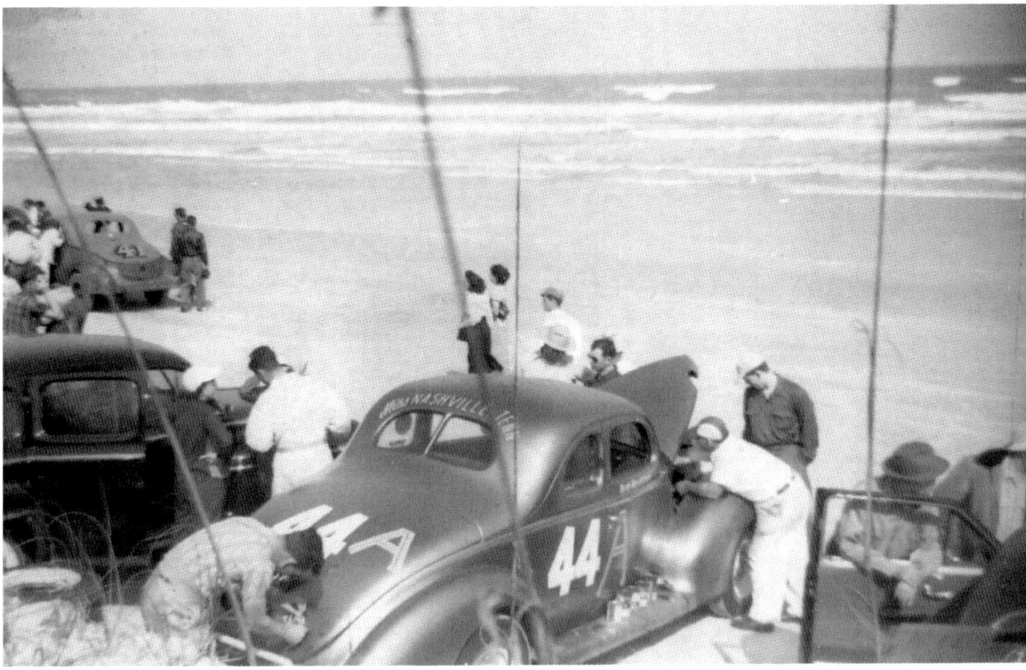

Everything must be checked and double-checked before the big NASCAR race on the beach course of Daytona, Florida. A good pit crew can make the difference between winning and losing a race. In the early days, the pit crews performed at a much slower pace, taking 30 or more seconds for a pit stop as opposed to 15 seconds or less today. (Courtesy of Russ Thompson.)

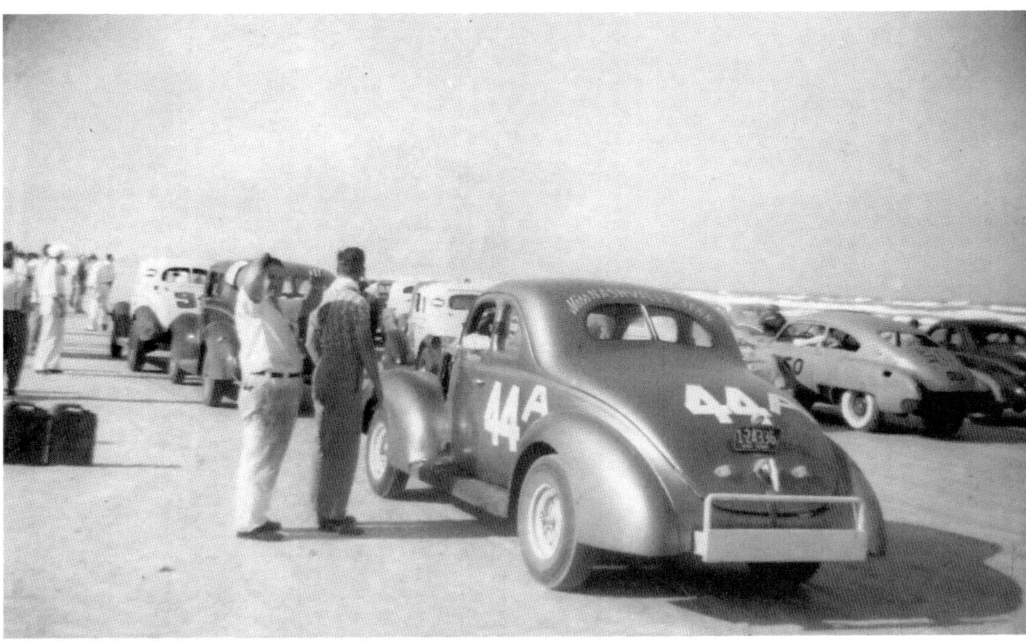

Bob Reuther is lined up and ready to race at NASCAR's Daytona Beach race course. (Courtesy of Russ Thompson.)

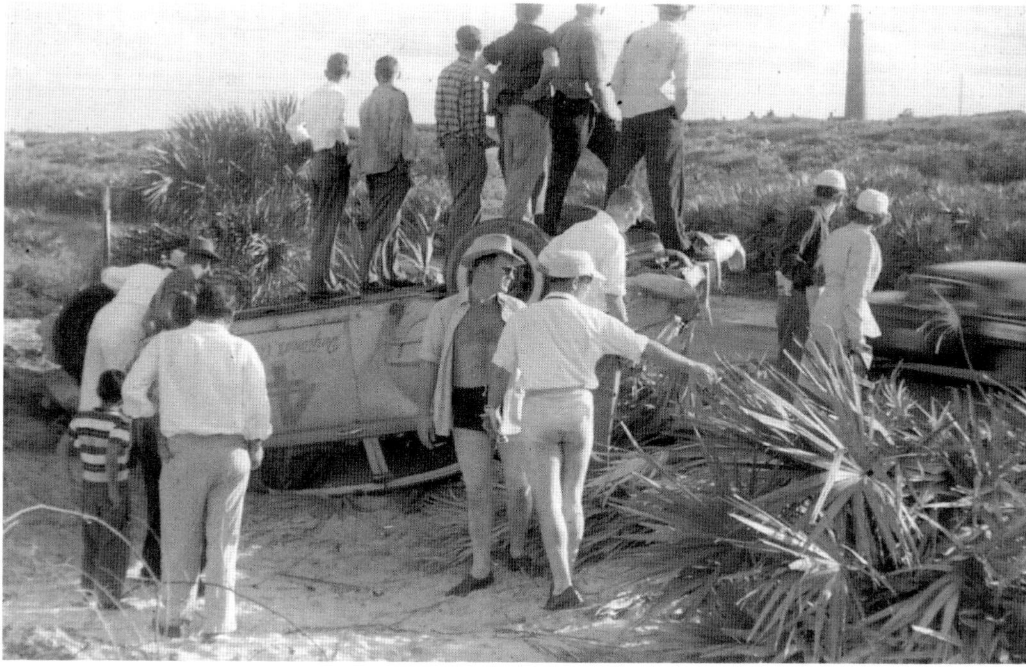

Racing is like life because things do not always go as planned. This driver has joined the "Upside Down Club." (Courtesy of Russ Thompson.)

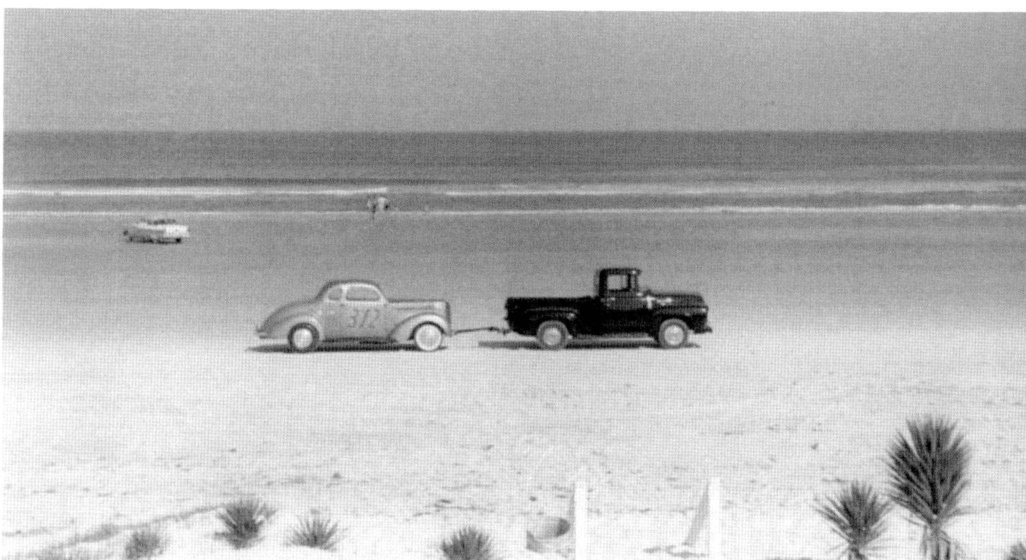

Bob Reuther is on the beach at Daytona, Florida, with No. 312, the car with which he set the lasting 1957 qualifying record for the "Measured Mile." The car is a 1938 Plymouth powered by a 1957 Chrysler V-8 with Firestone Bonneville tires, Halibrand quick-change rear-end, and a 1937 LaSalle transmission. The car hit 150.25 miles per hour, beating the previous record by 13 miles per hour. (Courtesy of Russ Thompson.)

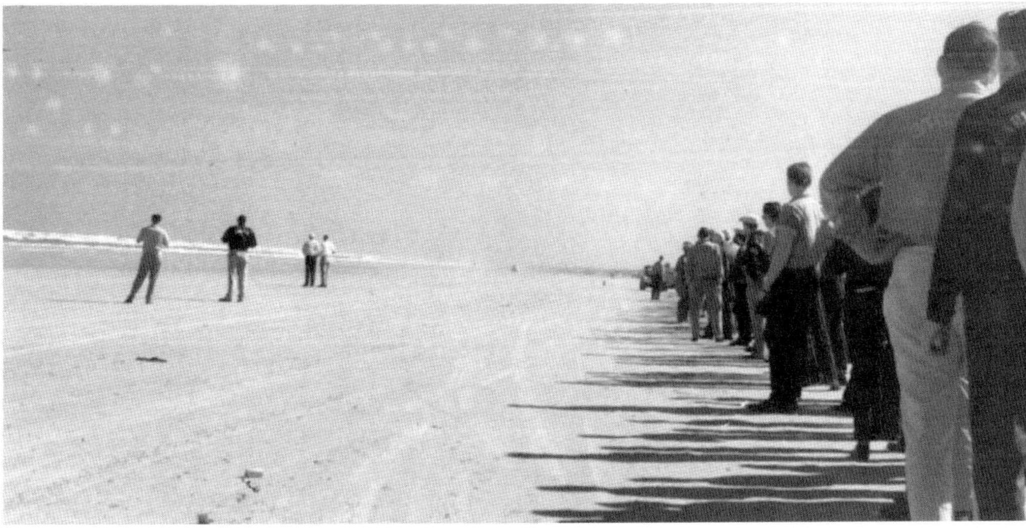

Fans are lined up on the beach to watch Bullet Bob Reuther run the Measured Mile. *Hot Rod Magazine* dubbed Reuther's 1938 Plymouth the "Birmingham Flyer," as it was owned by A. E. Burgess and built by Johnny Burell and Ed Samples, all of Birmingham, Alabama. Len Ashburn, writing in the February 2, 2008, issue of *Insider Racing News*, said he had hitchhiked to the beach course the day Reuther broke and set the Measured Mile record. Ashburn witnessed that Reuther's car "was pretty slicked out, had moon type covers on the wheels, and every crack and crevice taped with masking tape . . . We were mighty impressed." The car peaked at over 150 miles per hour. (Courtesy of Russ Thompson.)

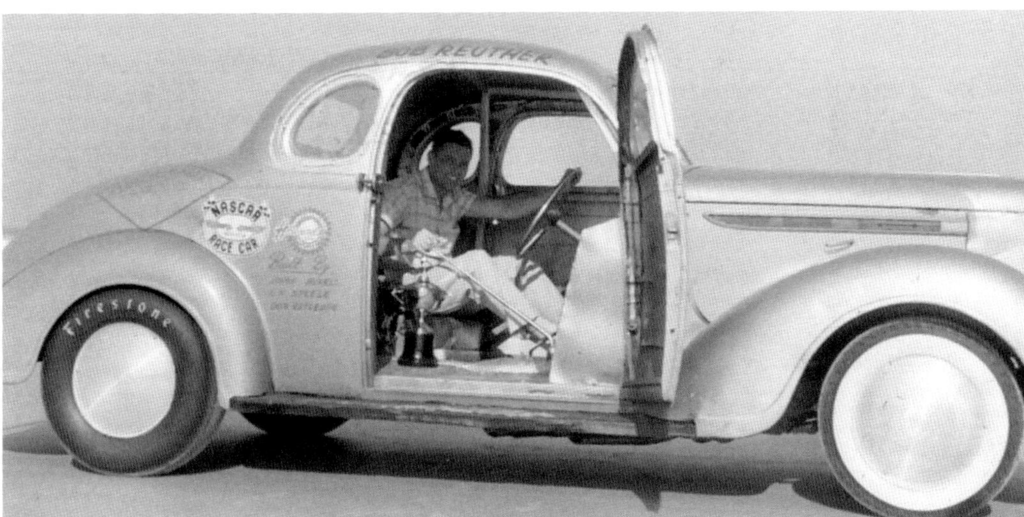

Bullet Bob Reuther sits with his trophy in the cockpit of his record-breaking 1938 Plymouth with a 1-mile qualifying run of 150.25 miles per hour. The 1957 Chrysler V-8 had a stock bore and stroke with Howard's cam and fuel injector, and a twin-chain driven McCulloch supercharger. The trophy is the reason men raced. Reuther once said, "We didn't race for money back then . . . We raced for the fun and excitement of it." (Courtesy of Russ Thompson.)

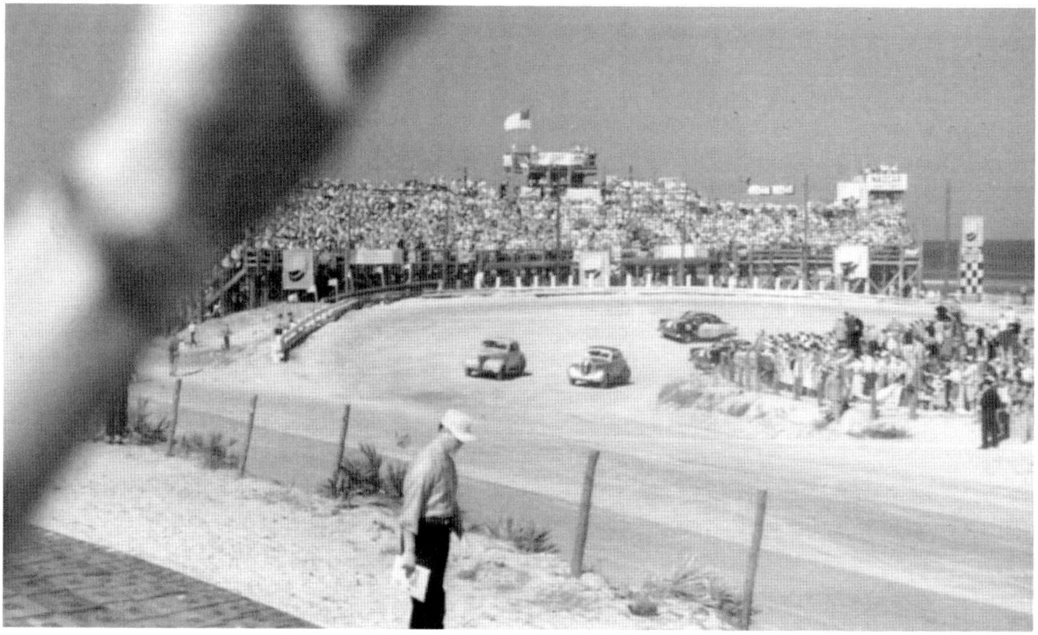

Coming out of turn four, Bob Reuther takes the inside as he attempts to pass Joe Wolf's No. 47, a 1939 Chevrolet called the "Backseat Bomber." The driver of No. 47 is one of the famous Flock brothers. Notice the NASCAR sign in the background right. (Courtesy of Russ Thompson.)

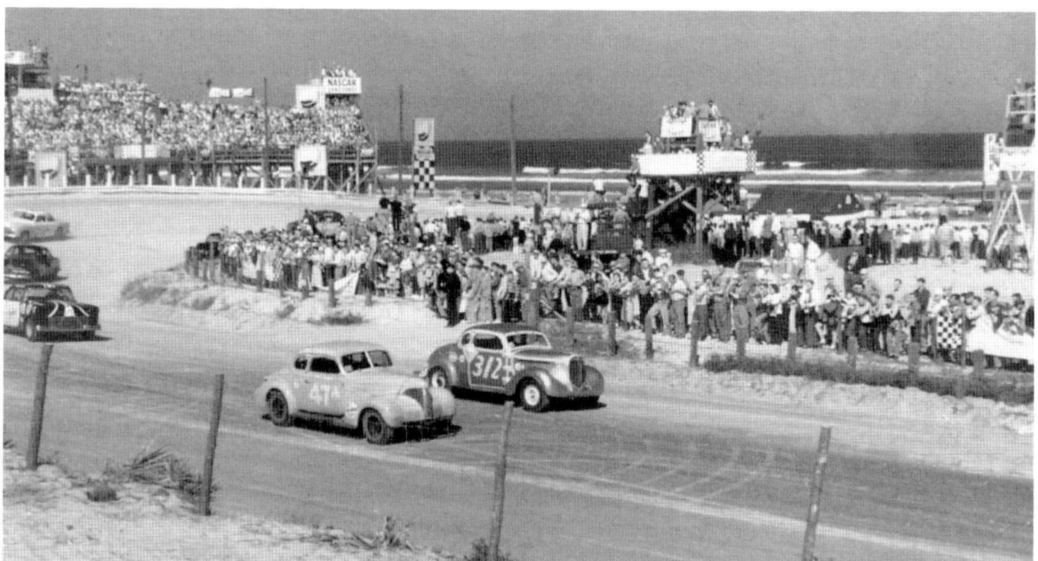

Reuther is pushing hard to get past Flock as they come onto the paved portion of the Daytona Beach course in 1957. Reuther's car set the qualifying record the day prior to the race. After qualifying, Bob asked when they were going to install the race motor, knowing that supercharged engines had a short life. The crew looked at him and said, "There isn't any race motor. This is all we've got." Reuther lasted four laps before the engine blew up. (Courtesy of Russ Thompson.)

Bob Reuther sits in the cockpit of Marty Robbins's No. 44. Outside looking in is Reuther's sponsor, country-western music star Marty Robbins, who was considered the best nonprofessional stock car driver on the NASCAR circuit in that era. (Courtesy of Russ Thompson.)

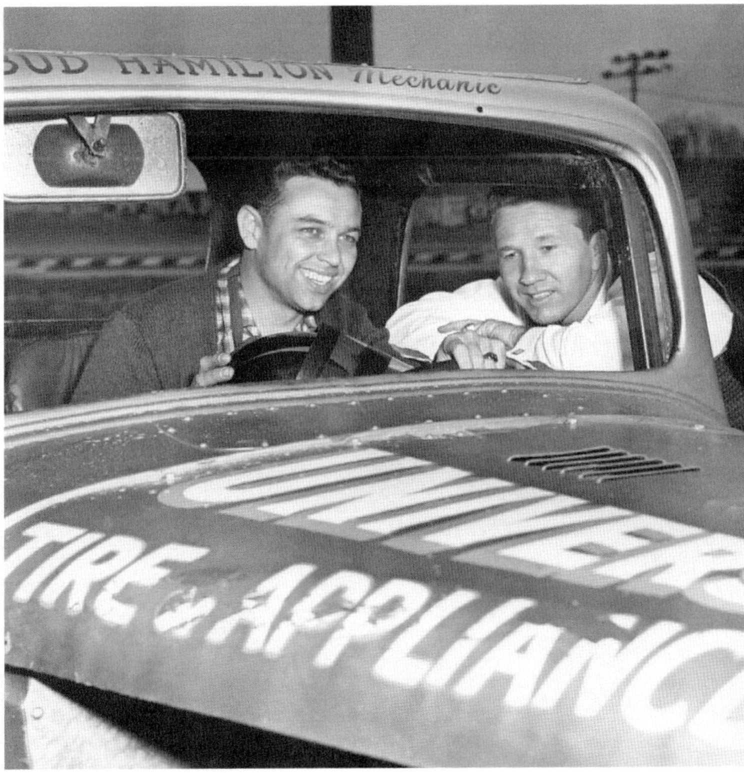

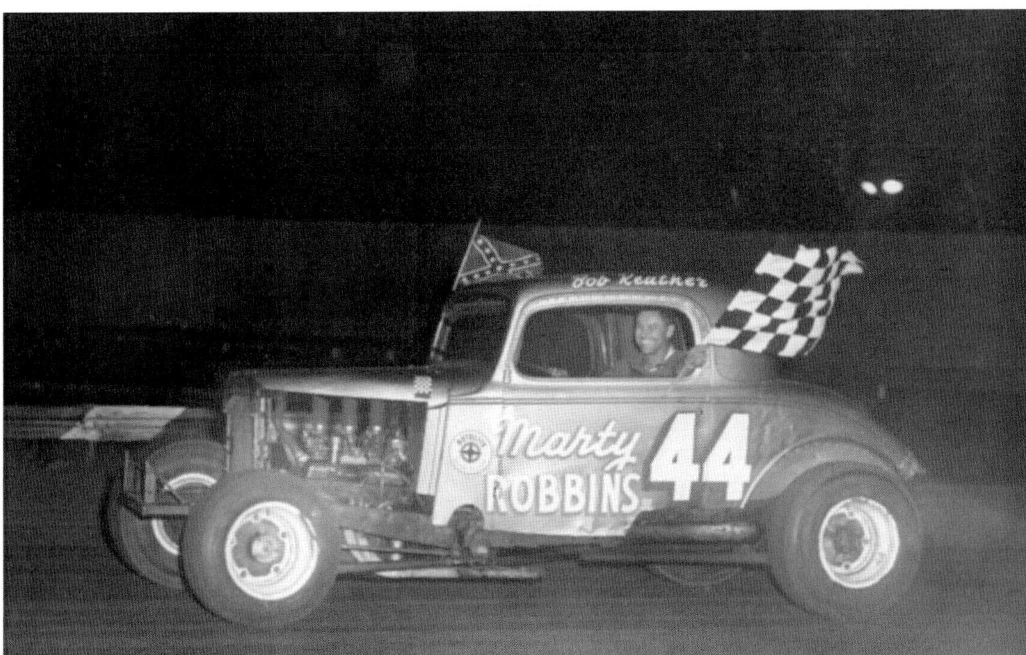

Bob Reuther is taking a victory lap. During his career, Reuther made a huge number of victory laps. (Courtesy of Russ Thompson.)

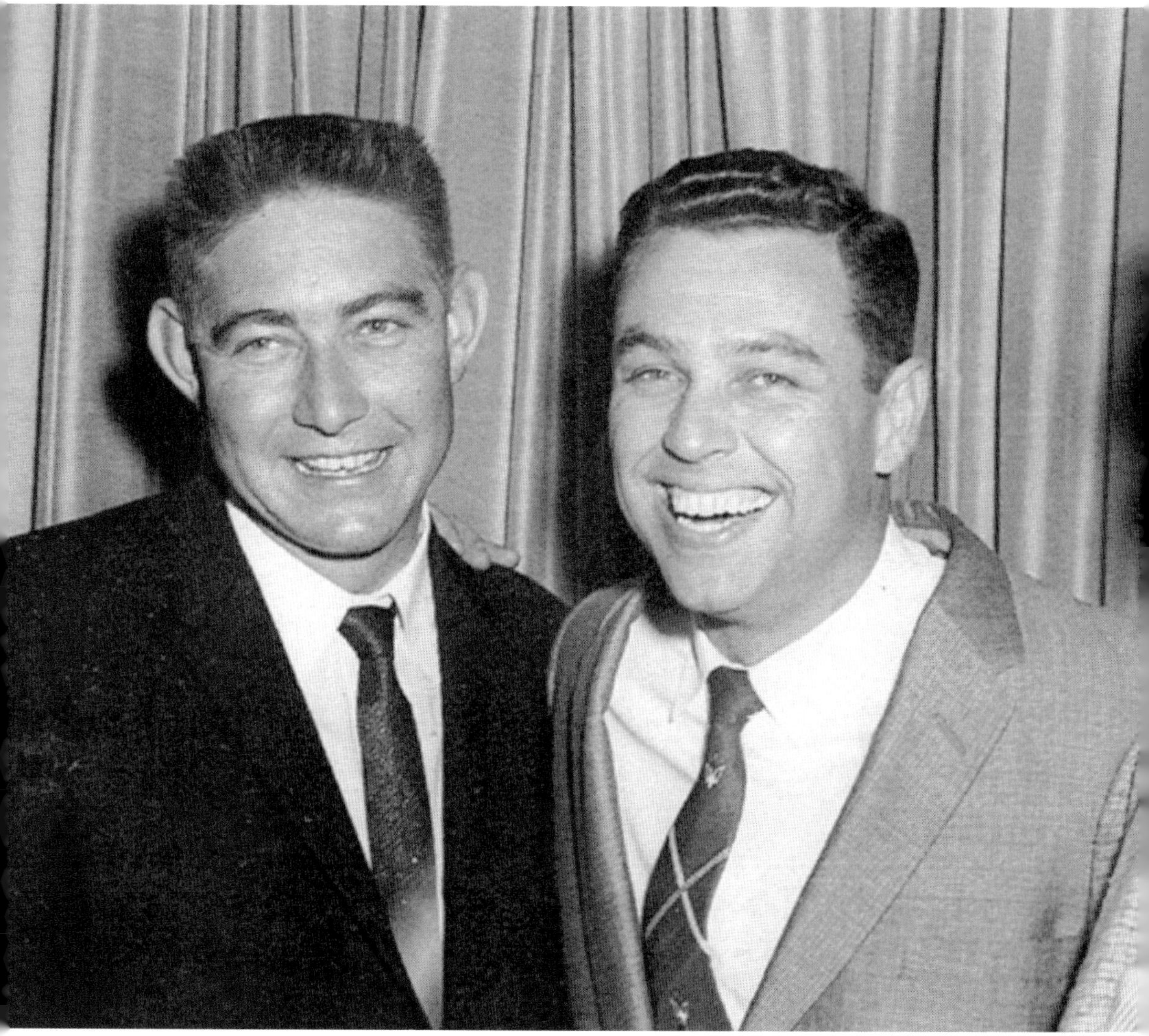

Bob Reuther (right) stands with his racing buddy, Glenn "Fireball" Roberts, arguably the top NASCAR driver of the 1950s era. Roberts earned his nickname, "Fireball," not from his driving style, but from his flame-throwing ability as a young baseball pitcher in high school. Sadly, Roberts was involved in a fiery crash at the World 600 in Charlotte, North Carolina, on May 24, 1964. Due to the injuries sustained from his burns, he passed away on July 2, 1964. His death led to the development of fire-retardant racing suits. (Courtesy of Russ Thompson.)

7

Beech Bend Raceway Park in the 21st Century

Beech Bend has been a Bowling Green attraction since 1898 when locals just wanted to escape the summer heat and enjoy the shade of the beech trees along the Barren River. In some ways, Beech Bend has remained the same, but in 1941 Charles Garvin expanded Bowling Green's vision of a summer escape and embarked on a quest to create a major amusement park. But even Garvin did not anticipate the crowds that descended on Beech Bend in 1951 as stock car racing became an obsession for most of Bowling Green. With each passing week that summer, Garvin was building additional grandstands to accommodate the fans.

With the addition of drag racing and the return of motorcycles to Beech Bend Park, the development of the Chevrolet Corvette Assembly Plant and the establishment of the Corvette Museum moved Bowling Green towards becoming the city of "speed." People from across the United States came to Bowling Green to discover the excitement tucked into the big bend of the Barren River.

Things have changed in the 21st century: Charles Garvin and Raymond McClard are gone, replaced by another promoter with a dream, Dallas Jones; Jim Baird sits behind the camera instead of Marshall Love Jr.; and all of the 1951 daredevils have been replaced by a new breed of stock car drivers, which today includes men and women. The dirt track is now asphalt and the cars are hotter but constrained by more rules. However, the men and women who race are the same determined, fearless, some might say reckless, demons of speed that the patrons of Beech Bend Park found at the racetrack in 1951.

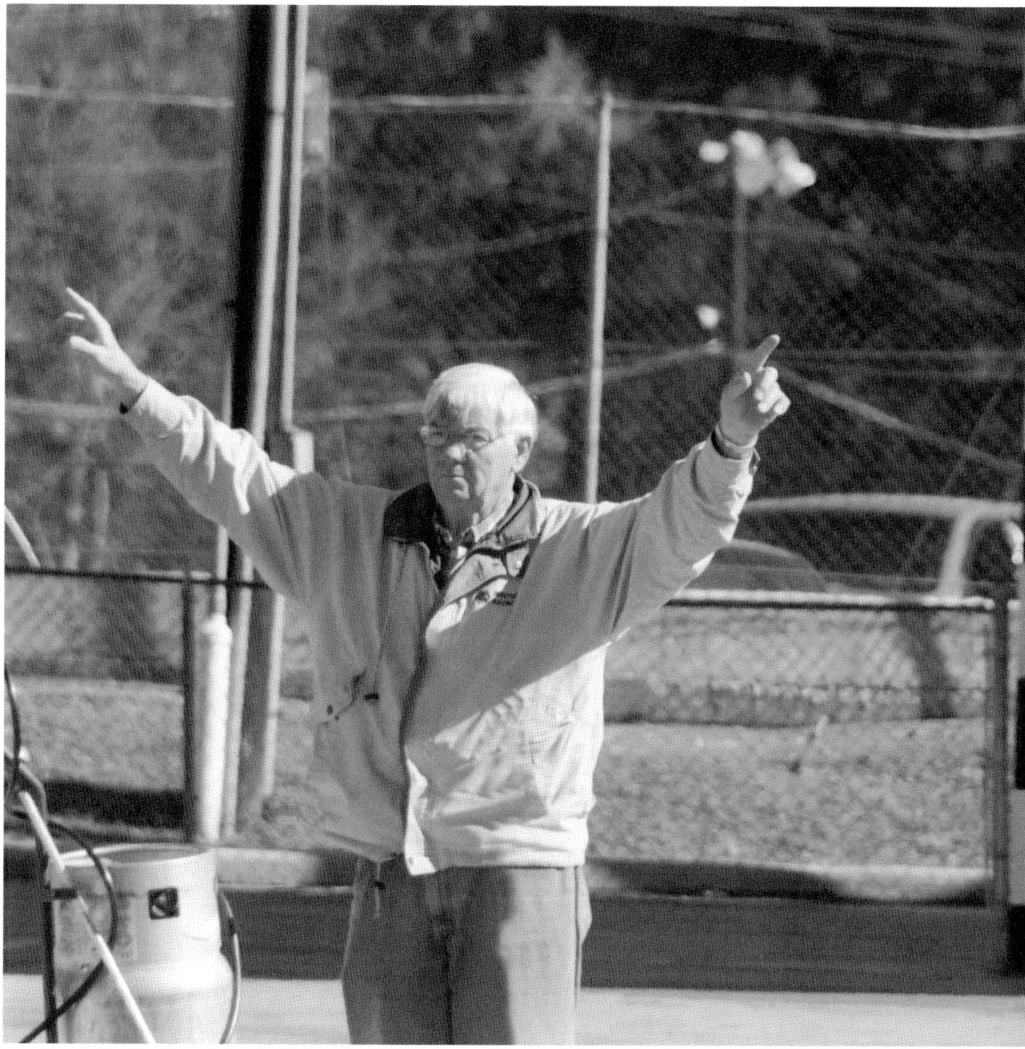

Dallas Jones, the owner of Beech Bend Park, is involved in all phases of its operation, especially the raceway. Jones has owned Beech Bend Park for the past 25 years and has expanded on Charles Garvin's dream. According to the local newspaper, the *Daily News*, Beech Bend Park pumps $42 million annually into the local economy, and Jones has announced a major expansion to the park in 2010. Progress comes in stages, and Charles Garvin put Beech Bend on a solid foundation for success. Now, Dallas Jones has his own dream, which will turn Beech Bend Park into a major tourist attraction. Jones announced that he is going to add to the park a 275,000-gallon wave pool, a 1,100-foot lazy river, and a four-story play structure with seven water slides. In addition, Jones will erect a new amphitheater and improve many of the existing facilities. The raceway, which draws the majority of visitors, will continue to be the park's major attraction. (Courtesy of Jim Baird.)

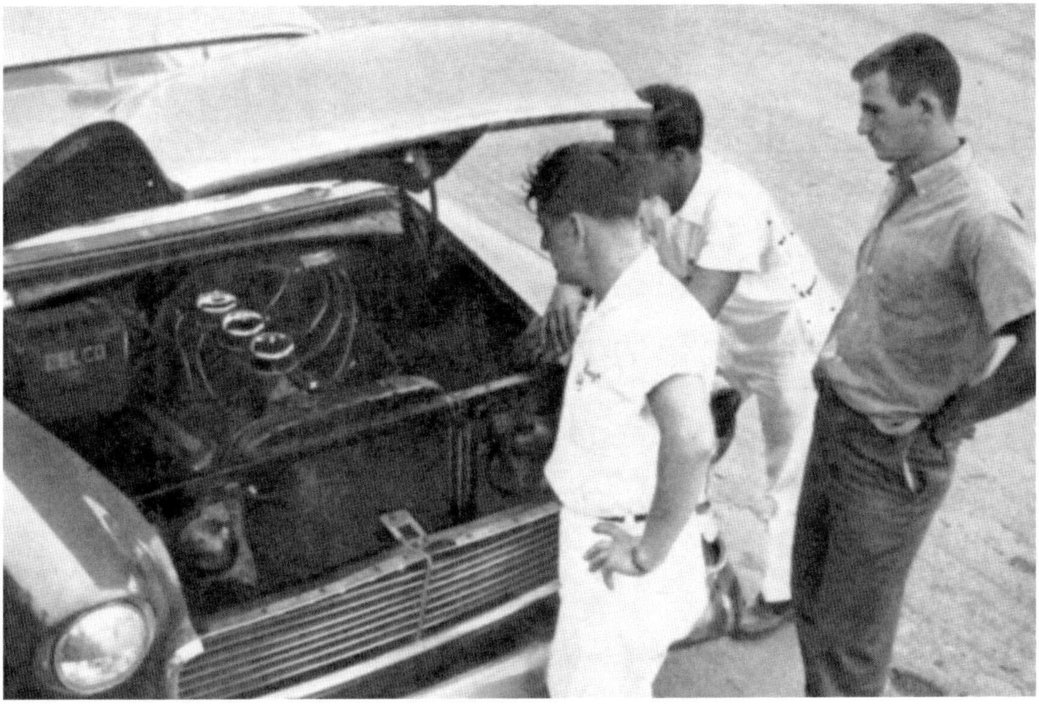

These unidentified men are checking out an engine that appears to be primed for drag action at Beech Bend Park. Drag racing became another overnight sensation for Charles Garvin; he had an innate ability to sense and act on trends. (Courtesy of David Garvin.)

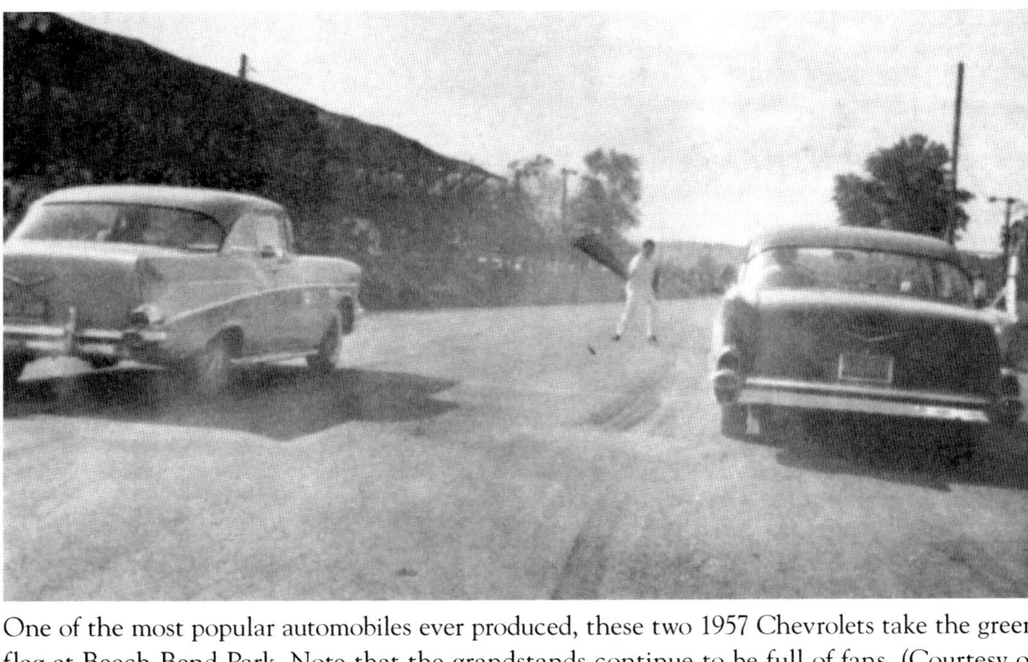

One of the most popular automobiles ever produced, these two 1957 Chevrolets take the green flag at Beech Bend Park. Note that the grandstands continue to be full of fans. (Courtesy of David Garvin.)

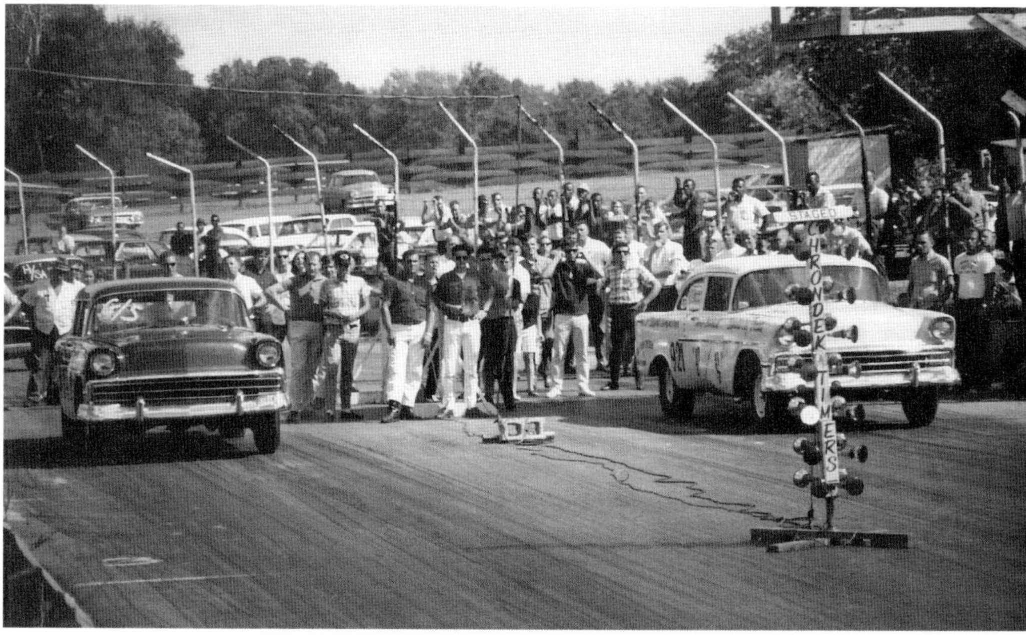

These two Chevrolets are waiting for the green light. Elmo Guy, who was one of the most dominating stock car drivers in the 1950s, made a smooth transition to drag racing and became a consistent winner. (Courtesy of David Garvin.)

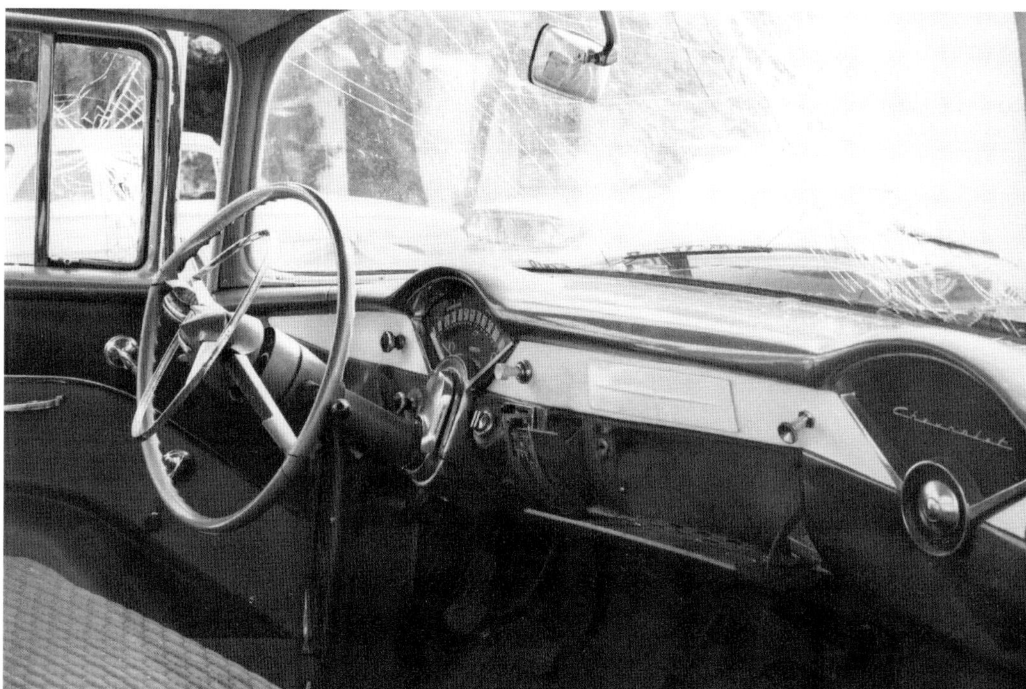

This photograph of the inside of a Chevrolet dragster shows that racing sometimes ends in disaster. (Courtesy of David Garvin.)

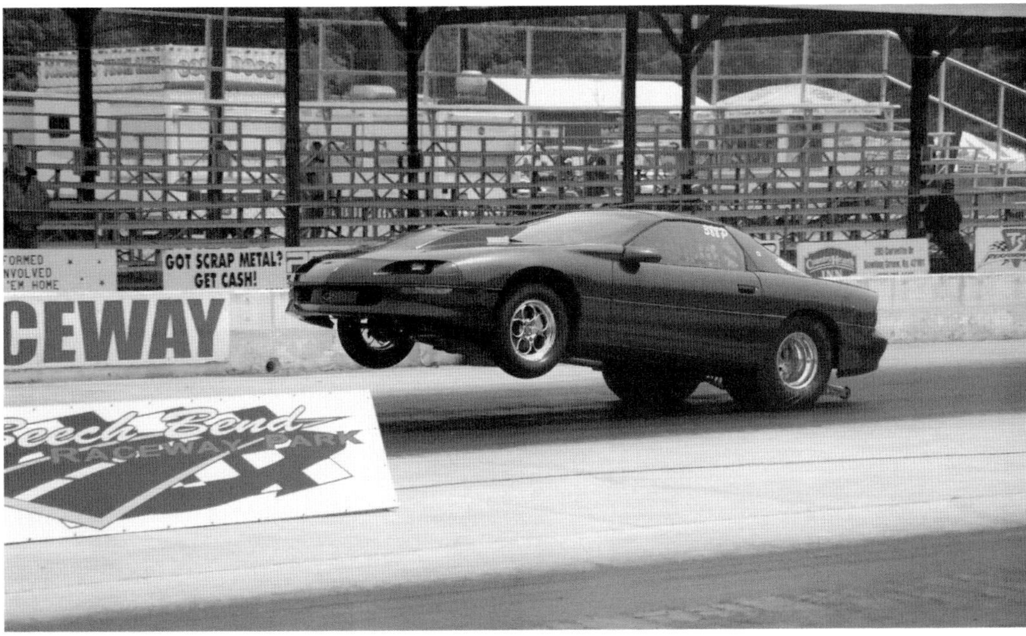

The modern era of drag racing is illustrated in this photograph that shows a sign signifying that the track is now known as Beech Bend Raceway Park. This high-powered dragster is just getting off the mark. (Courtesy of Jim Baird.)

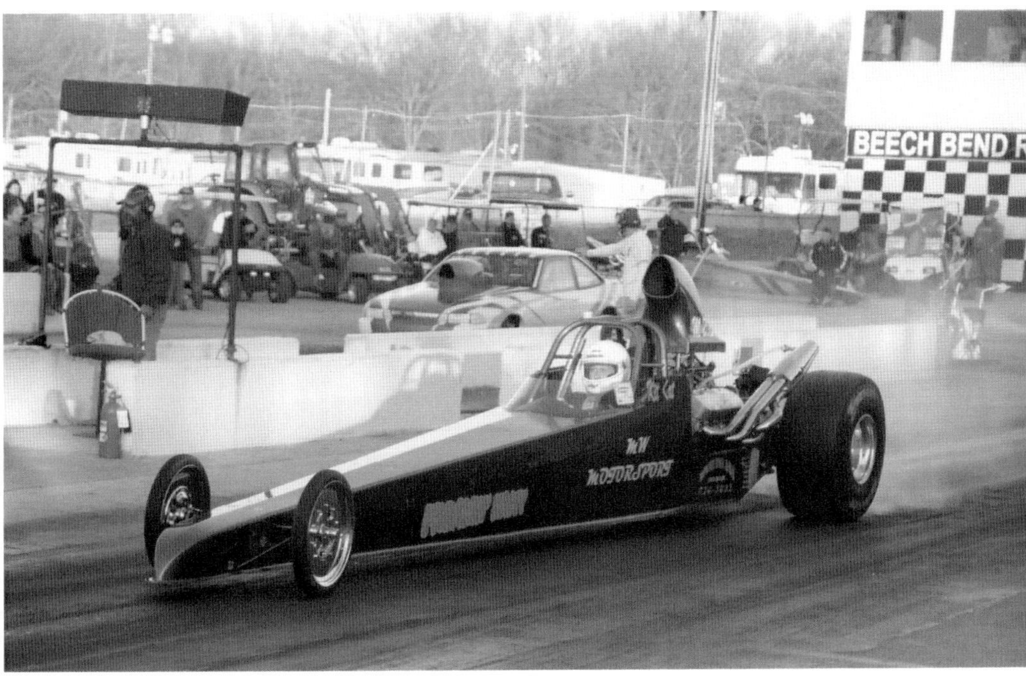

This rail car, known as "Freakin' Nasty," charges into action on a Sunday Bracket Program race. The wide tires on the back of the car denote a very high-powered engine. Today Beech Bend Raceway Park is sanctioned by the National Hot Rod Association (NHRA). (Courtesy of Jim Baird.)

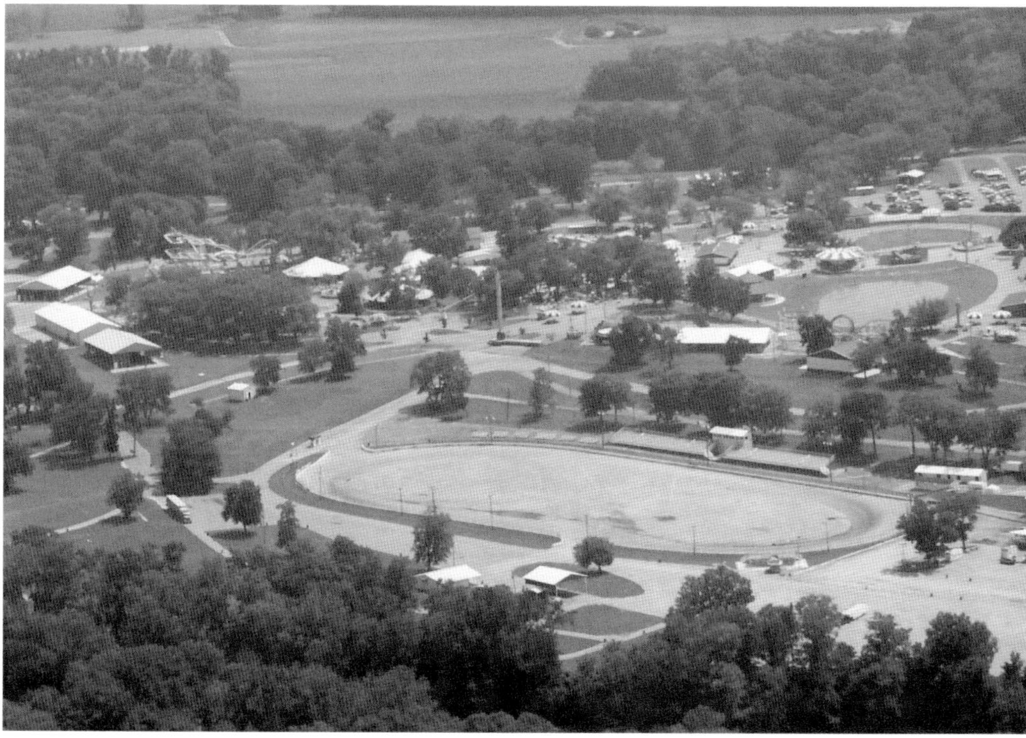

This photograph is a modern-day aerial view of the part of Beech Bend Park that focuses on the one-third mile asphalt oval track. (Courtesy of Jim Baird.)

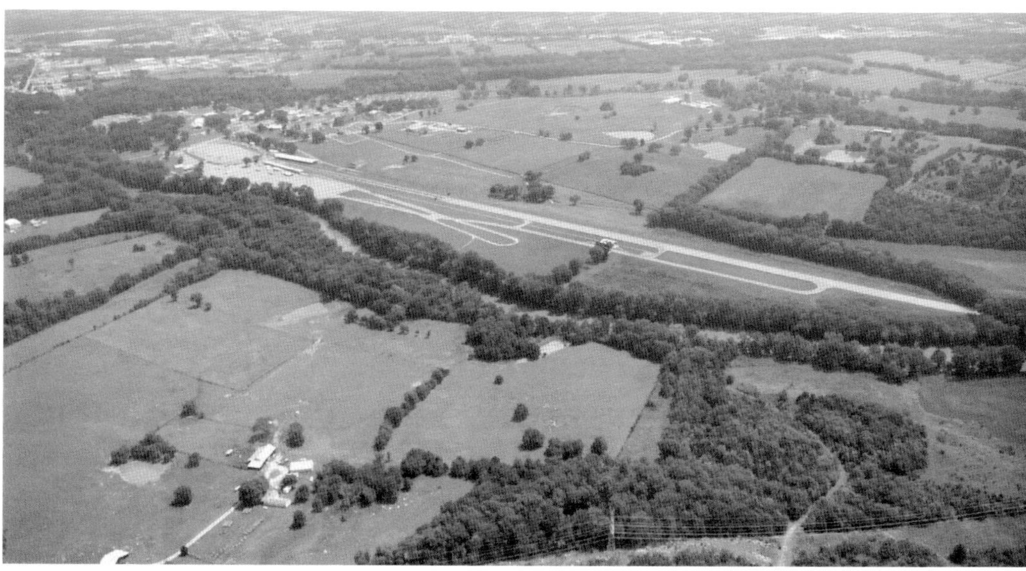

Beech Bend Raceway Park's asphalt oval track sits in the bend of the Barren River at the far upper left of the photograph with the drag strip extending through the entire center of the photograph. The Barren River curves around the oval track and runs parallel and just below the drag strip. (Courtesy of Jim Baird.)

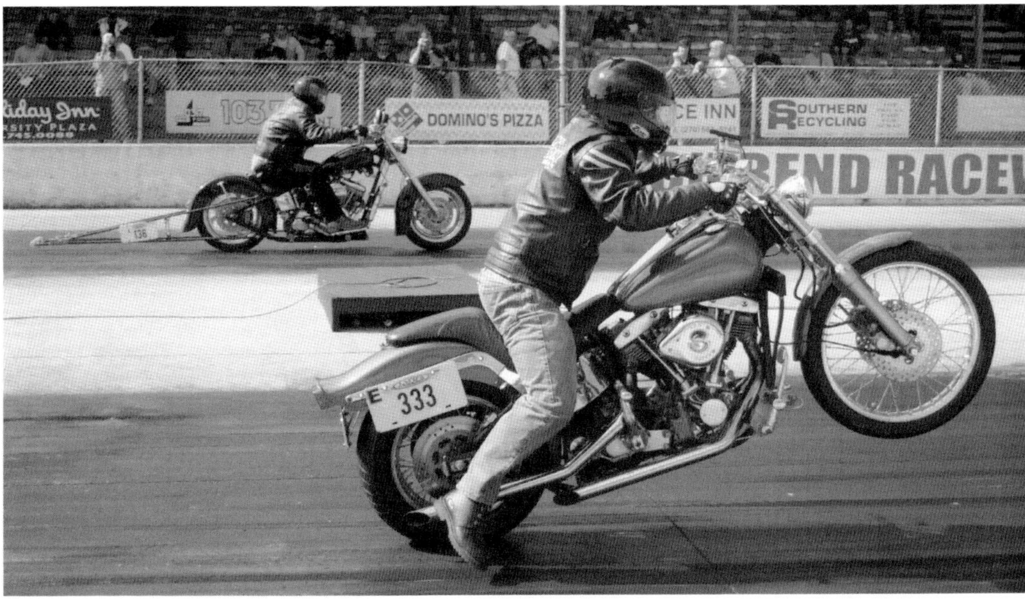

Motorcycle racing has come full circle and is back at Beech Bend Raceway Park. Today, however, it comes in the form of drag racing. In this photograph, a Harley Davidson racer pops a "wheelie." Notice the motorcycle racer in the background with the trailing rail, which keeps the bike on the ground. (Courtesy of Jim Baird.)

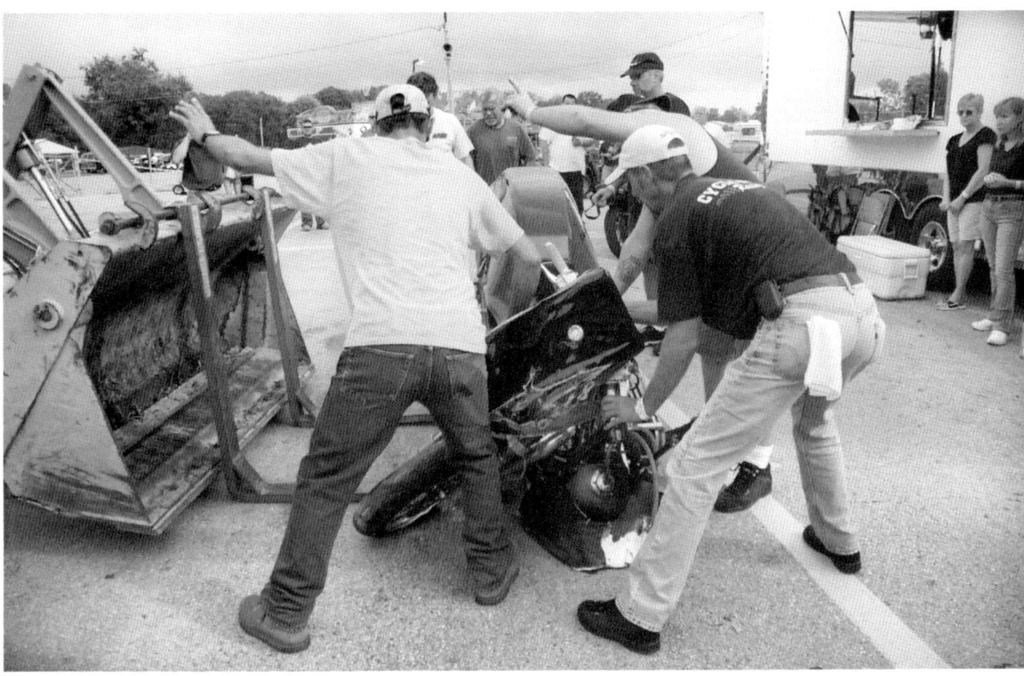

Sometimes one just has to scoop it up; luckily the rider of this nitro bike escaped with only scrapes and bruises at the American Motorcycle Racing Association (AMRA) season finals. (Courtesy of Jim Baird.)

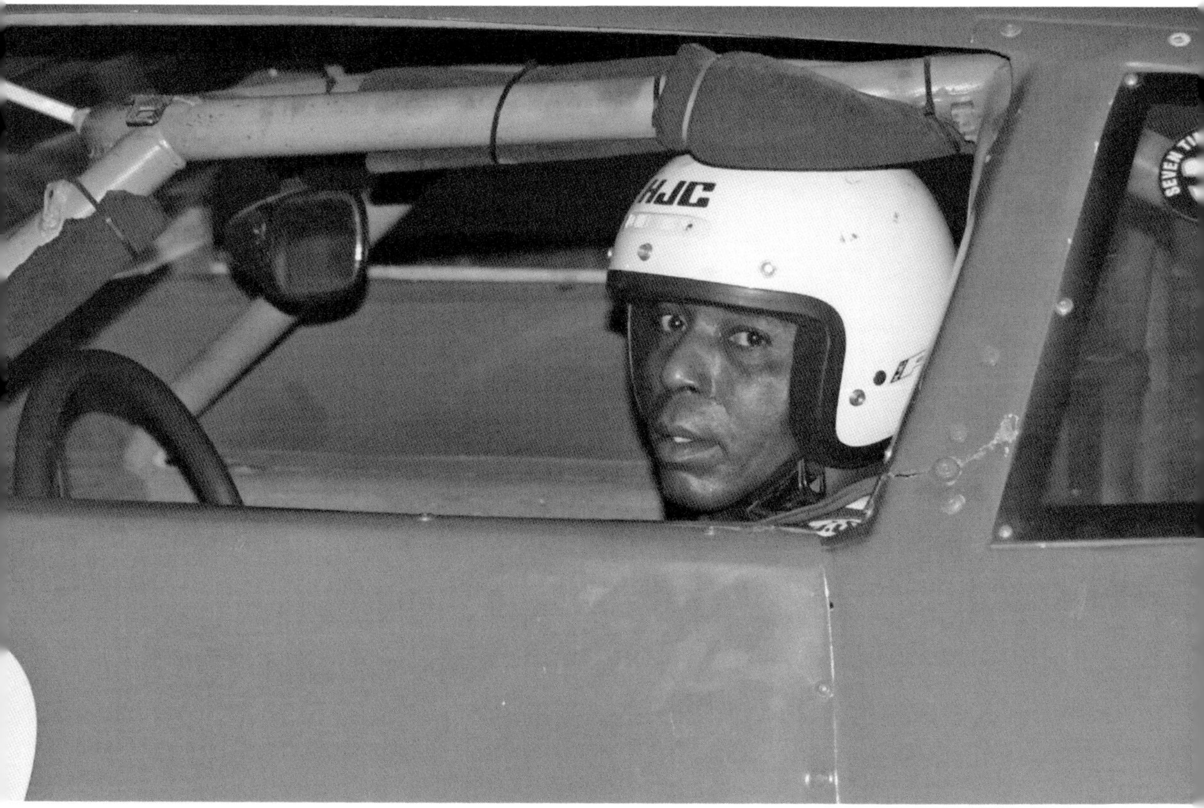

Tommy Lawrence looks relaxed in his "figure 8" car; however, figure 8 racing is not a situation in which any driver can ever get comfortable. Figure 8 racing means exactly what one would think when hearing the term. The cars race on a track in the shape of an "8," and the great danger comes when two or more cars arrive at the crossover at the same time. Fans love these types of races, but many people call the drivers "reckless, foolhardy, or crazy." (Courtesy of Jim Baird.)

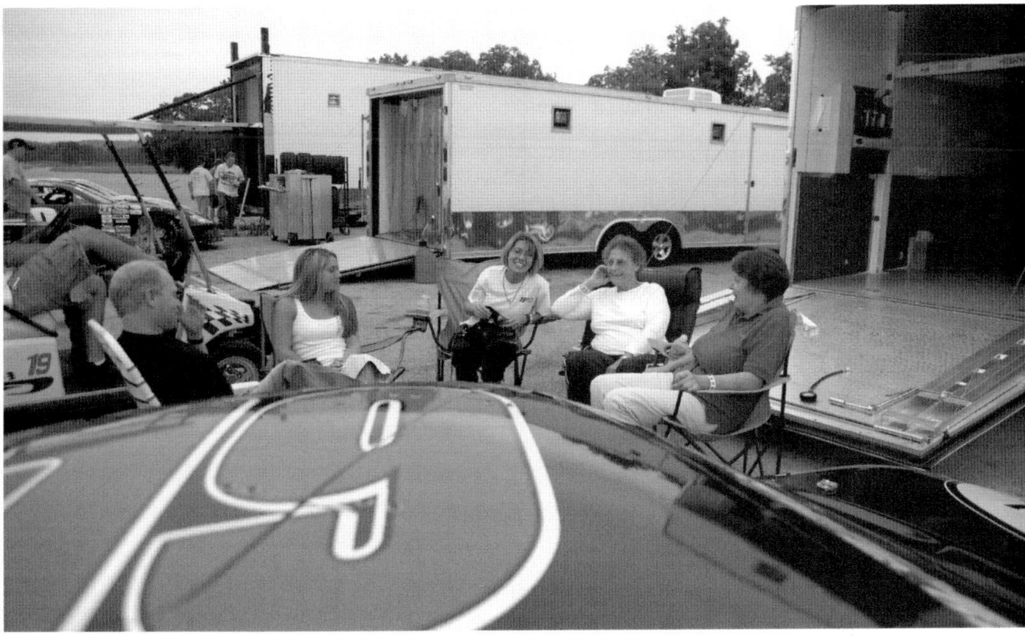

Bowling Green's 17-year-old Sportsman Division champion in 2008, Mary Daniels (second from left), is caught in a relaxing moment with her family. This will not last long as the tension will begin to build as race time nears. By the time Mary is strapped into her race car, the adrenaline will be flowing. Below, moving to the Late Model Division in 2009, Daniels will drive this late model car, No. 19, at this race event. Daniels is considered a young driver on the move. (Both, courtesy of Jim Baird.)

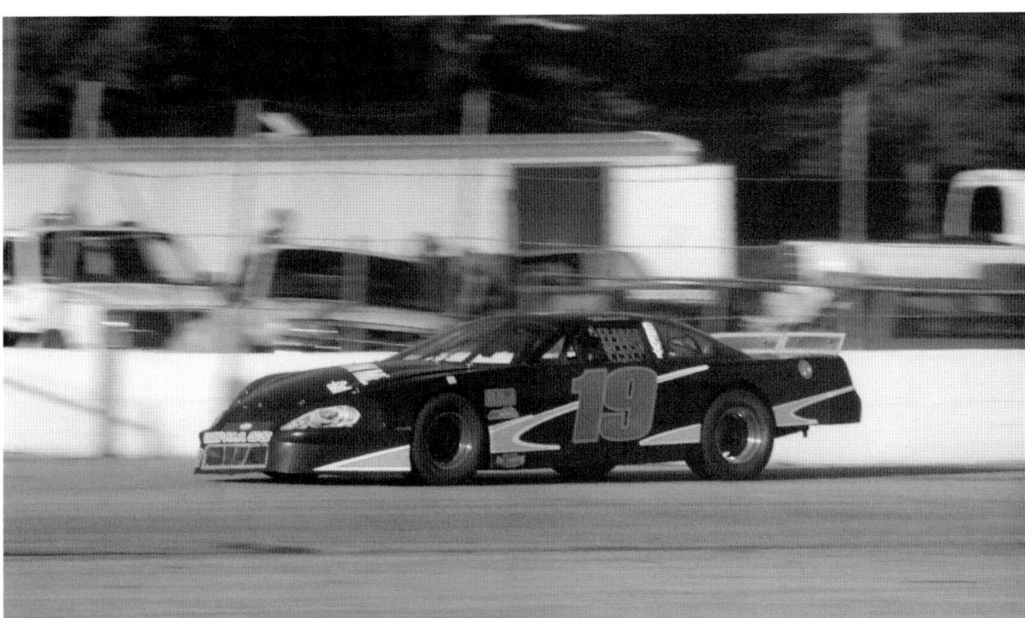

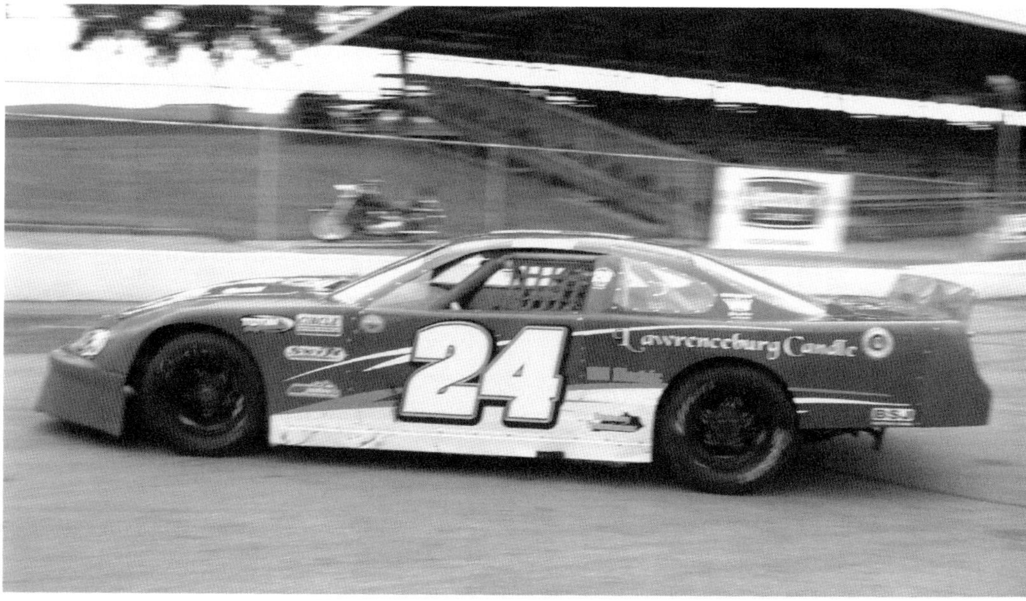

Brian Royalty warms up his No. 24 late model stock car at Beech Bend Raceway Park. Every driver wants to be a champion, but experience shows that a methodical approach to racing wins trophies. The problem to be solved is managing the necessary horsepower and equipment to behave in such a way that winning is possible. (Courtesy of Jim Baird.)

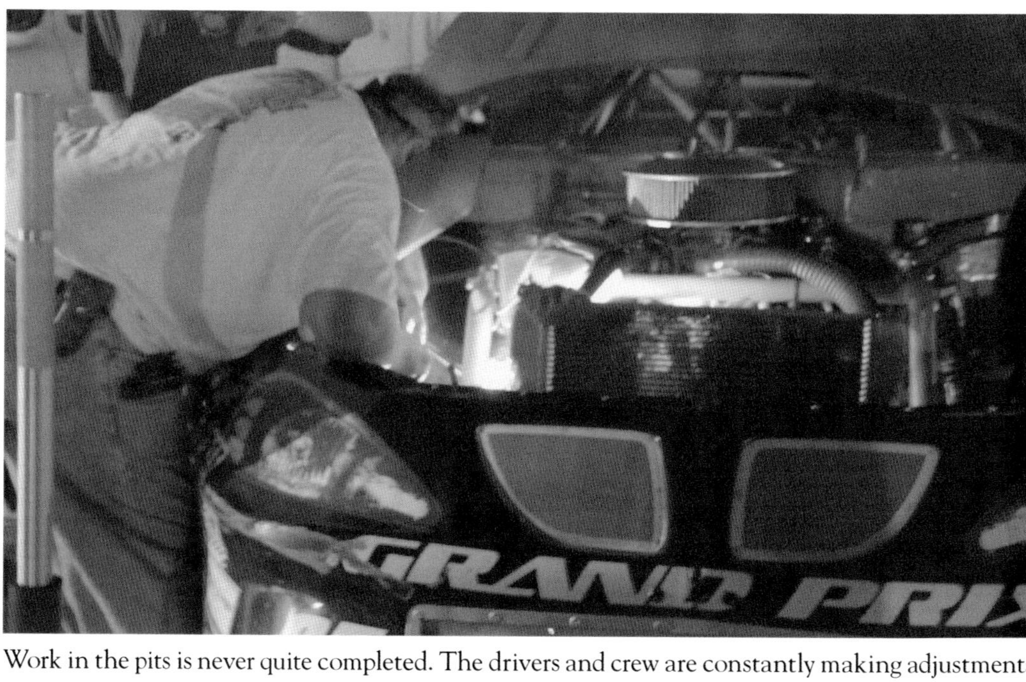

Work in the pits is never quite completed. The drivers and crew are constantly making adjustments in an effort to coax a little more power and speed or to make repairs on the spot. In this 2009 photograph, the welder is trying to put it back together in time for the next race. (Courtesy of Jim Baird.)

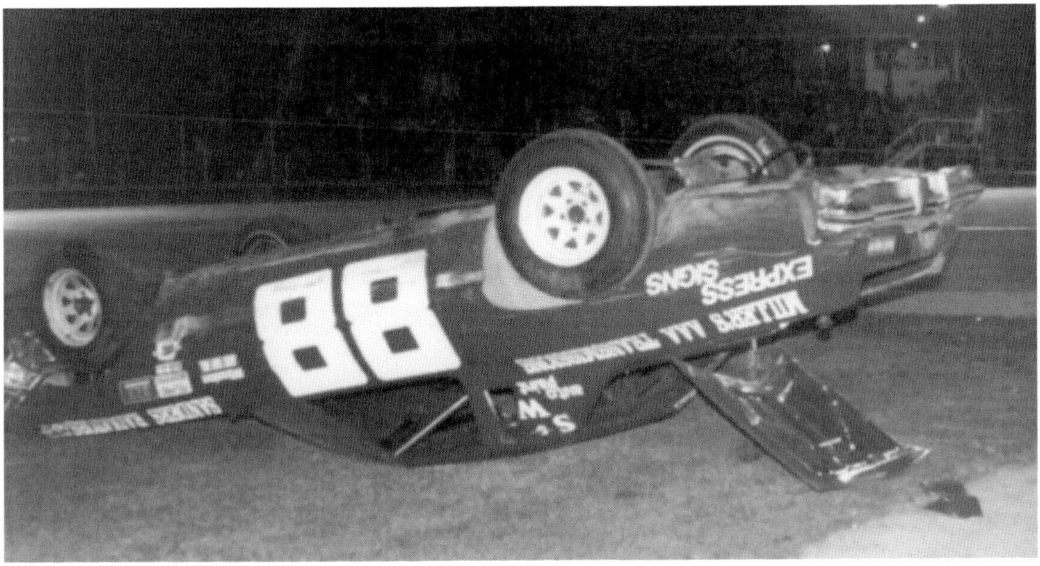

This photograph is from stock car racing at Beech Bend Park in 1988. Regardless of the type of track, speed and high-powered engines always produce an element of danger. Another stock car driver has become a member of the "Upside Down Club." (Courtesy of Dick Webber.)

"KP" Payne, Beech Bend Raceway's flagman, prepares to start a race. Everyone is familiar with the green, yellow, white, and checkered flag. Occasionally, however, the flagman pulls out the black flag (get off the track), red flag (stop the race), yellow stripe on blue background (yield right of way), or two rolled-up crossed flags (the race is at the half-way point). (Courtesy of Jim Baird.)

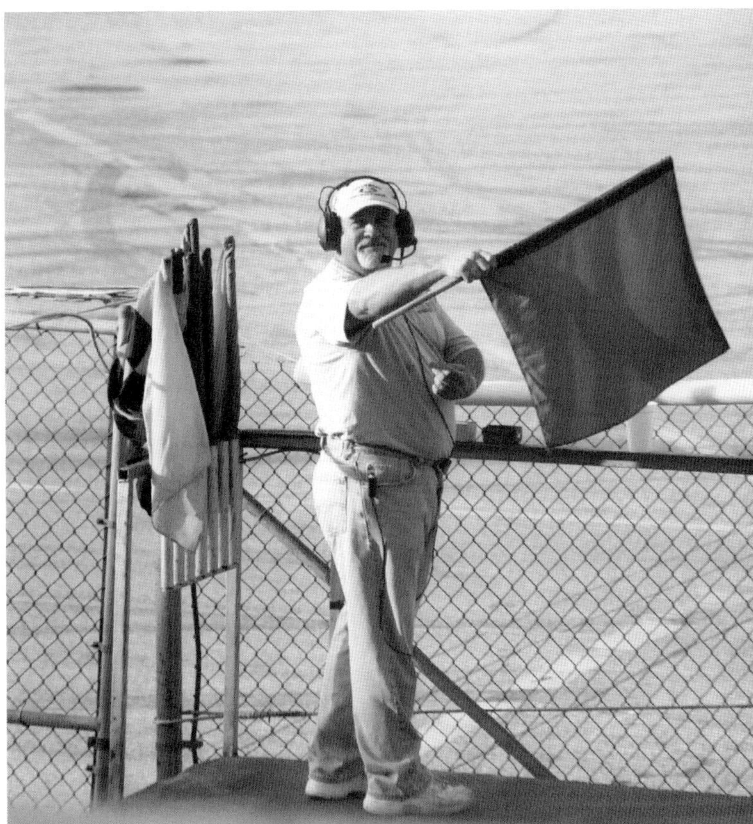

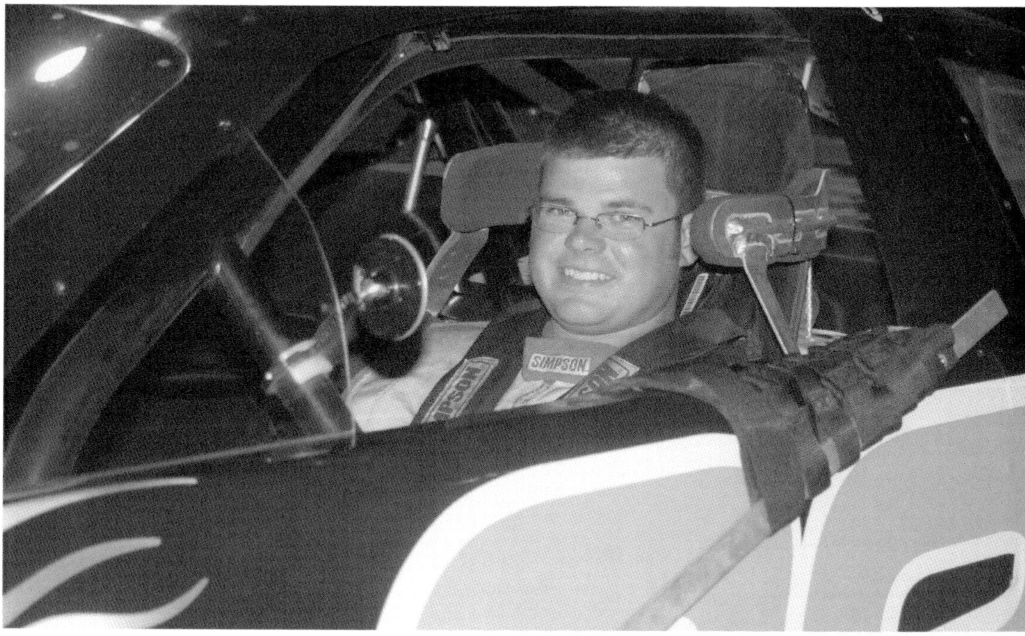

Brian Cherry, a Late Model Division driver, is strapped in tight. Once his helmet is in place, the only thing he will be able to move are his arms and feet. However, in an emergency, one tap of his hand on the five-point release of his harness will spring him free. (Courtesy of Jim Baird.)

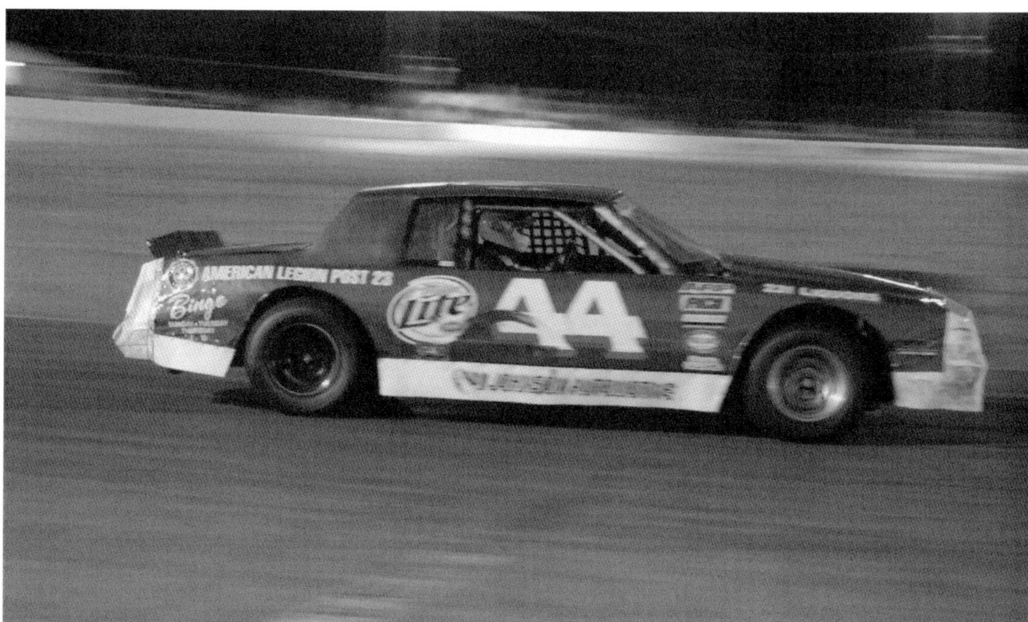

Phillip Akin warms up in his good-looking No. 44 Sportsman's Division entry. All racers know that good equipment and endurance pay big roles in chasing after a championship. A top driver with poor equipment will achieve mediocre results at best. Ultimately sponsors recognize talent and ensure that skilled drivers have good equipment. (Courtesy of Jim Baird.)

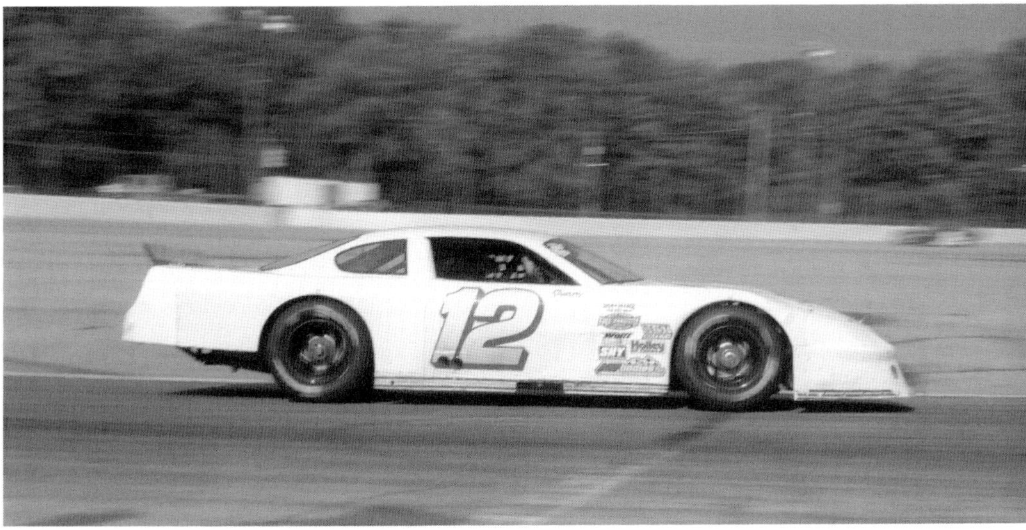

Sammy Sanders's 2008 Chevrolet Monte Carlo competes in the Late Model Division at Beech Bend Raceway Park and in the Ken-Ten Late Model Series, a touring series that runs at tracks in Kentucky and Tennessee. Sanders was the 2009 champion in the series and at Beech Bend Raceway Park. According to Sanders, he has no fear on the track but always worries about wrecking this beautiful stock car. Being born in Nashville, Tennessee, and growing up around men like "Bullet" Bob Reuther; Preacher Hamilton, father of NASCAR star Bobby Hamilton; and Bobby Hamilton himself, Sanders absorbed the influence of these men, which fed his passion to race. Sammy began racing in 1986 at age 18 and has raced off and on since that time. He is at the peak of his career and is a threat to win every time he is on the track. (Both, courtesy of Jim Baird.)

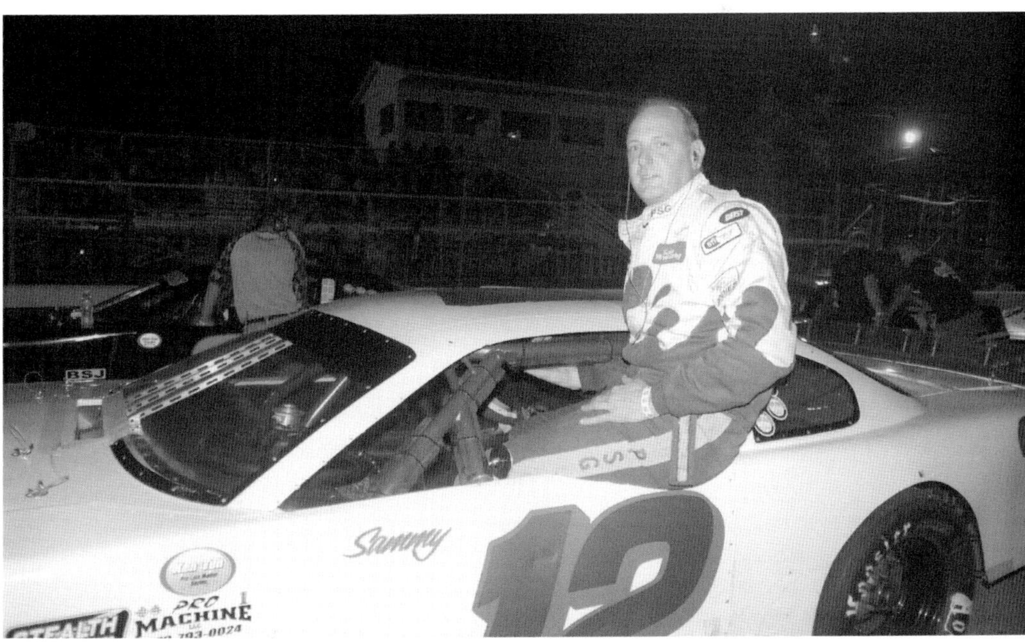

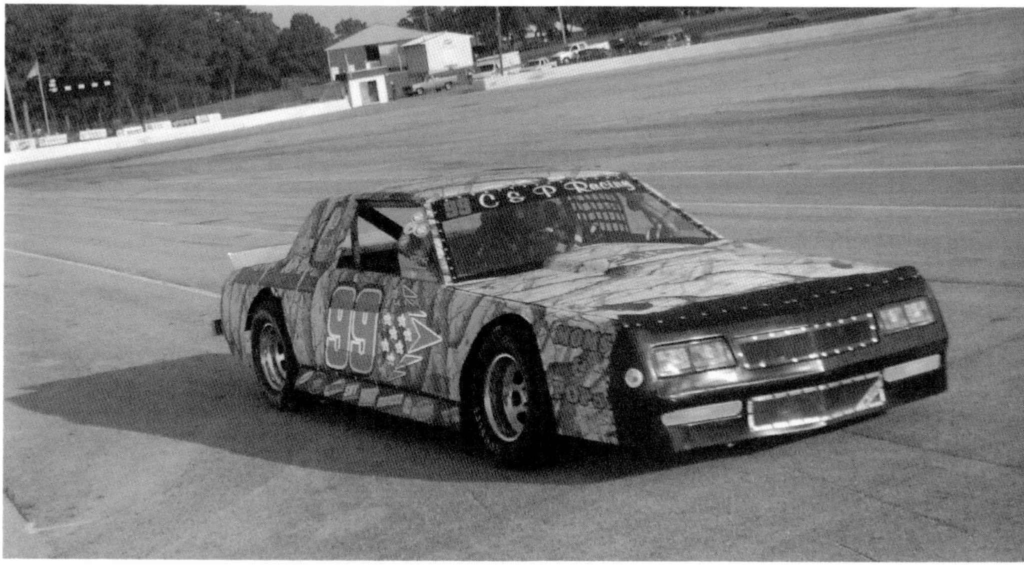

Robert Cohron of Bowling Green, Kentucky, drives this 1988 Chevrolet Monte Carlo Supersport, owned and built by his father, Jerry Cohron. Jerry Cohron is Robert's crew chief and is assisted by Jay Parrish. Robert won the 2009 Sportsman Division championship at Beech Bend Raceway after finishing second in 2008 and third in 2007. (Courtesy of Jim Baird.)

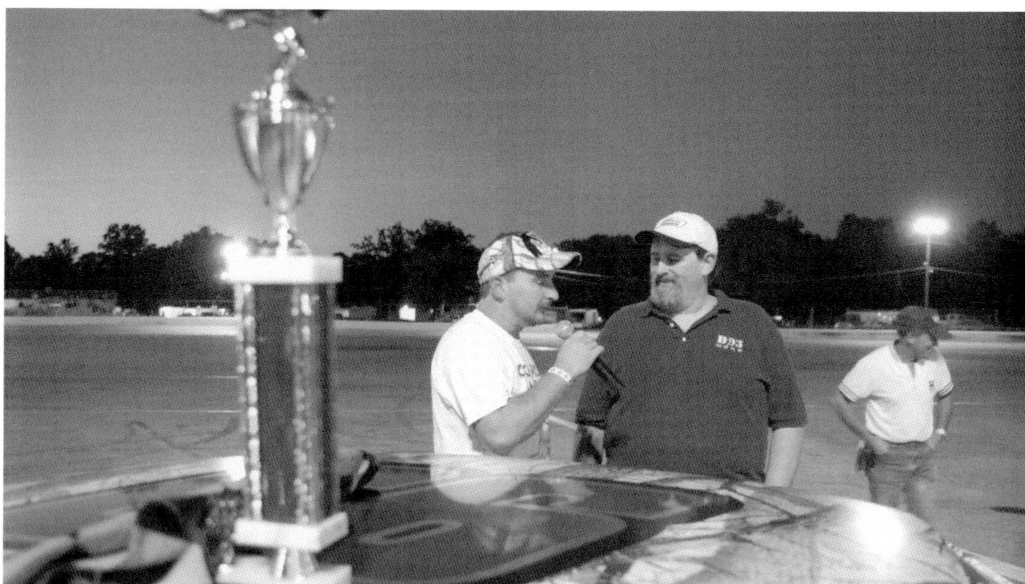

Robert Cohron, with the microphone, stands in victory lane with "Smokin Joe," the track announcer. Cohron began racing in 1990 before he had a driver's license. He learned to drive on the track. After a 12-year break, Cohron and his father, Jerry, came back to the track in 2007. After two good years of racing, Robert and Jerry set the track championship as their goal at the beginning of the 2009 season. They developed a strategy, made the money and time commitment required to win, and stuck with it. (Courtesy of Jim Baird.)

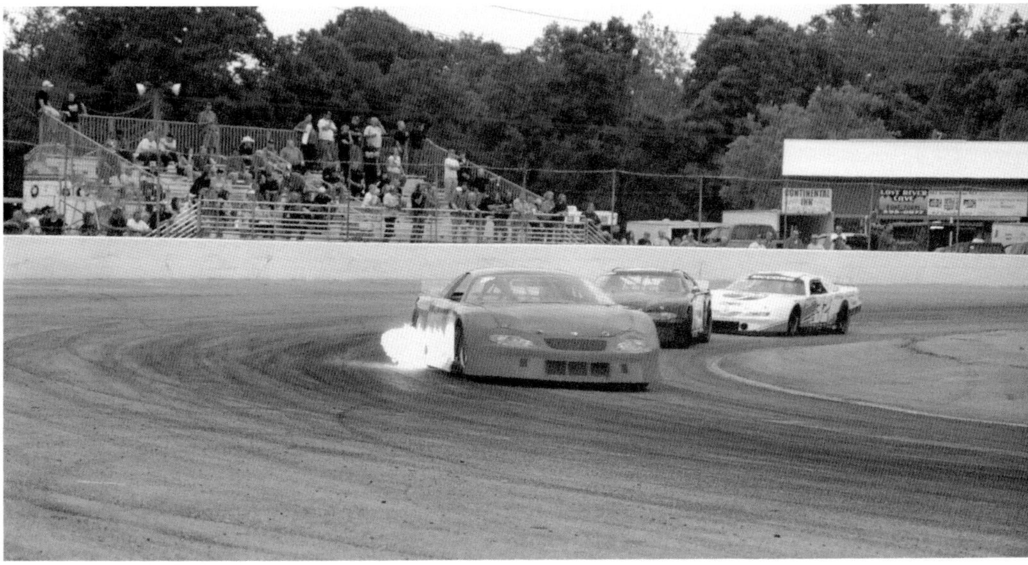

Beech Bend spectators get a thrill on Friday night from some hot action. At this point coming out of turn four, the driver is back on the gas, hoping the power is there to retain the lead down the front straight. The trailing car is trying to get the nose of his car inside the leader's back fender. If the driver is successful, the leader will be pushed to the outside going into turn one and lose the lead. (Courtesy of Jim Baird.)

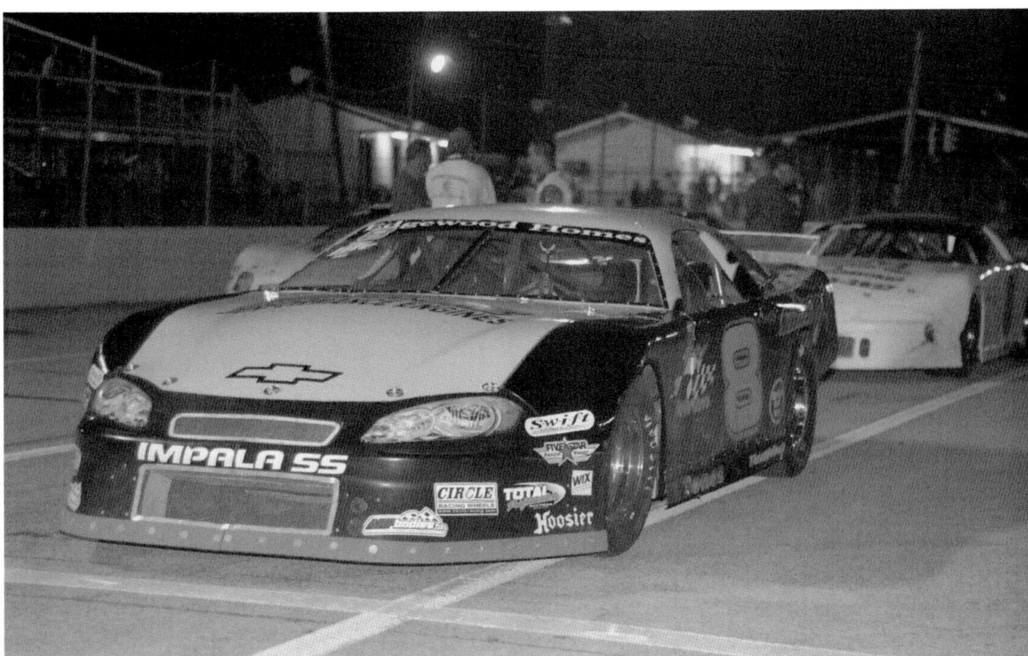

No. 8's driver is early to the staging area and has time to relax by visiting with other drivers and pit crews. It is a false relaxation because anxious nerves are inside the driver. This event consists of cars from the newly formed Ken-Ten League. (Courtesy of Jim Baird.)

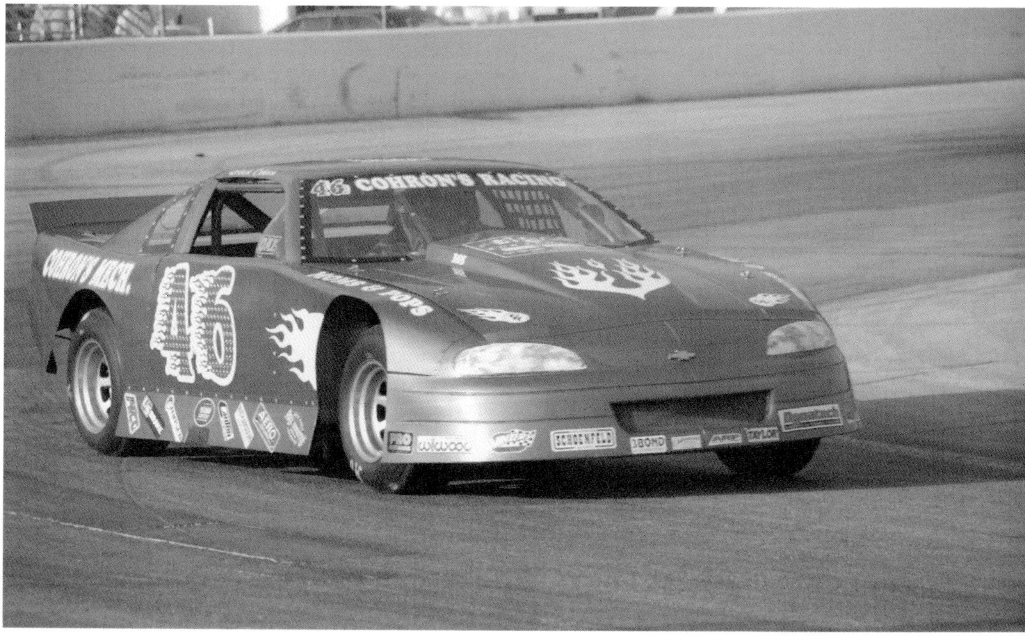

Robert Cohron is making the turn in his Sportsman's Division entry for 2008. Cohron finished second in the championship chase to Mary Daniels. Cohron won the division in 2009. (Courtesy of Jim Baird.)

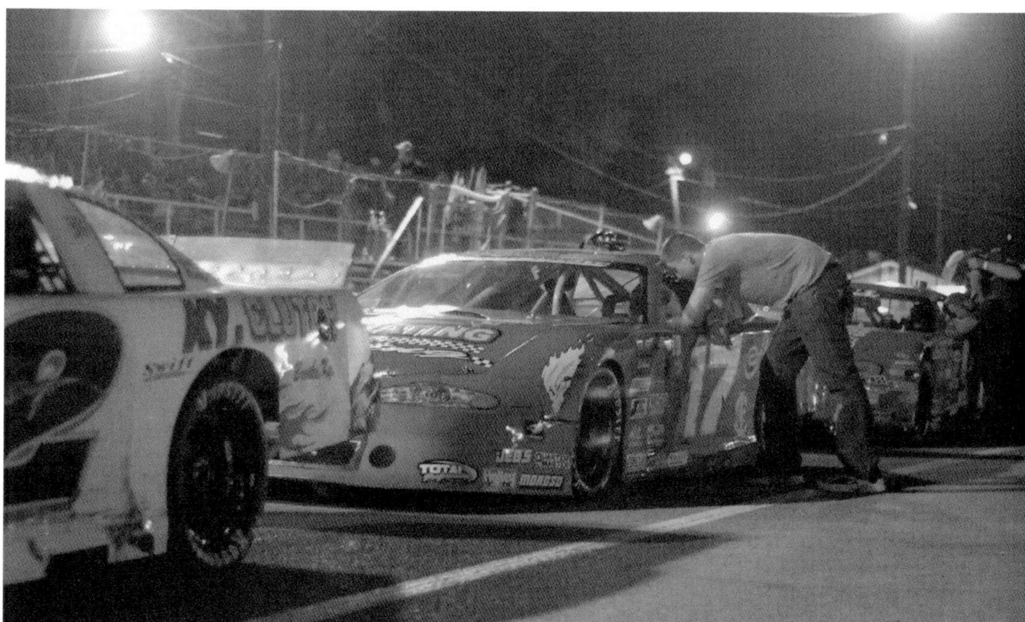

These Late Model Division cars are lined up for their introductions to the crowd. This is the moment when stress begins to peak in the drivers. Zipped up in double-layered fireproof suits and wearing gloves, shoes, and tight-fitting helmets, the drivers are experiencing triple-digit heat and humidity by the time the green flag flies. (Courtesy of Jim Baird.)

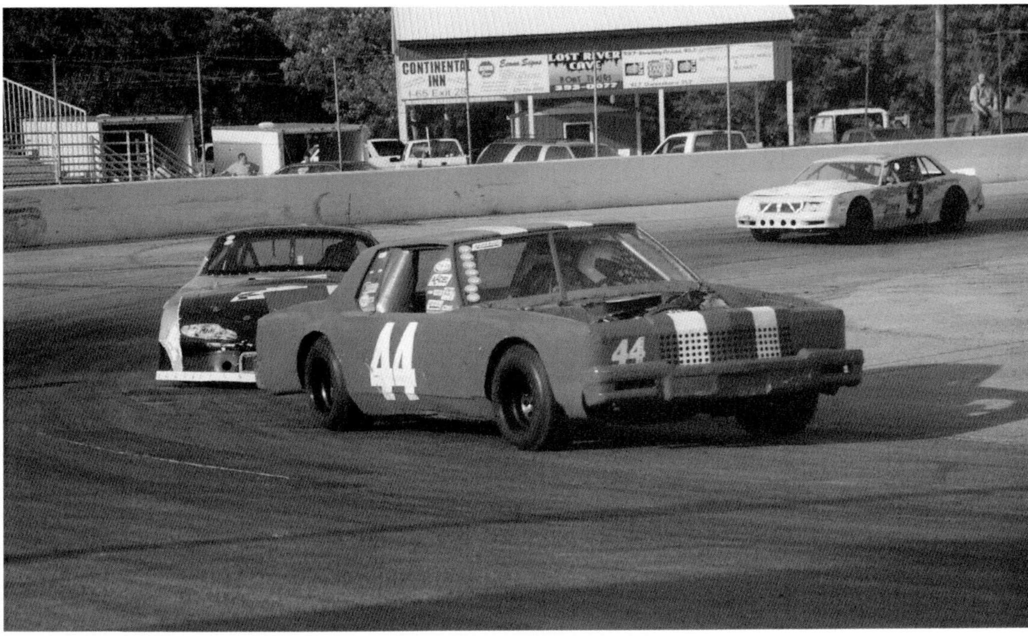

Running low protecting the track's inside line, Tony Rothe takes the lead in his No. 44. Sometimes a driver can gain momentum with a run that is high on the outside cushion because then the driver is able to slingshot out of a turn with enough speed to take the lead. (Courtesy of Jim Baird.)

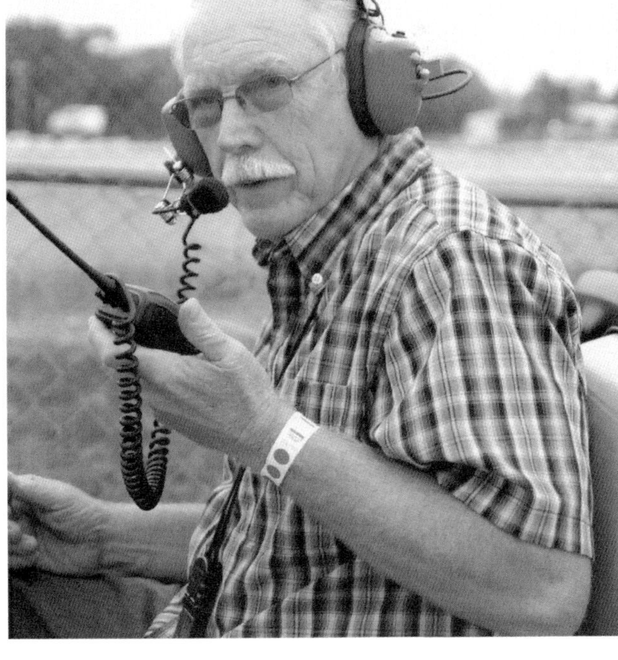

In the early dirt-track days at Beech Bend Park, drivers had no communication at all with their teams in the pits. Early cars did not even have a rear-view mirror. Today that has changed. This crew chief is conducting by radio an on-track strategy session. (Courtesy of Jim Baird.)

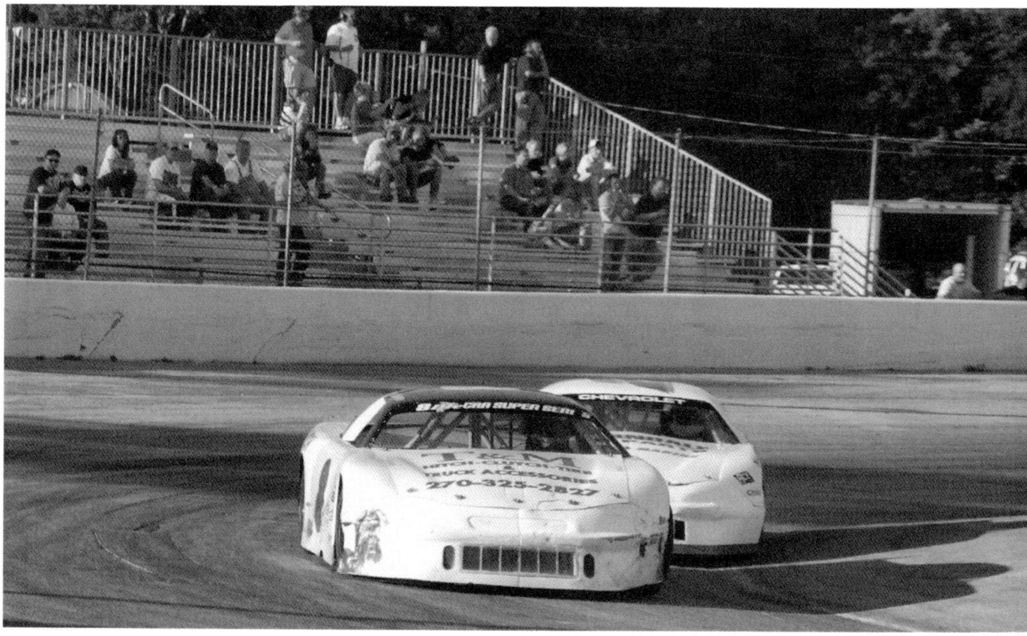

No. 8 races tight inside trying to hold off Mike Pruitt in the No. 2 car. Pruitt is going to keep the pressure on and never give the leader a moment without worry. If the leader ever gives Pruitt the slightest opportunity to get inside his back fender, the race will be over. Track position and knowing which line is working for one's car is the key to victory. (Courtesy of Jim Baird.)

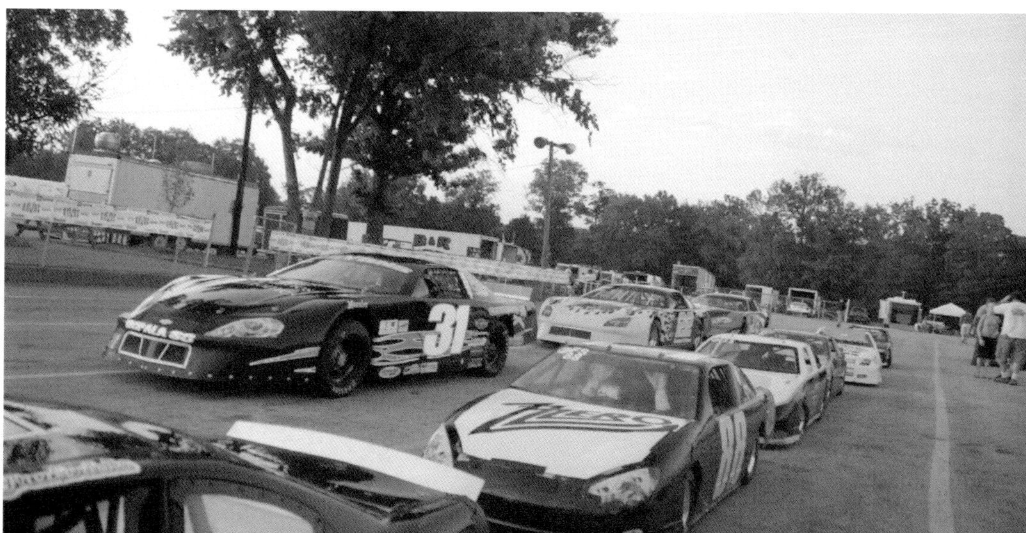

These Late Model Division cars sit in the staging area on a Friday ready for what might become a bare-knuckled brawl once racing begins. Unless one has been on the track, one cannot imagine the tension and excitement that is building inside each cockpit. Once these cars come off the parade lap in turn four, 20 drivers will punch the accelerator to the floor at the same time, creating a deafening roar as the cars barrel into turn one. (Courtesy of Jim Baird.)

Stacy Key works on his All-American Bomber. Key won the 2008 championship in the Bomber Division and finished second in 2009. He was also named "Mechanic of the Year." The Bombers are an entry-level class of cars designed to keep costs under control so that more drivers can participate in racing. Key runs a lean racing operation, stating that his "pit crew consists of me, myself, and I." (Courtesy of Jim Baird.)

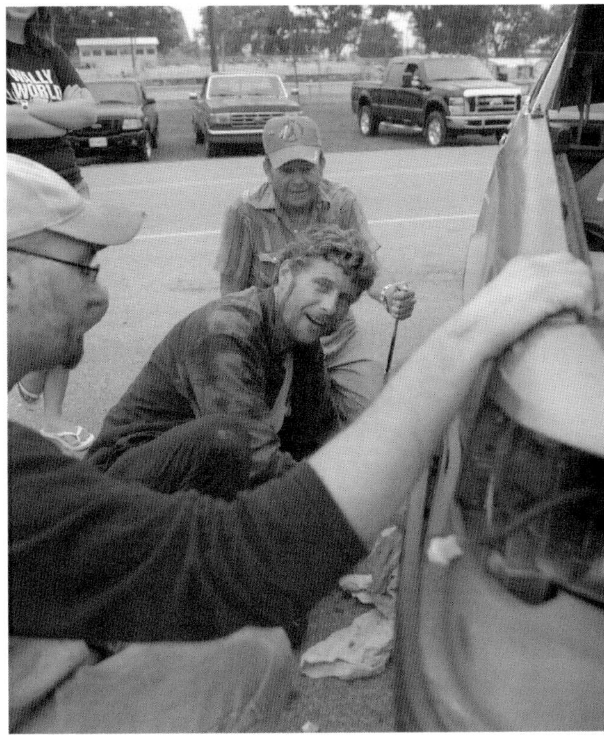

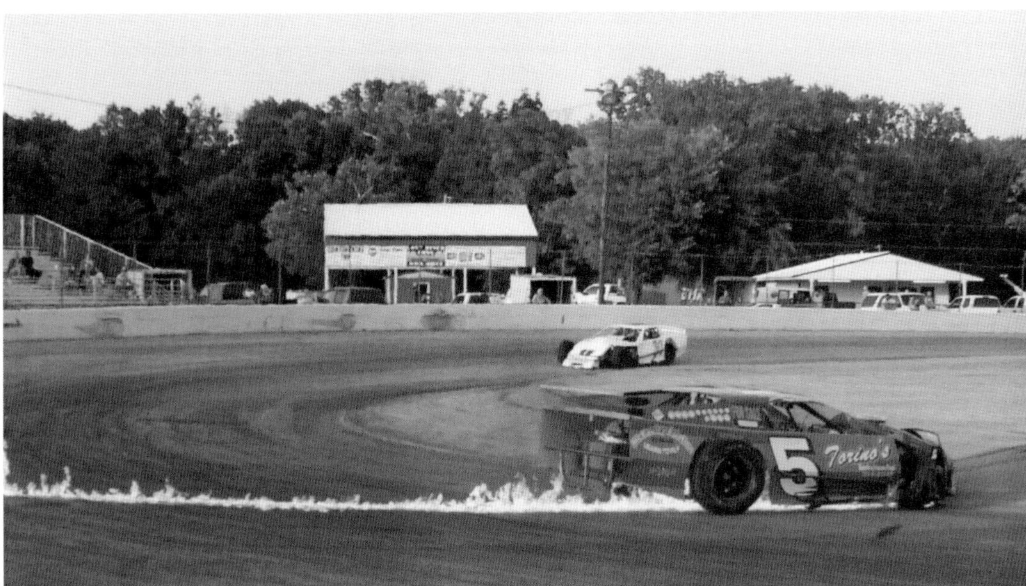

This open-wheel No. 5 catches fire after breaking a fuel line when it hit the wall. Fire is the greatest danger to a race car driver, and that is why so many safety features address this issue. In addition to the fireproof clothing, which only buys a driver a few extra seconds, other rules govern how fuel is contained within the car and how it gets to the engine. In the mishap pictured here, the driver escaped unhurt. (Courtesy of Jim Baird.)

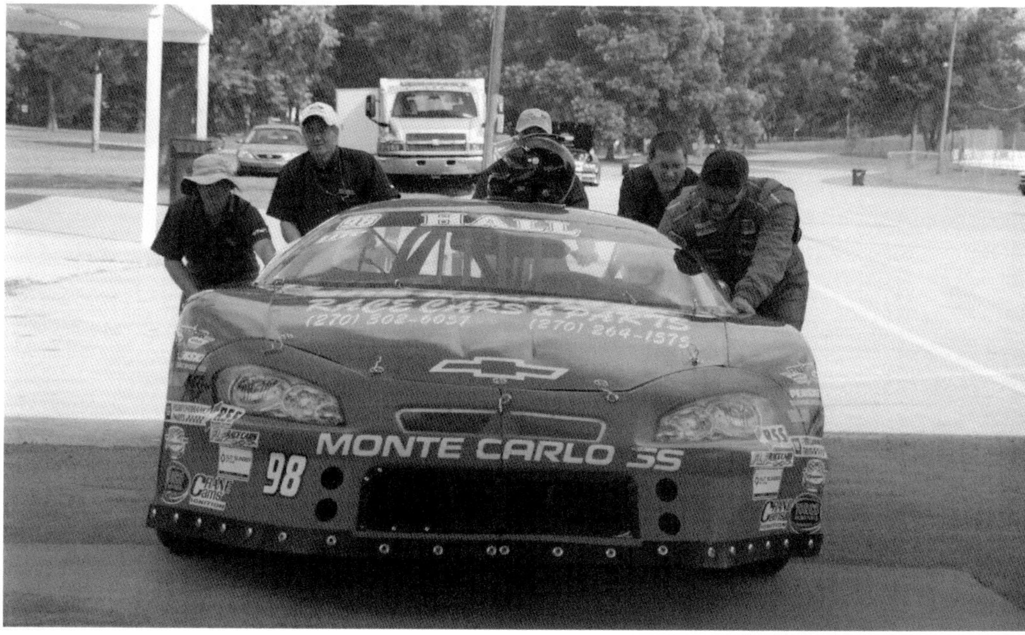

The driver and pit crew push the stock car to the scales after winning a race. Under current rules, the weight of the car and how that weight is positioned in the race car is controlled. After winning, cars are brought back to the scales to get reweighed, and that number is compared to their starting weight. (Courtesy of Jim Baird.)

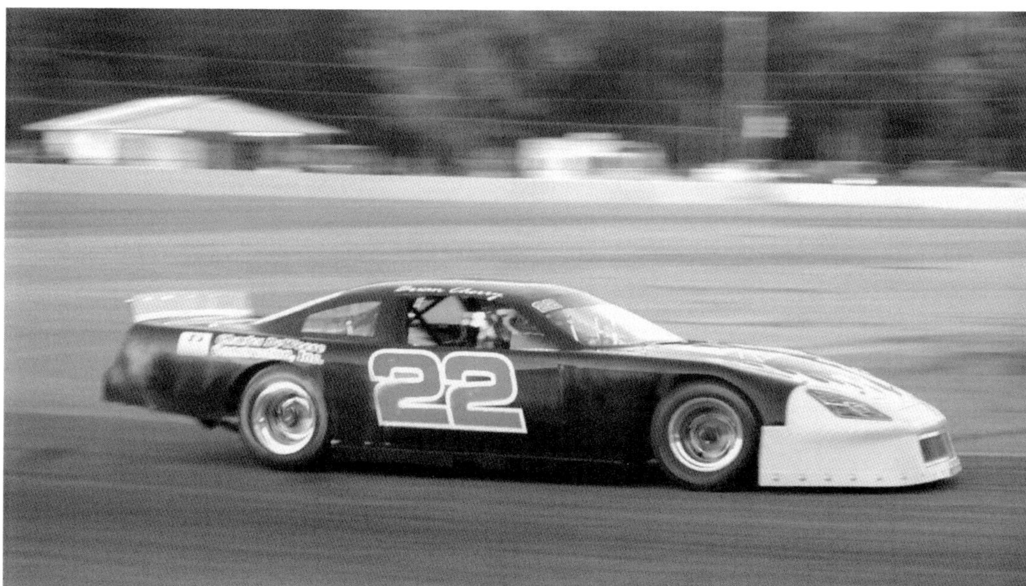

Brian Cherry is taking practice laps in his late model stock car. In the 1950s dirt track era, the track was watered at intervals to help control the dust. The stock cars warmed up by cruising around, packing the mud on the wet track. Today's stock cars warm up by cruising around the track and then ultimately going "hot," pushing the pedal to the medal. (Courtesy of Jim Baird.)

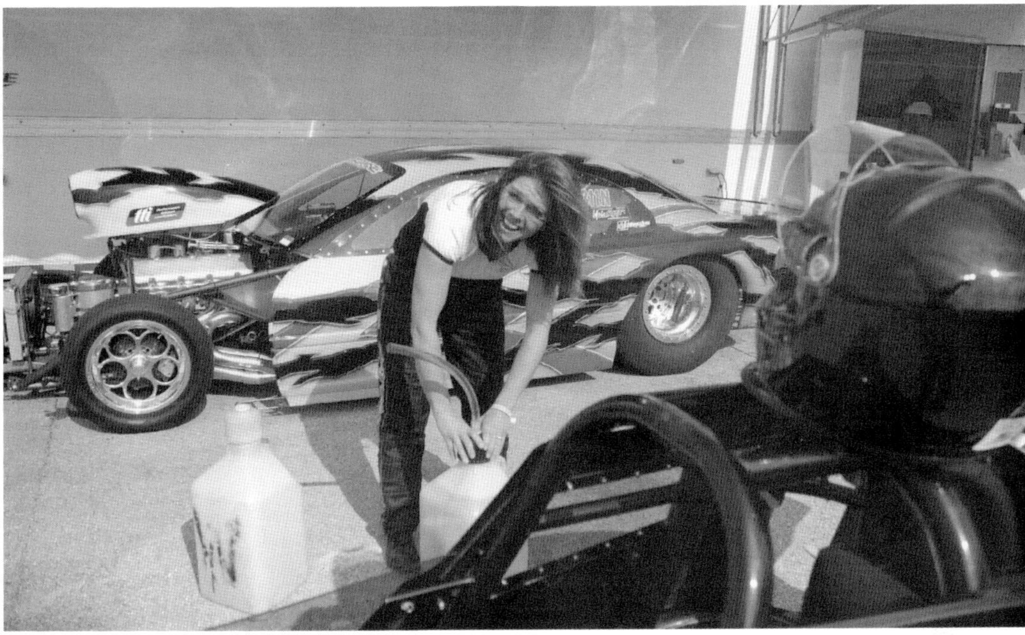

Charli Wheatcraft preps her dragster for another pass at the Chrysler Classic at Beech Bend Raceway Park. Racing out of Ohio, Wheatcraft is one of an increasing number of women participating in the sport. Charli runs at about 30 events per season, racing in Ohio, Pennsylvania, Michigan, Missouri, Illinois, and Nevada. With her car approaching 200 miles per hour in the Bowling Green event, Wheatcraft admits an addiction to speed. (Courtesy of Jim Baird.)

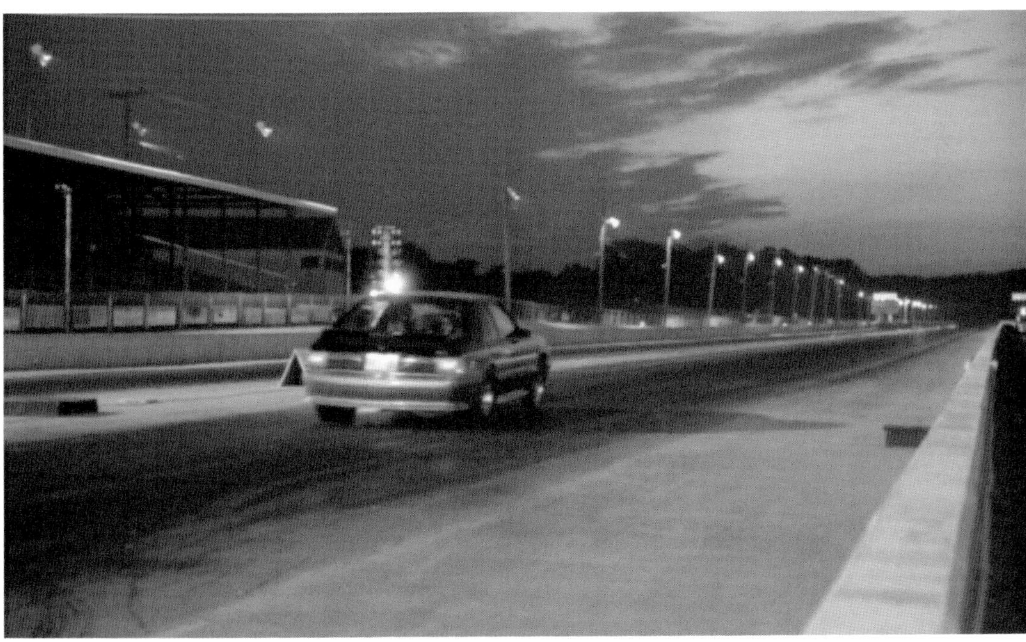

This dragster races into the sunset, making the last run before lights out. (Courtesy of Jim Baird.)